CHILDREN OF THE
Rich

Other books by William Davis

Three Years Hard Labour
Merger Mania
Money Talks
Have Expenses, Will Travel
It's No Sin to Be Rich
The Best of Everything (editor)
Money in the 1980s
The Rich: A Study of the Species
Fantasy: A Practical Guide to Escapism
The Corporate Infighter's Handbook
The World's Best Business Hotels (editor)
The Super Salesman's Handbook
The Innovators

CHILDREN OF THE
Rich

INSIDE THE WORLD OF
THE PRIVILEGED YOUNG

WILLIAM DAVIS

SIDGWICK & JACKSON
LONDON

First published in Great Britain in 1989
by Sidgwick & Jackson Limited

Copyright © 1989 by William Davis

ISBN 0-283-99791-5

Typeset by Hewer Text Composition Services, Edinburgh
Printed in Great Britain by Billing & Sons, Worcester
for Sidgwick & Jackson Limited
1 Tavistock Chambers, Bloomsbury Way
London WC1A 2SG

Contents

CONTENTS

List of Illustrations

Their Royal Highnesses The Prince and Princess of Wales with their children, The Princes William and Harry (Popperfoto/Reuter)

Gerald Grosvenor, Duke of Westminster (Popperfoto)

The Fords (Popperfoto)

4 June at Eton (Hulton-Deutsch collection)

Harvard Memorial Library (Rex Features Limited)

Christina and Athina Onassis (Rex Features Limited)

J. Paul Getty III (Rex Features Limited)

Patty Hearst (Rex Features Limited)

The Maxwells (Hulton-Deutsch Collection/Rex Features Limited/ Telegraph Weekend Magazine)

The Fortes (Popperfoto/Daily Telegraph Colour Library)

John and Marissa Wayne (Popperfoto)

The Picassos (Popperfoto/Rex Features Limited)

Donald Trump (Rex Features Limited)

Michael and Kirk Douglas (Rex Features Limited/Popperfoto)

Paolo Gucci (Rex Features Limited)

The Kennedys (Popperfoto)

Prince Albert and Princess Caroline of Monaco (Rex Features Limited)

Author's Note

I am grateful to all the children and parents who have talked to me so freely, and to Carey Smith of Sidgwick & Jackson for her helpful suggestions.

Introduction

The children of the rich are much envied. An accident of birth seems to have given them everything they could wish for. Others face a ceaseless struggle for survival and, if possible, success. They may reach their goal eventually, but most of them recognize that they will never enjoy the privileges that the rich seem to take for granted. Many never even try. They settle for what they have got, or for what they can get. It does not, however, prevent them from attacking fortune's children – in conversation, in the media, or in some form of political activity.

It is one of Margaret Thatcher's more notable achievements that, in Britain, this envy factor is much less obvious than it used to be. The principal reason, of course, is that her 'entrepreneurial revolution' and 'popular capitalism' have made many more people feel that, with real effort, they too can join the ranks of the rich. The newspapers, each day, are full of stories about entrepreneurs from humble backgrounds who have managed to make millions. Some, like Richard Branson, have become folk heroes. It inspires others to have a go. The number of small businesses started in the past decade has been quite extraordinary. The failure rate has been high, but there have been many impressive successes. The world of showbiz has also opened up great opportunities: pop singers like Paul McCartney and Mick Jagger have become wealthier than many of the people who owe their good fortune to an inheritance. We have moved much closer to the American view that everyone has a *right* to pursue wealth as well as happiness. Many of Mrs Thatcher's devoted followers would readily endorse Lee Iacocca's much-quoted remark: 'If little kids don't aspire to make money like I did, what the hell good is this country?'

But the envy persists – of people who make it look so easy and, more specifically, of those who seem to be able to get their hands on incredible sums of money without, apparently, making any effort at all.

The children of the rich tend to discover this at an early age. They learn at school that many classmates resent their privileges. If they invite friends to their homes they may have to endure disparaging comments on their opulent lifestyle. Later, at work, they have to cope with equally snide remarks about their supposed advantages. Many people will tell them that they find it hard to understand why they should want a job at all. Surely they do not *need* it? It will also be assumed that they have managed to secure their appointment because their parents have the right connections, not because they possess any merit themselves. If the business happens to be controlled by the parents, they will find it even more difficult to convince colleagues that they have anything worthwhile to contribute. It is taken for granted that they are there only because their fathers want them to be, and that they will easily make it to the top. They will be courted, in the hope that the flatterers will be able to hitch a ride, but they will find it hard to earn respect.

Many come to accept that, if this is how life is, they might as well make the most of it. Some undoubtedly enjoy the benefits of nepotism. They boast openly about their status and make it plain that, one day, they will be the boss. They relish the attention which goes with privilege. They flaunt their possessions and exploit their advantages.

Others find envy a hurtful emotion and become extremely defensive. They try to hide their wealth and do their best to seek jobs with companies that have nothing whatever to do with the family, even if it means performing lowly routine tasks. They long to be treated just like everyone else, and they go out of their way to achieve that objective.

Some even try to reject their inheritance. Abby Rockefeller recalls the difficult conversation she had with her father, David Rockefeller, when he informed her that she would one day inherit $25 million. 'When he was finished, I said that I thought I would prefer not to have it. I said that what I did not like was the idea of it hanging over me, affecting my future and my present, affecting my relations with people, and affecting my relations with him. I said it was just bad for relations.' Her father, according to Abby, looked 'stunned and upset'. He said: 'Well, I'm terribly sorry to tell you, but there is nothing I can do about it.' The money was in a trust fund set up by *his* father, and what she did with it after he was gone was her affair.

Such reactions to the news that one stands to get millions are the exception rather than the rule. It is much more common for the children of the rich to make some effort to show that it is not going to determine the course of their lives. They may back this resolve with an open denunciation of wealth and the habits of the rich. It is not unusual for them to join left-wing parties or become involved, in some other way, in causes which set them in direct opposition to the financial interests of their parents or other relatives.

Such opposition, not surprisingly, often becomes a major source of friction. The children feel obliged to make a stand, either because they genuinely believe in the cause or simply because they want to impress their friends. The parents see it as an act of betrayal or, at the very least, as an appalling display of ingratitude. Their children, they complain, have become 'champagne socialists'. They continue to enjoy all the good things that wealth can provide, while at the same time supporting those who seek to destroy that wealth and the process which creates it.

Wise parents recognize that most young people go through an idealistic stage and refuse to be goaded; they reckon that there is a good chance that, in time, they will learn to curb their rebellious instincts. But often the friction turns into a fire: the angry father may decide that, if his children are so firmly against all he believes in, and all that he has worked so hard to achieve, he might as well stop their allowances, or even disinherit them, and leave them to their own devices. Unfortunately for him, this response has become much more difficult because the creation of trust funds and other instruments designed to avoid tax and maintain control of the family business has given the children of the rich a greater degree of independence than they have ever had before.

What many rich children want, above all, is a real sense of personal worth: the feeling that they matter *despite* their privileged background. They do not want to be seen as mere appendages, as part of their parents' ego trip, as willing tools of people who are stronger than themselves. They dislike the idea that they have an obligation to play whatever role has been assigned to them.

Much of their discontent arises from feeling that they are being taken for granted, that they are deprived of choice, that their path has been mapped out for them without anyone bothering to ask what *they* want to do with their lives. You may well think that they should count themselves lucky: most people, after all, have less choice and have to make their way through life without the comforts available to the rich. But I suggest that one should at least try to understand why so many regard the accident of their birth as a mixed blessing.

In earlier times, the sons of wealthy families would often go into the army. This enabled them to put on a smart uniform, command men, and win glory on the battlefield. Their fathers might help them to become officers, but after that they were on their own. They *had* to prove themselves. But army life is no longer fashionable and there are few opportunities to gain the admiration of the world through acts of heroism. Today the sons of the rich are generally expected to prove themselves in business. Some do; some fail and give up; some do not even try because they think they have no hope of doing as well as their fathers or because they would rather do something else – or nothing at all.

An obvious alternative is politics. It offers the prospect of power and public recognition, and it can even help the family. Having money is useful, especially in America, where political campaigns at both state and national level have become so expensive that the rich possess an often decisive advantage over their less affluent opponents. Even in Britain it is a considerable asset because the children of the rich do not have to rely on a politician's salary, can employ assistants, and can afford to have homes both in London and in their constituency. If they lose their seats, they always have their fortunes to comfort them.

The Kennedy clan is the most famous example of political power won through the determined use of financial clout. Joseph Kennedy, who made his millions as a financier and real-estate entrepreneur, never got beyond the rank of ambassador, but he did his utmost to ensure that his children would be a force to be reckoned with. However talented he may have been, it is highly unlikely that Jack Kennedy would have made it to the White House without his father's money.

The Rockefellers, too, have shown a strong inclination to pursue political success. Nelson, the best known of the six children of John D. Rockefeller Jr, went to work for his father to begin with, but soon discovered that he had no taste for business life. He told an interviewer in his younger days: 'Just to work my way up in a business that another man has built, stepping from the shoes of one to those of another, making a few minor changes here and there and then, finally, perhaps at the age of sixty, getting to the top where I would have control for a few years – no, that isn't my idea of living a real life.' I very much doubt if it would have been as hard as all that, or taken as long, but it is easy to see why he found politics more exciting. He did not succeed in his four attempts to become the Republican Party's presidential candidate, but he served four terms as Governor of New York and was eventually nominated Vice-President of the United States by Gerald Ford. One of his brothers, Winthrop, dropped out of Yale and went to work as a roughneck in the Texas oil fields, but later became Governor of Arkansas. A grandchild of Junior's, Jay Rockefeller, was elected Governor of West Virginia and after two terms became a senator. Many of the younger Rockefellers have contributed generously to various political causes.

But, of course, the choice is not confined to politics or business. The children of the rich ought to be able to make their mark in many other fields – the theatre, painting, publishing, sport, and so on. They do not have to take a humdrum job (as so many people do) simply in order to earn a living. Money is no substitute for talent, but it buys time and freedom from the need to worry about paying the mortgage. That is the theory, anyway. In practice, many parents seek to control the activities of their children by keeping a tight rein on their finances, which means that they seldom feel truly free until they come into an inheritance or make some money of their own. Those who are wealthy at an early age often have another problem: because they have never had to try hard to succeed in anything, they lack the drive which propels less fortunate people forward. They may go into the arts or some other interesting field, but they tend to *play* at it.

Some of the children of the rich lead empty, aimless lives. They become alcoholics or drug addicts, or go off to distant places like India to 'find' themselves. Many indulge in an endless procession of love affairs and messy divorces. Because such behaviour tends to attract the attention of the press, particularly the gossip columns, it is widely assumed that the old cliché is valid: money does not buy happiness. The world wants to believe that it does not (it makes everyone else feel so much better about not being rich) and of course the world is right. But money does not necessarily buy misery either. It all depends on the individual.

There is no doubt that many children of the rich *are* unhappy. Many are emotionally insecure, for reasons which will become apparent in this book, or so spoilt by wealth that they cannot cope with the realities of everyday life. They are bullied by their parents, envied by their friends, resented by self-appointed critics, and exploited by ruthless opportunists. This is the other side of the golden coin, and I have dealt with it at some length because I find it fascinating. But it would clearly be wrong to give the impression that wealth is a recipe for failure. There are many children of the rich who lead happy, successful lives as adults. Some go on to build bigger empires than their fathers. So I have included a study of winners as well as of losers.

I

Old Money

There is a considerable difference between Old Money and New Money, between wealth which is inherited, and which has long been the basis of a distinctive lifestyle, and that which is created through entrepreneurial effort.

Old Money is handed on from one generation to the next; it is seen as a patrimony with a past and a future, literally or figuratively held in trust. It produces an income and a set of obligations – to the family and to causes held dear by the Old Rich, notably the perpetuation of a certain way of life. The children of Old Money know that they are going to be well provided for and they know that, in return, they are expected to conform to a code of behaviour. Their wealth protects them from many of the tiresome facts of life, but it also carries responsibilities, including a duty to preserve the inheritance for *their* children.

Not all of them succeed: fortunes are sometimes dissipated through careless administration, unwise marriages, social upheavals, and other damaging events. Europe has numerous scions of Old Money – princes, dukes, counts, princesses, baronesses, knights and ladies – who can no longer call themselves rich. The Russian dukes vanished with the Revolution, the hand-kissing Austrian counts were impoverished by wars, and the English lords are struggling to protect their crumbling ancestral estates from dry rot. (For many of them, the inheritance is more of a burden than an asset.) Their children have had to fend for themselves and many have ended up in plebeian jobs. Earl Nelson of Trafalgar, descendant of the heroic admiral, became a policeman.

Other nobles work in advertising and public relations. Many are salesmen.

In America, too, many rich old families are finding it hard to maintain themselves, and their children, in the style that is expected of them. Previous generations may have spent their money too freely, or the family business which provides the income may have gone into a steep decline, or their own parents may have given away the bulk of their fortune to charity instead of passing it on to the next generation. Some have managed to replenish their fortunes by forging marriage links with New Money, but many have discovered, to their dismay, that the survival of lofty dynasties cannot be taken for granted.

Nevertheless, enough families have held on to their heritage (and, in some cases, substantially increased it) to ensure that Old Money remains a major force. Indeed, some people insist that it is still the backbone of the so-called 'ruling class'.

I doubt if they have given it much thought. No one could seriously argue that politics and business, on either side of the Atlantic, are dominated by Old Money. President Bush may have a patrician background, but Ronald Reagan was an actor and Jimmy Carter a peanut farmer. Most political offices are held by the New Money (or No Money) crowd. In Britain, we stubbornly go along with the pretence that the Queen is the 'ruler', but everyone knows that real power is in the hands of a grocer's daughter. The Lords have a splendid chamber, and provide the nation with some good entertainment, but the House of Commons makes the laws.

Old Money is the backbone of a *social* class, which is a very different matter. It tries to exercise guardianship over taste and manners; it seeks to impose its views of 'correct' behaviour not only on its own but also on society as a whole, including the upstarts of New Money. Its allies are time, tradition, continuity.

In Britain, Old Money is fortified by the existence of a royal family and of titles which still have some meaning. A Russian prince may no longer be of consequence, but a British duke or lord retains a certain aura. In America, the brahmins of cities like Boston and Philadelphia reckon to be their equal. In the absence of titles, many Old Money families like to indicate their lineage by the use of Roman numerals – John D. Rockefeller IV, Harvey S. Firestone III, Pierre S. du Pont IV, and so forth. (The record may be held by Marshall Field VI, the great-great-great-grandson of the department chain of the same name.) It instantly identifies them as members of a dynasty and is a great deal more prestigious than the more common label, 'Junior', which is generally pinned on second-generation offspring who hope to join the Old Money set.

The shared financial interests of these dynasties are generally given concrete form by devices like trusts, holding companies, and family offices. The Rockefellers, for example, maintain a family office which employs over two hundred clerks, accountants, lawyers and financial advisers. The chief purpose of these institutions is to protect the dynasty's accumulated wealth, but they also tend to bind the family fortune.

Trust funds play a particularly important role in this. They have long been a popular method of preserving Old Money, and are nowadays also used extensively by New Money people. The legal instrument is older than most of the families who use it. It goes back more than seven hundred years, to the thirteenth century. Its first use, ironically, seems to have been as a holding device for donations to the Franciscan order, whose vows of poverty forbade its members to 'own' wealth. The trust was to own it for them.

A wealthy individual may create a single large trust for the benefit of all of his descendants. More often, a few key family members serve as the trustees of a series of separate trusts for the benefit of many different family members. They tend to bristle with clauses and stipulations designed to meet any contingency. Many are so-called 'generation-skipping' trusts. Under these arrangements the children are usually entitled to receive all the income for life; the grandchildren, who are generally the remaindermen of the trusts, receive these assets only after the death of the last surviving beneficiary. When principal is paid out, it is often in dribbling instalments throughout the recipients' lifetime. It is a ploy which was developed primarily to protect fortunes from gift and estates taxes, but it also helps to prevent the dissipation of capital through the exercise of immature judgement. The first generation cannot disturb the principal and the next generation does not get all of it – or sometimes any of it – until its members are quite advanced in age. At that point many of them lock the principal back in new trusts for the benefit of the next two generations.

Trusts sometimes lead to bitter family feuds (see Chapter 14) but by and large they have served Old Money well. Much of it is tied up this way. The children of the rich may not have freely available capital (as most of us tend to assume they have) but they are provided with a handsome income. They do not have to get a job, start a business, or do any of the other things to which the less fortunate devote their lives. If they wish, they can simply sit back and collect the dividends. There is no financial incentive to do anything else. Unless the trust is accompanied by a family enterprise that requires the personal attention of some of its members, it makes almost no demands on its inheritors. It is this state of affairs, envied by the outside world, which so often results in an aimless existence. Because there is no need for effort, it is all too easy to become lethargic, or to devote one's life to the frivolous pursuit of pleasure.

Many Old Money families recognize the danger, and do their best to involve their children in work which, although it may not produce financial rewards, is nevertheless of value to the clan or to the community. This is where Old Money's concept of duty comes into play again. It may mean the preservation of a stately home or estate, or a close involvement in one or more of the family's philanthropic enterprises.

Family foundations are not as old as trusts, but they have come to play an increasingly important role in the management of wealth. The rich would like them to be seen as a contribution to society, an attempt to put something back. We are expected to applaud their generosity. In practice, their motives are rarely as altruistic as they like to pretend. One of the main reasons why so many family foundations have been created over the years is that they have enabled the rich to avoid estate taxes without relinquishing control of their corporations. Although a family loses the ownership of any stock it donates to a charitable foundation, it does not necessarily lose control of this stock. As long as family members are able to control a foundation, they are able to control the stock in its investment portfolio. As trustees, they can use it to elect family members as directors of the corporation. They can also refuse to sell the stock to other companies who may have their eye on it.

It is a neat solution to several problems: the rich can remain in charge of the family business, minimize taxes, and at the same time

counter the attacks of their critics with the argument that they are
using their wealth for the benefit of society as a whole. As trustees,
the children can be a force in all kinds of agreeable activities –
museums, art galleries, colleges, medical research, conservation
programmes, evangelical crusades. It buys them the one thing
which Old Money claims to value above all else: cultural and
social capital.

Control of a foundation enables members of a family to extend
their power and prestige beyond the economic sphere and into
the realm of community affairs. They can decide who should
benefit from their support, and they can bask in the gratitude of
those who have been chosen. Even a small foundation can have
a considerable impact at the local level.

They can also, if they wish, seek to influence public policies
by funding impressive studies and other activities. When the
Ford Foundation, set up in 1946, became a major player in the
1950s it laid out five grandiose programmes: the establishment
of peace: the strengthening of democracy; the strengthening of
the economy; education in a democratic society; and research
into individual behaviour and human relations. Nothing much
wrong with that, you may think, but the way the Foundation
chose to implement these programmes attracted a lot of criticism
and it was forced to change direction. Today there are no longer
any family representatives on the board of trustees. Henry Ford
II resigned in 1978 because he disagreed with the Foundation's
more liberal approach. In his letter of resignation, he complained
that it failed to appreciate the virtues of the capitalist system that
was responsible for its very existence. It might have been wiser to
have stuck to old Henry's more modest original aim of supporting
local causes: once a foundation becomes too obviously powerful
on the national scene, it can easily get out of hand.

Because the accumulation of cultural and social capital is considered to be of such importance, Old Money families devote
much time and effort to ensuring that their children understand,
accept, and implement the code of behaviour which has been
passed on with the fortune. Good manners, the right accent,
sportsmanship (i.e. the ability to lose with good grace), and
a talent for presiding over social functions and making endless
small talk without appearing to get bored, are all part of the
Old Money curriculum. Expertise in the arts is not essential, but

children should be able to convince others that they appreciate opera, the ballet, painting and literature, even if they have never set foot in an opera house and cannot tell the difference between a Klee and a Picasso. Servants and tradesmen should be treated with courtesy, but one should never make friends of them. (Nannies are an exception: they are employed to keep the children on the right track and often act as surrogate mothers. Many children retain a life-long affection for their nannies.)

The children must learn to do all this without seeming to put in any effort: the essence of Old Money behaviour is a capacity for making everything look easy, natural, casual, nonchalant. One must dress well, but not *too* well, except on formal occasions like society balls and weddings and at Ascot. Eccentricity is acceptable and even encouraged; it is widely regarded as a further sign of good breeding, though heaven knows why.

The code, of course, also applies to the next stage – attendance at a prestigious boarding school, probably the same one that looked after their parents and grandparents. Everything they have been taught at home is reinforced at Old Money establishments like Eton and Harrow, and in America at the boarding schools of New England. (F. Scott Fitzgerald called them St Midas.) Here, too, they are led to believe that the Old Money way is the only way – at least the only one that matters. They are carefully shielded from outside influences, though not always successfully.

There is a nice story about the child of a wealthy banker who, in her first year, was asked to write an essay on poverty. 'There once was a very poor family,' she began. 'Everyone in the family was poor. The butler was poor, the chauffeur was poor, the maids were poor . . .' Apocryphal, perhaps, but it is not difficult to imagine how a sheltered upbringing, continued at school, can lead to a false perception of everyday realities.

Lord James Russell, youngest son of the Marquis of Tavistock, once asked some people who were entertaining his family to lunch: 'Now can we go and see your lions?' Woburn Abbey, the stately home where he was born, has a safari park and the ten-year-old assumed that it was a perfectly normal thing to have in the back garden.

Love of animals is another well-known Old Money trait. Not just any animal, naturally. Lions may be a bit too exotic for most of the children, but they generally adore ponies, horses, and good-looking aristocratic dogs. Girls, especially, learn to handle horses at an early age. Brought up on country estates, they find it hard to believe that there are people in the world who do not have their own horse.

At school, the children of the rich are usually introduced to one or more sports. The girls may play hockey: the boys may be asked to tackle rugby. In America it is more likely to be football and baseball, but there are certain sporting activities which are popular with Old Money on both sides of the Atlantic – competitive riding, boating, tennis, fishing, polo. The aim is to toughen them up, but there is a second reason: these are the kind of activities they are likely to be called upon to take part in as adults. They do not necessarily have to be very good, but they must be familiar enough with them to acquit themselves honourably on future occasions. In Britain, Old Money still clings to that well-worn cliché: 'It matters not who won or lost, but how you played the game.'

Learning to sail a boat is obviously useful, because the offspring will probably be called upon eventually to handle Daddy's ocean-racer or yacht. As boys grow older, they will also be introduced to another Old Money pastime – shooting. British aristocrats have an insatiable passion for shooting birds of all kinds, and their heirs are expected to become reasonably proficient at this controversial sport: fathers take great pride in the ability of their sons to bag an impressive number of pheasants, grouse, or ducks. In addition, they will probably be taught to hunt foxes, an equally controversial pastime which has managed to survive despite the militant protests of the lower orders.

Jousting tournaments and other medieval events are, nowadays, staged mainly for the benefit of tourists. But horsemanship is taken every bit as seriously as it was hundreds of years ago. The children of the rich tend to excel at guiding their mounts over hurdles, and many still take up the 'sport of princes', polo. It is the most aristocratic of all the sports, and one of the most expensive. It requires all the knightly virtues which Old Money values so highly, notably good horsemanship and courage to the point of recklessness. Britain's aristocratic families were delighted when the heir to the throne, Prince Charles, became a player who could put up a 'good show' on the polo fields of the world.

Children of both sexes, of course, are also expected to become well-versed in that great indoor recreation, dancing. The main objective of a dance is to enable them to meet 'suitable' young men and women: it is the parental alternative to dangerous places like discos, where they are liable to team up with undesirables like plumbers and secretaries from working-class areas. Old Money people recognize that they have to move with the times, but they feel the need to draw the line somewhere. Bankers, lawyers, and stockbrokers are acceptable; plumbers, carpenters and clerks are not.

Suitable partners may find themselves invited to a weekend house party, which in London generally means going off 'to the country'. It can be anywhere from fifty to a hundred miles away. There may be about a dozen guests, which gives parents the opportunity to study the friends of their children without being too obvious about it. They must not seem overly impressed by the splendour of their surroundings (the 'right people' take such things for granted) and they must not plead ignorance or lack of skill if asked to participate in Old Money sports or in parlour games like charades. Proficiency in bridge or chess is also considered a useful asset, though it is impolite to beat one's hosts.

The conversation usually ranges round the shared interests and grievances of the rich: horses, gardens, the evils of socialism, the impertinence of trade unions, servant problems and so on. Occasionally children will be tempted to express a dissenting view, but upsetting one's hosts and fellow guests by a spirited display of independence is bad form and they generally avoid doing so. The most serious offence, however, is to talk openly about money.

Old Money families are as interested in the subject as everyone else, but it simply is not done to discuss it in a brash vulgar way. You do not boast about your family's wealth (it is assumed that all the guests have money, even if they do not) and you do not mention your latest deals, even if you have made millions. Nor do you indulge in the habit, so common among New Money people, of talking about the *cost* of everything – property, cars, boats, air travel, hotels, clothes. The children of the rich are well aware of such matters, but they have been taught that it is ill-mannered to mention them. It goes against the code of behaviour: one's public attitude to money should be the same as to all the other facts of life: casual, nonchalant.

This convention is also rigorously upheld in the 'gentlemen's clubs' which the sons of the rich are expected to join as soon as they are old enough. For as long as anyone can remember, these clubs have prohibited 'shop talk' – conversations about business and money. Briefcases must be left at the door, and if someone has the audacity to produce documents (or, heaven forbid, a pocket calculator) at the lunch table or even in the library he will find himself sternly reprimanded by another member. Persistent offenders are reported to the committee and may suffer the ultimate disgrace: exclusion from the elite circle. The club has always been intended to provide a civilized *milieu* in which like-minded men might meet, talk, read, play cards, or just doze in a comfortable leather armchair. There have always been overtones of privilege, and the archetypal clubman is the aristocrat who used to enjoy sitting in the bow-window of his St James's club on rainy London afternoons 'watching the damn' people get wet'.

Every club has its own special atmosphere, a function not only of its architecture and furnishings but more especially of its membership. The Duke of Devonshire insists that you can judge a man's character by the club to which he belongs. He has some expertise in this regard, since his paternal grandfather used to sit in the hall of his club (Brooks's) using a heavy walking stick to strike across the shins of any member he disliked.

Although the gentleman's club originated in London, it is also one of the legacies of Empire around the world. India, Hong Kong, Singapore, Malaysia and, of course, the United States all have their own versions. In venerable establishments like the Racquet Club in New York, silver-haired Republican mandarins of stupendous elegance may be seen studying the *Washington Post* or the *New York Times*, a glass of chilled Chardonnay ready to hand. Old Money people become very attached to their clubs and, of course, try to put down their sons for membership as early as possible. (Women are, nowadays, permitted to dine but most clubs still try to prevent them from actually joining, a fact which infuriates ardent feminists.) Many have long waiting lists and applications are carefully vetted, but the right family connections remain a formidable asset.

In London, Old Money can mainly be found in clubs like White's, the Athenaeum, Brooks's, and Boodle's. The Athenaeum is widely regarded as the ultimate British club. Behind its Attic façade, presided over by a statue of Athene, the goddess of wisdom, there are great drawing-rooms and a magnificent dining-room. It is notoriously stuffy: *Punch* once defined an imaginary conversation as 'anybody speaking to anybody in the Athenaeum'. The food is nothing to write home about, but Britain's Old Money families have never been as obsessed with food as, say, the French. Members may complain now and then, but they generally do so without passion. (One of the more memorable anecdotes recalls Sir Edward Lutyens's description of a dinner as 'a piece of cod which passeth all understanding'.)

It is, by and large, Old Money behaviour which, for most people around the world, represents what they regard as 'British style'. My American friends know exactly what they mean by it. To them, it is not just a matter of clothes, or possessions, or pageantry – though, of course, all are part of it. British style, they say, is mostly a matter of attitude.

As they see it, we have an enviable capacity for understatement. We do not boast about successes; indeed, we often seem to take an odd pleasure in failure. We do not feel a compelling need to have the 'biggest' of everything. We do not go for exaggerated praise: we tell people that something is 'not bad' rather than 'great'. We are reserved: we do not call people we have just met by their first names or ask in lifts: where are you from? We do not hustle, we do not push, we are not aggressive. We are formal: we keep our jackets and ties on even when it is very hot; we dress up for dinner; and we call our enemies in parliament 'honourable gentlemen'. We do not worship the new merely because it is new. We hang on to the old because we are used to it, like it, and believe in tradition. Our judges wear wigs; the Queen rides about in an ancient coach; our aristocrats continue to live in stately homes and castles. It is all delightfully quaint.

It is difficult for anyone living in the East End of London, or in a northern working-class area, to accept that such generalizations add up to a realistic portrayal of Britain in the 1980s. They know better. Even the average self-made millionaire or City yuppie would almost certainly reject the whole thing as absurdly superficial. He boasts, he hustles, he praises, he loves the new. It may not be Old Money style, but it is assuredly British. Look at the aggressive deals we make, the American companies we buy, the goods we ship abroad. How *dare* anyone say that we prefer failure to success?

I know that many Americans are equally irritated by the sweeping generalizations we make about them – the portrayal of the United States as a nation of grasping, selfish, pushy people who care only about material things. It is especially annoying to Old Money Americans who reckon that, when it comes to civilized behaviour, they are as polished as any of the British or other European families, if not more so.

They are right: the Old Money code is standard on both sides of the Atlantic. Old Money families in America find the brashness of New Money just as distasteful as their counterparts in Britain and elsewhere. They are willing to acknowledge some of the better features of New Money people – their energy, alertness, and willingness to take risks – but they despise, or profess to despise, what they regard as the ugly side of the coin: the greed, the ceaseless struggle for advantage, the vulgarity, the lack of sensitivity, the disloyalty shown to people who are supposed to be friends. They feel that, although they may not be able to compete financially, they have an obligation to civilize the New Money crowd, to show the *nouveaux riches* that money isn't everything, that one cannot and should not leave society at the mercy of market forces. This is what they believe, and this is what they try to teach their children so that they may continue the good work.

2

Little Princes

The royals are at the apex of Old Money. This is especially true in Britain, where they still play a major role in public affairs. They may not have the power they once had, but they retain considerable influence.

Prince Charles and Princess Diana have two young children, William and Harry. The first-born, known to the royal family as Wills, will one day be king. Some people question whether the monarchy can last that long, but at present it looks a safe bet.

It may not mean much to him yet. As Charles himself once said: 'I didn't wake up in my pram one day and say "Yippee!" I think it's something that dawns on you with the most ghastly, inexorable sense. Slowly you get the idea that you have a certain duty and responsibility. And I think it's better that way, rather than somebody suddenly telling you.' William is long past the pram stage and it has probably dawned on him already; he certainly knows that photographers regard him as someone of importance and has become quite adept at giving a royal wave to the cameras. But it is doubtful whether he has got round to thinking of it as a 'ghastly' prospect. When Charles made his comment he was an adult and fully acquainted with the demands and frustrations involved in the job. His son may come to feel the same, but it is much too early to tell.

Meanwhile, his parents are doing their best to strike a balance between normality and nobility. Princess Diana comes from an aristocratic family, but she has had an opportunity to find out what life is like outside the Old Money set. When she and Prince

Charles got engaged, the press hailed it as a fairytale come true. She may not have been Cinderella, but she had shared a flat with three girlfriends, shopped in the local supermarket, and worked as an assistant in a children's nursery. She relishes spending time with William and Harry, playing with them, reading them stories ('It's terribly important that parents should do this', she says) and dropping them off at school on many mornings. The little princes' two nannies and three security men have been encouraged to take them to play – with the children of commoners, even – in public parks and to other amusements such as the London Dungeon, where the boys spent an hour oohing and aahing over grisly exhibits of medieval torture instruments. When their mother took them to see *Snow White and the Seven Dwarfs* at a Leicester Square cinema, she treated them to a lunch of hamburgers and ribs at the Chicago Rib Shack, an American-style restaurant in Knightsbridge.

But it is difficult to bring them up as ordinary children. Despite all the efforts of their parents to make them feel 'normal', the reality is that the princes' lives, in the end, will be dictated by their birth. They are destined to be set forever apart. Having gone through the same process, Prince Charles is all too well aware of what awaits them.

His own parents also wanted their offspring to grow up as far as possible like other people's children. The Queen and Prince Philip were anxious to get away from the stiff-upper-lip training that was the lot of earlier generations of royals. They realized that they could never lead a 'normal' life, as the rest of us understand it, and they certainly did not want them to abandon the basic principles of the royal code of behaviour, which is even more strict than the Old Money code. But they wanted them to have a happy childhood; the obligations would be imposed soon enough. So Charles, too, was taken to public parks and London's museums, and he became the first heir apparent ever to go to school. He remembers visiting Harrods at the age of seven and asking Father Christmas for a bicycle.

Although he had become heir apparent at the age of three, when his mother succeeded to the throne, it took him some time to discover what it meant. His biographer, Anthony Holden, says that a few weeks before his fourth birthday Charles met a private secretary in a Palace corridor and asked his usual question: 'What are you doing here?' The secretary explained that he was going to see the Queen. 'Oh, yes?' said Prince Charles. 'Who's she?' On being told that the Queen was his mother, he appeared extremely puzzled. According to Holden, the courtier felt a qualm of guilt, 'as if I had given away the secret of Father Christmas'.

Prince Charles's life was far from ordinary. The family had several luxurious homes, including Buckingham Palace and Windsor Castle, and he had his own car with his own chauffeur. He also had a footman, a Palace servant called Richard Brown. 'Why haven't you got a Richard?' he innocently asked when out to tea with a friend one day.

It soon became clear to him that he was someone special, even if he was not sure why. Games in the park became impossible because they attracted the attention of the press, and his father once spanked him for sticking his tongue out at the crowd watching him drive down the Mall. He had to join the family on the Palace balcony, on special occasions, to acknowledge the enthusiastic cheers of his mother's subjects. His parents often went away on royal tours, and it was explained to him that the Queen had a duty to be with her subjects in other countries. He followed their journeys on a globe given to him by his nanny.

There were dancing and piano lessons at the Palace, but the Queen and Prince Philip decided that Charles should also have a formal education at suitable schools. They chose, to begin with, an exclusive day school for boys in Knightsbridge. One fellow pupil was the grandson of the new Prime Minister, Harold Macmillan. Charles put on his uniform and became number 102 on the school roll of 120. The staff were instructed to address him as Prince Charles, but he was plain Charles to the other boys. Inevitably, though, photographers and sightseers began to gather outside the school each day as news of his presence got around. His parents seriously considered abandoning the whole experiment, but the Queen's press secretary called the editors of all the newspapers and they agreed to co-operate. Charles stayed.

At the age of eight, he was sent to a private boarding school, Cheam, in a village near the Hampshire Downs. Prince Philip had been there before him, and he and the Queen felt that their son would benefit from a continued association with children outside the royal circle. Cheam was an old and exclusive school, so there was little chance that he might mix with anyone from a working–class background, but for the first time in his life he had to make his own bed, clean his own shoes, and wait on others at table. Again, the press snatched as many pictures as possible of the heir apparent, and again the Queen's secretary called the editors asking them to desist. If they failed to do so, he warned, she would have to leave his education to tutors behind the Palace walls and they, the editors, would be to blame. Charles had little more trouble during his four years at the school.

He was an average pupil, but his parents, happily, did not set any great store by academic achievement. Prince Philip had (and still has) strong views on the 'art of education'. It is, he once said, to 'combine a formal training with as wide a variety of experiences as is possible, including some which involve a calculated risk. I think education is intended to produce intelligent, morally strong, self-sufficient human beings willing and capable of improving the machinery of living which man has created for his enjoyment.' The Old Money view in a nutshell.

The royals' next choice surprised everyone: after finishing his spell at the preparatory school, it was announced, Charles would go to Gordonstoun in Scotland. Philip had been there, too, but he and his son had different personalities: Philip was outgoing and Charles introspective. Gordonstoun was known to be a tough school, with an unusual emphasis on outdoor and physical attainment. Would Charles be able to cope?

Prince Philip later told his biographer, Basil Boothroyd, that his son had been fully consulted. 'I said, here are the alternatives: you've seen Eton, you know the place, it's right on our doorstep (at Windsor), you can more or less come home any time you like. Its disadvantages are that every time you hiccup you'll have the whole of the national press on your shoulders. Also, Eton is frequently in the news, and when it is it's going to reflect on you. If you go to the north of Scotland you'll be out of sight, and they're going to think twice about taking an aeroplane to get up there, so it's got to be a major crisis before they'll actually turn up, and you'll be able to get on with things . . . and we had a general discussion and I said, "Well, it's up to you." '

Prince Philip, I suspect, was being deliberately naive about the press: he must have known that, if there are good pictures to be had, the prospect of 'taking an aeroplane' would not deter the ambitious photographers. The effect which the school's curriculum would have on his son was infinitely more important. It was, above all, designed to build strength of character: Gordonstoun's motto was *Plus est en vous* (There is more in you). But Charles took the bait.

Life at Gordonstoun was very different from that at the royal family's palaces. The accommodation was spartan and the boys were expected to follow a rigorous routine, which involved getting up at 7a.m., taking a cold shower, running round the garden before breakfast, and taking part in all kinds of games and physical tests. He was miserable at first, and asked his grandmother to intercede with his parents to take him away from this dreadful place. Although she was fond of him, she refused to do so. It would not be fitting for the heir to the throne to flinch from a challenge – what would people think? (It was a typical Old Money response: ordeals must be faced in order to demonstrate moral and spiritual superiority over the common people.)

To his credit, Charles adapted himself and even developed a genuine enthusiasm for outdoor pursuits, especially shooting and fishing. But the introspective side of his nature also led to a keen interest in the arts. He learned to paint and to play the cello, and when the school staged a production of Shakespeare's *Macbeth* he was delighted to be asked to play the leading role.

The Queen had promised Australia that her son would visit the country when he was older, and in 1966 he took a break from Gordonstoun and went to Geelong, a prestigious school which has a country outpost, Timbertop, some two hundred miles north of Melbourne. At Timbertop, too, the emphasis was on outdoor activities and he enjoyed himself immensely: he stayed for six months and later said that it was 'the most wonderful period of my life'. He felt that the Australians, who have a penchant for 'cutting down tall poppies', liked him for what he was, not just for *who* he was, and he thought that was great.

When he returned to Gordonstoun, he got down to the serious business of studying for the A-level examinations, so that he could qualify for a university place. He passed and chose to go to Trinity College, Cambridge. He told the Master that the subjects he was particularly interested in were archaeology and anthropology. He applied himself diligently, but royal duties kept getting in the way: his investiture as the Prince of Wales and as a knight of the Garter, and grand occasions like the State Opening of Parliament. On the lighter side, he was given an opportunity to take part in Trinity's drama productions. He showed a talent for comedy and made his debut in a satirical revue. He also joined the Cambridge Union and attended some of its debates. He eventually gained a degree – the first heir to the throne ever to do so. He then went into the armed services where he became the first heir to have captained a ship, the first to have flown helicopters and jets, the first to have made a parachute jump, and the first to have trained as a commando.

When he left service life, at the age of twenty-eight, I asked him for an interview. I was then the editor of *Punch*, a magazine he liked, and he had already written an article for us – a review of a book by one of his favourite people, Harry Secombe. We had told him that it did not have to be a comic masterpiece, to which he had responded: 'What do you mean it doesn't have to be a comic masterpiece? People have wandered feet first into the Tower for less than that . . .' I had also invited him to become a member of the *Punch* Table, and he had come to lunch and carved the initial 'C', surrounded by the Prince of Wales feathers, on the famous piece of furniture, as every member was required to do. So I felt that, despite his well-known suspicion of the press, I had a reasonable chance of getting him to talk about his experiences. He readily agreed, but said that he would like to set down his thoughts in writing, prior to the interview. The Palace duly sent me 3,000 words, which he had written in longhand but which someone had turned into a neat typescript. (The Palace is very conscious of the fact that an original MS by the Prince of Wales is a document that would fetch a good price at an auction.)

He said that he was glad that he went to Gordonstoun: 'it was an education which tried to balance the physical and mental, with the emphasis on self-reliance'. That, and his time in Australia, had imbued him with a love of adventure. 'I enjoy violent exercise of all sorts and relish an outdoor existence. I also enjoy trying something new and challenging – like diving under the Arctic ice not long ago. It was a fascinating and rewarding experience and I would never have forgiven myself if I had shirked the opportunity to dive. I think the appeal is basically to conquer one's fear of the unknown. There is enormous satisfaction in achieving something which is potentially hazardous and which requires concentration and self-discipline.'

In the services, he had particularly liked flying and he intended 'to try to continue my flying for as long as I'm medically and technically fit. I'm afraid I always prefer to do things rather than watch someone else doing them.'

At heart, he said, he was a complete countryman. 'I could be very happy occupying myself as a farmer.' But he accepted that it was not the life mapped out for him. He went on at length about the need for conservation. 'Unlike previous generations,' he said, 'we live in an age of immense and rapid change where "progress" tends to pressurize our lives almost to breaking point. Conservation, I believe, should be the result of a sensible, rational compromise between the need to progress and the need to "conserve" those things we value highly. Of course there are many occasions when it's impossible to compromise, but on the whole it is the conservationist's duty to draw people's attention to what beautiful things surround them and to make them aware of past mistakes so that we can all learn from other people's experience.'

He said that one of the things that kept him going was a sense of humour. 'I honestly cannot believe that there is a single occasion in life when it proves to be a handicap. It may turn out to be something of an embarrassment, such as when a wave of hysteria overcomes you when the atmosphere is meant to be serious, but that is slightly different. As far as I'm concerned, a sense of humour is what keeps me sane and I would probably have been committed to an institution long ago were it not for the ability to see the funny side of life.'

Monarchs and their heirs, alas, are paid to keep a straight face in public. Prince Charles has, since then, managed to curb his urge to laugh when he finds himself confronted by some pompous, red-faced, be-medalled official who insists on boring everyone with a tedious, cliché-ridden declaration of loyalty. He still manages to work jokes into his speeches, but he has become a much more serious person. He continues to campaign actively on behalf of conservationist causes and has become a much-quoted and controversial critic of modern architecture. But the most frustrating thing for someone once described as 'Action Man' is the fact that an heir to the throne does not really have a proper job. Charles carries out numerous public engagements each year, but they ceased to be a challenge a long time ago.

When we met after I had read his manuscript, he talked enthusiastically about a new charitable organization he had set up, called the Prince's Trust. Its aim, he explained, was to give practical assistance to deprived and disadvantaged youth, especially ethnic minorities. 'I cannot help feeling,' he said, 'that there is a great deal of untapped enthusiasm amongst young people in this country who want to involve themselves in the more challenging and adventurous aspects of community service but who find it difficult to know where to begin.' The Trust still exists, but it has not made the impact he had hoped for.

Now past the age of forty, Charles is locked into a way of life from which he knows there is no escape. He often envies others their freedom. When I gave up the editorship of *Punch* in 1979 he expressed surprise. Why had I done it? I said that I had been editor for ten years and felt it was time for a change: one should always try to do something new every ten years. 'That's all very well for you,' he said. 'What about *me*?'

It will be fascinating to see what happens to his children. Will they learn to share his love of the countryside, his concern for causes like conservation, his fondness for classical music? Will they, in time, develop the kind of passion for adventure their father had in his younger days? Will William feel as frustrated by the limitations of the role of heir apparent if and when Charles succeeds to the throne?

Prince Philip clearly had a strong influence on Charles and it seems reasonable to suppose that Charles, in turn, will also guide his children with a firm hand. They have already been to nursery school and in 1987 William joined the strict Wetherby school, reputed to tame boisterous boys. It is unlikely that either of them will be sent to Gordonstoun, unless they expressly wish it, but Charles will no doubt find other ways of teaching them at least some of the things he learned there. And he will surely want them to go to university. Charles has said that he hopes William will learn a lot by just hanging around with his dad, 'rather like a farmer's son picks up things by following his father around the farm'. But he knows that he will also need a formal education.

William and Harry live with their parents in Kensington Palace, a child's paradise with vast hallways and splendid gardens. Their collection of toys would be the envy of most other children: aside from the usual stuffed animals and jigsaws, there is William's troop of foot-high soldiers, a magnificent rocking horse (a present from Nancy Reagan), and his £30,000 miniature replica of his parents' XJS Jaguar (a gift from the manufacturers). Weekends are spent at Highgrove, the family's elegant country house in Gloucestershire, where they have their own Shetland ponies.

William is more outgoing than his younger brother, though this may change. Before he went to Wetherby, he was frequently reprimanded (usually by his nanny, but sometimes by his father) for his exuberant behaviour. Shouting orders at the Royal Highland Fusiliers and threatening them, 'my Dad is going to be King one day!', poking his tongue out at photographers, guzzling cherry pop in the royal larder, and dangling his brother out of the window were just some of his jolly japes that ended in tears by bedtime.

Princess Diana loves to give parties for them. They begin around 4.30 p.m., after school, and she usually invites eight or nine other boys and girls. She provides the kind of junk food all children love and usually hires an entertainer. She also buys little presents for everyone, which they happily carry away with them after the high-jinks are over.

William and Harry get pocket money, which they are expected to spend carefully. One day, though, William will be very rich. Prince Charles has a large income from the Duchy of Cornwall, which owns more than 127,000 acres of land and controls numerous tenancies in nine counties. He has never had to worry about mundane things like a mortgage: indeed, he has never even bothered to carry cash. When he inherits the throne, he will get most of the Queen's vast personal fortune. William will, in due course, get the Duchy. In manners of finance, as in so much else, he will be far from ordinary.

3

Royal Lives

Prince Charles may envy others their freedom, but there are plenty of people who would love to be in his privileged position. They include former monarchs like Constantine of Greece, who lost his throne in 1967.

Constantine – nicknamed Tino – has close links with other royal families. His sister is the Queen of Spain and he is a cousin of Prince Philip; his wife Anne-Marie is the sister of Queen Margrethe of Denmark.

His early years were unusual. When Germany invaded Greece during the Second World War, his mother took the children to the island of Crete, and later to Egypt and South Africa. The family went home after the war and in 1947 Constantine's father became king. The boy's future seemed settled and he was groomed accordingly. In 1964 King Paul died and Constantine succeeded him. He was twenty-four. Three years later, though, he fled Greece after staging an abortive counter-coup against the right-wing colonels. A subsequent referendum showed 69 per cent of Greeks in favour of a republic and 31 per cent for the monarchy.

Ex-monarchs are awkwardly placed: they are generally unwelcome in the land of their birth and they cannot easily find suitable employment elsewhere. Who, these days, needs a king? Constantine was more fortunate than others, like the Shah of Iran, in that he could at least make a new life in a country where he had friends and relatives: Britain. He already spoke excellent English (the children had a British nanny) and he moved to London. He is now based in Hampstead Garden Suburb. He and his wife are frequently on the Buckingham Palace and Windsor Castle guest list, and often stay at Balmoral and Sandringham. His loyal subjects still address him as 'Your Majesty'. The family has been helped financially by royalist shipowners and he has been allowed to keep property in Greece. This has made it possible for him to lead a comfortable life, and to send his own five children to a good school. But the Greek Government officially does not recognize him, which causes some embarrassment at diplomatic functions. He would like to return, but there seems little chance that he or his children will get the throne back.

Still, you never know. Spain gave up the monarchy when General Franco became head of state and absolute ruler, but it has since been restored. In today's turbulent world anything can happen.

There are many scions of royal families whose chances are much worse. The Comte de Paris, for instance. He is the great-great-grandson of Louis-Philippe, the last king of France, and the pretender to a throne which was abolished long ago. Indefatigable royalists would like to see the family restored to its former position, but they are very much in the minority.

The Comte is in his eighties, but he appears to have hopes for his 24-year-old grandson, Jean d'Orléans. In 1986 he named him as his successor after disinheriting his eldest son, the Duc de Clermont. The Duc's offence was to have divorced his wife, of whom the Comte was particularly fond. The elevation came as a surprise to Jean, a none-too-successful chocolate salesman, who had described his grandfather's followers on previous occasions as clowns. 'I'd rather stay in chocolate,' he had then declared.

Some of Europe's other royal houses have produced successful businessmen: they have long ago come to terms with the fact that the old days are over and have made the best of whatever the world has to offer. But there are also many cases of aimless, wasted lives.

Old Money people were shocked last year when they heard that Prince Ludwig Rudolph of Hanover and his wife, Princess Isabelle, had met self-inflicted ends. They had celebrated their wedding only thirteen months before at an Alpine castle in Austria, home of the bride's family. A son had been born soon afterwards. They were rich, and they had several splendid homes. What had gone wrong?

The answer, it emerged, was that the couple had king-size drug problems. At the time they became engaged, in fact, friends had commented: 'Now the hash princess has found her hash prince.' Both Isabelle and Ludwig were known to run with Germany's *Schickeria*, the chic crowd of investment bankers, rock musicians, and bored blue bloods among whom use of cocaine is fashionable. On several occasions, police had investigated the couple's drug connections, but had run up against a wall of silence among their titled friends.

Prince Ludwig was a great-grandson of Kaiser Wilhelm II. His family's wealth, based on immense ancestral landholdings, probably exceeded $200 million. He had no wish to play a part in public life: indeed, he showed little interest in any kind of work. He talked about a possible career as a rock producer, but most of the couple's time was devoted to having fun.

On the night of 28 November, their friends turned out at the family's magnificent summer residence in Austria to celebrate Prince Ludwig's thirty-third birthday. In the early hours, he found the 26-year-old Isabelle in their upstairs bedroom, lying prostrate on the bed. He tried for an hour to revive her before calling an ambulance, but his efforts were in vain. Isabelle was dead. Her death was later attributed to an overdose of cocaine.

When the police arrived, Ludwig had disappeared. A search was begun and they finally found him at dawn, sitting at the wheel of his blue Mercedes coupé, which had been parked in the nearby forest. He had shot himself with his hunting rifle, putting the muzzle into his mouth and pulling the trigger. The fun was over.

It was not the first royal suicide and I dare say it will not be the last. But I can well understand why Europe's aristocracy were shocked: they do not expect that sort of thing from their own kind. Royal children may go off the rails now and then, but their upbringing is supposed to protect them from such excesses.

It is, of course, easier if you are still part of a family with a clearly defined role. You know that you are in the public eye and that you cannot let the side down. Even those who are well down the line of succession recognize that they have certain obligations. Many keep busy by undertaking official engagements and getting involved in good works. Princess Anne, sister of Prince Charles, is a prominent example. She is a high-spirited lady, but she has inherited a great deal of her mother's dedicated sense of duty.

In her younger days, she attracted as much attention as her brother. Britain wanted a fairytale princess and she was the obvious candidate. But she never felt comfortable in the part. She was much too competitive and her abrasive wit often upset other people, especially the press.

Princess Anne became an expert rider while still in her teens and at the age of twenty won the European championship in her chosen field, the three-day event. It had nothing to do with her royal birth: she made it on her own. Understandably she took great pride in that – and still does. 'No one,' she once told me, 'ever thought that I was going to be in the least successful. Yes, I'm competitive. What's wrong with that? When I go into a competition I want to prove that I am as good as anyone else.' In 1976, she became the first British royal to compete in the Olympic Games.

The Princess married a commoner, army captain Mark Phillips, who shared her love of horses. (He, too, has represented his country in the Olympics.) They farm a 1,260 acre estate in Gloucestershire and have two children, Peter and Zara. She maintained her sense of humour: asked, on the BBC's Wogan show, what she would have liked to have been in another life she replied: 'A long-distance lorry driver'.

In recent years she has become well known for her diligent work on behalf of the Save the Children Fund. She became president in 1970, but the appointment did not make much of an impact at the time. Most people assumed that she would be a figurehead. She later added other honorary posts: Commandant of the Women's Royal Naval Service, Colonel-in-Chief of several regiments, Commander-in-Chief of the Ambulance and Nursing Cadets, and so on. But she said she would be a 'working president' and she has kept her promise.

The Fund is Britain's largest international children's charity. It will always come to the rescue of children in areas of natural disaster, but its main efforts are for the longer-term welfare of those in hunger, sickness, and need anywhere in the world, regardless of nationality, race, colour, or creed. The Princess has not only helped to raise large sums of money but has also travelled all over the world, visiting relief centres and clinics and displaying an encyclopaedic knowledge of their work. Staff and journalists who have accompanied her testify to the gruelling conditions that she endures on these journeys. She has been both moved and inspired by her encounters with children barely alive, or with grim prospects for the future, who can scarcely believe that she has come all this way to see them. An average month consists of more than fifty engagements, many on behalf of the fund. She may not have the good looks of her stylish sister-in-law, Princess Diana, but she is justly admired and respected.

Not long ago, I interviewed another determined royal lady – Princess Chulabhorn, youngest daughter of the King of Thailand. She has a doctorate in (of all things) organic chemistry, and spends a great deal of time in her laboratory at the University of Bangkok, or giving lectures at home and abroad. She is closely involved in her father's many community projects and heads a royal medical unit (she originally studied medicine) which makes frequent trips to remote villages. Astonishingly, the Princess has also made several hit records. She even wrote the words.

'I like to keep busy,' she said when we met at the moated Chitralada Palace. 'It means you don't have time to worry about anything.' Her husband is an air force pilot and they have two young children, who play happily in the palace grounds. In her spare time the Princess looks after several large fish ponds – ever practical, she raises carp which she sells to Japan and other countries.

This is the positive side of royal life. There is no reason why royals should not all try to keep busy. The lesser royals, and their children, generally have far more scope in their choice of activities than those at the very top. The one thing asked of them is that they should not bring the institution of monarchy into disrepute. They cannot afford to get drunk in public, tell dubious jokes, or be caught with drugs. In countries like Britain, they are also expected to steer clear of politics and of people who seek to exploit their titles. Business is one of the more difficult areas. Many corporations like the notion of having a royal on their board, and indeed people like Prince Michael and the Duke of Kent have accepted directorships. But all offers are carefully vetted by officials. It would never do to have a member of the royal family involved in a financial scandal.

It happened once, long ago. George I enthusiastically agreed to become a governor of the South Sea Company, which provided the ramp for Britain's first stock market boom, and for its most spectacular stock market crash. When the South Sea Bubble burst, furious shareholders rounded on both the King and his Cabinet Ministers. The lesson has not been forgotten. The royals may tour factories, and declare overseas trade fairs well and truly open, but they are not going to lend their names to fancy financial schemes or do anything as vulgar as promoting deodorants on television. The same unwritten rules apply to their children. Charity work is fine, and no one really minds these days if they join the board of a reputable company. They may even make television documentaries on non-political issues like architecture, as Prince Charles has done. But TV commercials are *out* and they should not be allowed to endorse New Money pastimes like take-over fights and asset stripping. It is a thin line, but there is always some royal adviser who will sternly remind them that there are some things which simply are not *done*.

They may, of course, ignore such advice. The only sanction available to the monarch is exclusion from the royal circle. In practice, that seldom happens. The royal code is understood and accepted by everyone who really matters.

The institution of monarchy itself is an anachronism, but it supplies a sense of unity, continuity and history. As long as the royals live up to expectations, and adapt themselves to changing circumstances, it has a remarkable capacity for survival. Europe still has seven reigning monarchs – those of Britain, Belgium, Holland, Denmark, Sweden, Norway and Spain. In addition, there are hereditary rulers of several principalities, including Monaco and Liechtenstein.

One of the most surprising survivors is the King of Sweden. His country has a strong republican following, and many people thought the monarchy would be abolished when King Gustav VI Adolf died in 1973. But his grandson, who succeeded him at the age of twenty-seven, has managed to hold on. He willingly agreed to changes in the Constitution, two years after the old man's death, which reduced his role to a merely ceremonial one.

Carl XVI Gustav had all the normal trappings of a progressive modern royal education: boarding school near Stockholm, followed by two and a half years training in the armed forces, and a special one-year course at Uppsala University, where he studied history, sociology, political science, fiscal law and economics. But thereafter his grandfather insisted that the young man involve himself in almost every aspect of Swedish daily life. He attended government sessions, served a tour of duty at his country's UN mission in New York, and worked for a while at the embassy in London.

In those early days, Carl Gustav acquired a reputation as something of a playboy. He was handsome and charming, and in the late 60s and early 70s he lived what seemed to the outward eye a more than pleasure-loving life. But he settled down after his marriage to the daughter of a German businessman, Silvia Sommerlath. They had met at the Munich Olympics, where she was working as a hostess. Silvia was not only an attractive young woman but was also endowed with a great deal of common sense. She told an interviewer: 'I don't have the impression that I am abandoning my professional life in becoming queen. I have simply changed one job for another.' The Swedish people took to her at once, and the couple have become very popular. They live a simple, unstuffy, non-pompous existence and they have three children to complete the picture of a modern young family. They seem almost consciously to act out their parts as 'ordinary people'. The only observable ruffle in this sea of calmness appears to have been back in 1979 when their only son, Prince Carl Philip, was born and automatically supplanted his older sister, the Princess Victoria, as heir to the throne. It was too much for Sweden's *avant garde* Government and Parliament. They immediately passed a new Act saying that henceforth the first-born would always succeed, irrespective of sex. The baby prince was in turn supplanted by the child princess. Carl Gustav was reputed to have been strongly opposed to this down-grading of his infant son, but he was careful not to vent his feelings in public.

The Government has since passed another new law, giving the monarchy the same rights as ordinary citizens to prevent their photographs being used for commercial purposes without their permission. The faces of the royal couple and their children were being exploited by all manner of companies to promote just about every product under the sun, from tins of sardines and pork sausages to brassières. Even Sweden's socialists felt that the line had to be drawn somewhere.

The Danish monarchy has also endured through adaptation. Queen Margrethe II first learned of her destiny in 1953, when a referendum overturned the Salic law which said that only males could inherit the throne. It sent Margrethe, then thirteen, into a rigorous programme of preparation for her future role. 'My first reaction was utter terror,' she later said. 'Then my parents made me see there could be no higher service that I could render to my country. Now my job never ends. It involves me 24 hours a day, 365 days a year, and will last my entire life.'

While studying at the London School of Economics in the mid-sixties, Margrethe met French diplomat Count Laborde de Monpezat and they got to know each other better in Scotland. They decided to get married and he is now the Prince of Denmark. The Danes were not too sure about him at first. 'Some people,' he recalled when I interviewed him in Copenhagen, 'thought it was an insult to Danish manhood that the heir to the throne should marry a Frenchman. So they were quite aggressive to begin with. It was easier to attack a woman. They criticized the colour of my tie, the length of my hair, and my poor command of the Danish language. I said at the time that I had the most difficult job in the world, and I meant it. Things are much better now, but it is still a difficult job because it is not a definite job.' He has done a lot of work for the Red Cross and has helped to promote Danish industry abroad. He also looks after his family's vineyards in France. He and Margrethe have two boys, and like the Swedish royals they try to live like an 'ordinary family' – though, obviously, they can never be quite like the rest of us.

Crown Prince Frederik is twenty and his brother is nineteen. The Queen startled her subjects recently when she told an interviewer that she had been a poor mother. 'I was not with them nearly often enough,' she said. 'There simply wasn't the time. I neglected them and have felt guilty ever since.' Happily, the 'neglect' appears to have caused them little harm. They are high-spirited young men whose love of fast cars has earned them the popular nickname 'the Turbo-Princes'.

The transformation from commoner to royal can be particularly hard on consorts, because they are not trained for it and because, as Queen Margrethe's husband said, they do not have any precise function. Not everyone is prepared to take it on, as Prince Charles discovered. Some of the girls he went out with prior to marrying Diana made it perfectly clear that they had no wish to become the future Queen.

Queen Elizabeth herself did not become heir to the British throne until her uncle abdicated, when she was ten, and her father took his place. She has never complained about her fate, but there must have been times, over the long years, when she has regretted that life did not take a different turn.

Juan Carlos of Spain had even less reason to believe, as a young child, that he would one day become his country's head of state. His grandfather, Alfonso XIII, had been forced to cede the throne of the Spanish Bourbons to the ill-fated Republic of Spain, and Juan Carlos was born in exile. He did not see Spain until the age of nine. General Franco was the undisputed ruler after the Civil War, which ended in April 1939. Franco said that the monarchy would be restored eventually, but he did not name a date and it was not made clear who would be king. Juan Carlos was not next in line; his grandfather had renounced his rights in favour of his third son, Don Juan, the Count of Barcelona and father of Juan Carlos. Franco, however, did not want Don Juan to succeed him. He was too liberal, thought to be too British (his mother had been a British princess) and, in any event, too long out of Spain. So the ageing dictator took the boy prince under his wing, with the somewhat reluctant consent of his father, and groomed him as a possible successor – though it was not until 1969, when he was thirty, that he was officially declared heir to the throne. Franco remained at the helm until his death six years later. When Juan Carlos became King, he immediately gave most of his prerogatives to the Parliament in a gesture of allegiance to democracy.

Sofia, who married him in 1962, has said that he was 'a very lonely child'. He saw little of his family after Franco took control of his life, and the General certainly did not act like a father. He was sent to Madrid's oldest private school, and thereafter to the Military Academy and to the city's university. He was shy and introverted, but he has since come out of his shell. When, one evening in 1981, extremist right-wing Civil Guards seized the entire Spanish Cabinet gathered in Parliament and General Milans del Bosch ordered the tanks into the streets of Valencia in a would-be revolution in the name of the King, it was Juan Carlos who preserved the democratic process by ordering the arrest of the officers responsible.

Yet, for all his strength of purpose, he is very casual about the surface appearance of power and status. He and Queen Sofia decided to stay in their home on the outskirts of Madrid, instead of moving to the Royal Palace, and their summer house in Majorca (where Charles and Diana have been frequent guests) is no more grand than many another large villa on that agreeable Mediterranean island. Their three children have grown up and lead their own lives; the Crown Prince spent time in the armed forces before going on to university and takes a keen interest in astronomy.

The longest apprenticeship of any of the present generation of monarchs was served by the new Emperor of Japan, Akihito. He became heir to the throne on the day he was born in 1933, but he had to wait fifty-five years before becoming Emperor.

During the war he was sent to a mountain resort, well away from the capital, and when it was over he went to a private school for the Japanese elite. He began English studies in 1948 with Elisabeth Gray Vining, an American teacher from Philadelphia, who was hired to make him aware of the need to internationalize the monarchy. This period of his education has received both praise and criticism from Japanese scholars: supporters have seen it as a modernizing element in the imperial system while critics have argued that it has made him too fond of Western ways.

He spent eight months in Europe before completing his studies at Gakushkin University. Various marriage partners were presented to him at this time, but he was determined to make his own choice – which turned out to be a commoner who had beaten him in a tennis competition. The union captured the imagination of the Japanese people, and they were delighted when, in the years that followed, they produced three children, including a son who is now known as Crown Prince Naruhito.

During his long years as heir, Akihito did a great deal of travelling, attended official events, and continued to be an avid tennis player. He also wrote traditional Japanese poetry and, like his father, developed an interest in marine biology. He has written many articles and a book on the subject. His life will inevitably be more restricted in future but it is unlikely to be as rigidly formal as that of his controversial father.

I would not want to swap places with any of them, but I would not have minded being born into a family like the Grimaldis, who have ruled the sunny playground of Monaco for generations. They have an easy task: their principality is smaller than New York's Central Park. The world finds them amusing, but it does not regard them as important. They can go where they please, and do pretty much what they like. Their subjects can be relied upon to stay loyal as long as they continue to produce heirs and help to attract tourists and the tax-dodging rich.

Prince Albert has inherited the dashing good looks of his late mother, Princess Grace, and has a free-wheeling lifestyle. He is a keen scuba-diver and powerboat-racer. Educated at Amherst College, Massachusetts, he has prepared himself for his future task by learning banking and international law in New York – appropriate subjects for the ruler of a tax haven.

Princess Caroline, one year older, is an olive-skinned beauty whose exuberant behaviour has made her the darling of the gossip columns. In 1978 she married social-climbing Paris entrepreneur Philippe Junot, seventeen years her senior, but quickly regretted it. They got a divorce, and she later took up with handsome Italian oil heir Stefano Casiraghi, five years younger than her. They married in 1983, and have three young children. More responsible now, she acts as Monaco's First Lady and is involved in various cultural activities, notably the Monte Carlo Ballet. Graceful and self-assured, she leads a full and happy life. Home for the family is a very private, spacious house with an interior garden that Caroline was given by her father Prince Rainier and which she decorated herself. The children do not have titles: they are simply Casiraghis and that is how they are being brought up. She hopes to have more. 'I love being a mother,' she says.

4

From Cowboy to Duke

The royals have the grandest titles, but some of the lesser members of the aristocracy have bigger fortunes. In Britain's Old Money circles, Queen Elizabeth is well ahead of the rest of the field. None of the other members of the royal family, though, are as rich as a young man who, in his teens, worked as a cowboy and who at one time wanted to be a professional footballer. (He even had a trial for Fulham.) Instead he presides over a global property empire which is reckoned to be worth £2 billion.

Gerald Cavendish Grosvenor is one of the small band of British dukes. Some are royal but others are not; the title is the highest honour the Crown may bestow on a person not of royal blood. Some of the present company had ancestors who, like Marlborough and Wellington, won great battles for their country. Others owe their exalted status to men who performed outstanding services in political and public life. There are fewer of them than in the past because, since 1900, only members of the royal family have been added to their ranks. The Government can do without them these days; the last duke to be prime minister was Wellington in 1828.

The basis of ducal fortunes has always been land. Original grants were augmented by well-planned marriages to owners of other estates or heiresses with ancestral acres of their own. Estate taxes have played havoc with the system in the twentieth century, but several dukes still own more land than the Queen.

Grosvenor is the sixth Duke of Westminster, Marquess of

Westminster, Earl Grosvenor, Viscount Belgrave, Baron Grosvenor, and fifteenth baronet of Eaton. His family has owned property in Cheshire for 900 years and in London for 300 years. Its prize possession is a large part of fashionable Mayfair and the whole of Belgravia, which was marshland when one of the Duke's ancestors acquired it in 1678. It has also kept the estate in Cheshire, added another in Lancashire, and built up other property interests in many other parts of the world, including farmland, office blocks, and shopping centres.

The Duke, nicknamed 'Himself' by his peasantry, is an amiable, boyish-looking six-footer who travels many thousands of miles each year on business. He was born and bred on a farm in Northern Ireland, and first learned that he was going to inherit the Westminster money when he was fifteen. It had actually been put in his name much earlier, but no one had seen fit to tell him. (He is still grateful rather than annoyed: it meant, he says, that he had 'an infinitely happier childhood'.) To minimize death duties, the legendary four-times-married second Duke had drawn up a canny will before his death in 1953. It bypassed the elderly heirs, who became third, fourth, and fifth Dukes, in favour of baby Gerald.

His formal training for the role was virtually non-existent. His father never even sat down with him to discuss it. He attended Sunningdale and Harrow, but only managed to get two 'O' Levels and left school at eighteen to work on ranches in British Columbia and New Zealand. When he returned to London he worked for a short time with a firm of estate agents, but then his father had a stroke and Gerald assumed the reins at twenty-one. He was about as well-qualified for the task as the office boy, but happily there were older, very experienced trustees to guide him.

In 1978 he married nineteen-year-old Natalia Phillips, a former *Vogue* secretary, and their honeymoon was spent touring the various overseas estates. A year later he became Duke of Westminster in his own right. All those early longings for fame on the football field were discarded – though not, perhaps, forgotten. He joined the Queen's Own Yeomanry as a part-time soldier, which was not quite as glamorous but more suitable for a duke. 'I love it,' he told an interviewer. 'You know, it was Winston Churchill who said that the only time the Grosvenors were any good was when they were at war. I suppose there's a lot to be said for that.' In earlier times he might have gone on to lead his troops into battle, which he would clearly have enjoyed, but he settled readily enough for wearing an officer's uniform on weekend exercises and spending his weekdays as a business warrior.

Like most Old Money people, he does not feel that the inheritance is his to spend. He firmly believes in the principle that his mandate is to hand over to the next generation a family estate that is in better shape than the one he was given. (His great sadness is the absence, so far, of a son to carry on the title. He and Natalia have two daughters. The Grosvenors have a bad record in producing male heirs, but he is confident that this feat too will be achieved, all in good time.)

'The pull of history is very strong,' he says. 'People tend to ignore it or just think it's something to commercialize, but it's a very stabilizing factor. And it's my duty to continue it.' To that end, he spends his days functioning largely like the chairman of a major multinational corporation. The estate is run by a board of six trustees, of which he is the head. He is proud of the fact that, in the past decade, the emphasis has been on aggressive expansion.

The Grosvenors have long benefited from Britain's peculiar leasehold system. Instead of selling the freehold of a property they have been able to sell only the lease for a specified period of time. They have usually limited this period to 99 years, which has enabled them to capitalize on rising real-estate prices. Some of London's best-known establishments are on land owned by the duke, including Claridge's, the Connaught, and even the American Embassy. He is, officially, the landlord of many thousands of people – myself included. In 1967, however, the Government passed a Leasehold Reform Act, which gave tenants the right to buy their freeholds. This has since been endorsed by the European Court of Human Rights. The estate has, therefore, been forced to sell more than it would like and the next generation will own less of Mayfair and Belgravia. But the millions released by these sales are being used to buy and develop other interests. The Duke has built a dozen major shopping centres and has extended his overseas holdings, notably in the United States. The Leasehold Reform Act may be irritating, but it is not causing him any sleepless nights.

Home for Gerald and Natalia Grosvenor is the 13,000-acre family estate just outside the pretty little town of Chester, about two hundred miles north of London. His house, Eaton Hall, is the only modern 'stately home' to be found in the English countryside. Designed by British architect John Denys in 1973, it is a vast marble and glass structure which has been compared unflatteringly to an office building or a mausoleum. The Duke says that when the decision was made to build a new residence they did not want a mock Georgian mansion; they wanted to 'leave something of this architectural period for future generations'. They may or may not appreciate it; his ancestors would probably have hated it.

Gerald spends roughly a third of his time in Chester, a third in London, and a third in various places around Britain and the rest of the world. He had another home in London, and commutes between the two in his own helicopter, bearing the ducal insignia. He says that he does not see as much of his children as he would like, and that he sometimes wonders if he has got his priorities right. It is a good question. 'Now and then,' he says, 'I find myself struggling for an answer.' He claims that he 'howled with laughter' when a recent *Sunday Times* survey put his fortune at £2.3 billion and insists that the figure is 'not actually madly relevant'. But he acknowledges that he is the richest man in Britain. He certainly doesn't *have* to work. Challenge is the thing, he says, that and the satisfaction – 'however trite it might sound' of doing it right.

From the outset he knew, above all, that he wanted to stay in England. 'All sorts of people were urging one to push off, but I have yet to meet a tax exile who is happy.' He had a vision – 'I knew what I wanted to achieve, and I knew the traditions I wanted to protect – the historical assets as much as the commercial side. The task was to try and run a modern business, without compromises to the values of the past. That was the challenge, and I must say I relish it.' The business will continue to grow, he says, 'but I hope with sensitivity. If the returns or investment aren't as sexy as they could be, because there are things that need to be done, irrespective of profit, we can afford to be choosy – that's my privilege. There are no shareholders breathing down one's neck.' He is patron of some 140 charities, but business comes first. 'One's brain is buzzing,' he says.

5

Children of the Sun

'I would prefer,' the Maharajah of Kashmir told me at his home in Delhi, 'if you called me *doctor* Karan Singh. Any moron can be a maharajah; not every moron can be a doctor.'

Karan Singh talked at length, and without regret, about his remarkable childhood. He was born during a family holiday in Cannes (his father had checked into the entire third floor of the Martinez) and he recalled that that event 'triggered off an almost delirious wave of enthusiasm' among the people of Jammu and Kashmir, then the largest princely state in India. The next three days were public holidays, all children were given sweets and told to pray for the long life of the prince, and when his father brought him home there was a 'staggering array of feasts, receptions, illuminations, free cinema shows, and sundry festivities'. He made his first speech at eleven, was married six years later to a Nepalese princess of thirteen, and became regent at eighteen.

This was, at the time, the customary lot of the heir to one of the great fortunes in one of the poorest countries in the world. The birth of a son ensured the continuity of the dynasty. Fathers could – and did – die at an early age. Daughters were of no consequence, but the eldest boy had his future mapped out for him from the day he emerged from his mother's womb. He was as important a figure as a Prince of Wales is in Britain today. He might be called upon to become a ruler of his people while barely out of the cradle. So a lavish debut was considered essential.

One maharajah's arrival was celebrated with such a sea of champagne that, for the rest of his life, he would be known as

Bubbles. The Gaekwar of Baroda received officials of the Raj at the age of twelve wearing jewels worth millions of dollars. He would probably have preferred to show off his toys, but it simply was not *done*. The ostentatious display of wealth was an essential part of the elaborate effort to demonstrate the natural superiority of princely children.

The British, of course, understood the game and were keen to help: by manipulating the vainglorious maharajahs and their offspring they could establish and maintain control of a vast country with a comparatively small number of people.

India's princes had a long history of bloody infighting, not only with the rulers of other states but also with members of their own families. A famous example was that of Shah Jehan, creator of the sublime Taj Mahal. When he fell ill in 1657, four of his sons went to war to decide the succession. Within a year, one of them emerged, took the throne, and imprisoned his ailing father. He beheaded one of his brothers, wrapped up the head, and sent it to Shah Jehan, who opened the package eagerly, thinking it a present.

Britain later exploited these divisions, but did not simply take over. Many of the princes went on ruling in splendour, under British supervision. They kept their palaces and their jewels. Their egos were gratified in all sorts of ways. One of the more absurd (or so it seems today) was the allocation of gun salutes. The rajahs were at the lower end of the scale of bombardment – nine guns. The maharajahs could expect to be saluted by thirteen guns or more, and the most important princes (including Dr Karan Singh's ancestors) were entitled to twenty-one. Official pleasure or disfavour could quickly be registered by adding or subtracting a couple of guns. The princes were so jealous of their noisy privileges that it turned out to be a very effective means of getting them to toe the line.

They were encouraged to send their children to public schools like Eton, where they were shown how to become English gentlemen and usually went on to Oxford or Cambridge. On their return, they stoutly defended the English way of life. Many princes added knighthoods to their already formidable list of titles. They acquired a fleet of Rolls-Royces, and during the summer they would visit Britain for Ascot or the Derby.

All this was threatened when India gained its independence. At

43

first, the princes were merely stripped of power. In 1971, they also lost what remained of their incomes and privileges, including the titles themselves. They still visit Britain, where they can usually count on a warm welcome from British aristocrats, who are often old school friends. But the days of glory are over.

Karan Singh was elected head of his state and carried on for another eighteen years. But in 1967 he decided to go into politics and, armed with his doctorate in philosophy, went into Parliament. He voluntarily renounced his privy purse (the only former ruler to do so) and eventually became a minister in Mrs Gandhi's government. When we met, he told me proudly of his ability to attract vast audiences.

'One doesn't want to be respected for one's past,' he said. 'One wants to be respected for what *one* is. I am a writer, a philosopher, and a social reformer. I am deeply interested in the problems of the nuclear age.' He gave me some of the books he had written and talked enthusiastically about his association with various cultural institutions. He said that one of his former palaces, in Srinagar, has been turned into a hotel and his palace in Jummur had become a museum and a library. He was not as wealthy as his father had been, but that did not bother him: 'I am not obsessed with money.' His own sons, he added, would have to work for a living.

The next day I went to see the former Maharajah of Jodhpur. Dr Singh had been modest by maharajah standards, but Jodhpur was even more unassuming. There was, however, no attempt to display any love of democratic labels. 'His Royal Highness will see you now,' an aide informed me after a short wait.

'His Royal Highness' readily admitted that he enjoyed the privilege still attached to the title. 'The Government may no longer respect it,' he said, 'but the people do.' He was born in 1948, so he never really knew the days of princely splendour. Having to give them up, he said, 'was more a blow to my mother'. He went to Eton and Oxford, and remained abroad for many years. For a time, he was India's High Commissioner in Trinidad.

I asked him if he would have liked to have been a ruler. 'It's hard to say,' he said. 'There is a lot to be done under the present system, and I would like to play my part.'

Like Karan Singh, he had to decide what to do with his main legacy – an immense palace of marble and red sandstone in Jodhpur, designed by a British architect best known for his

English town halls. He concluded that it should become a hotel, 'to keep it running and to provide employment for my staff'. He also has a house in the delightful hill resort of Abu, but still likes to make regular visits to England. His two sons had their names put down for Eton at birth.

Was he still a millionaire? 'In what currency?' he replied. He went on: 'I'm not wealthy by international standards, and even in India there are some industrialists who have far more money than I have. They have liquid assets: we have dead assets. Our palaces look impressive, but they don't produce a large income and no one wants to buy them. My palace now belongs to a charitable trust. I also have some investment income, and I run a farm about thirty miles from Jodhpur – but if you have ever tried farming, you know what a risky business it can be.'

'His Royal Highness' said that he was keen to preserve India's architectural heritage. 'But there is so much of it, and there are more important priorities in a poor country.' He thought that people were more inclined these days to respect what remains of the past – there was less vandalism – and tourism had undoubtedly helped. But many former princes had been forced to give up the struggle, especially those whose homes were away from the main communication routes.

The children of the maharajahs are growing up in a very different India, an India which has become one of the world's leading industrial nations, with its own space and nuclear programmes, computer manufacturers, steel plants, and offshore oil rigs. New Money now sets the pace. In Bombay, the financial capital, ambitious young men dream of becoming millionaires – and some of them do.

Bombay's leading industrial enterprises are, for the most part, dynastic concerns. But they have been built by men who, in the old days, would have had to be content with minor roles. Dhirajlal Ambani is a notable example. The son of a rural schoolmaster, he started as a small-time trader. He has since built up a synthetic yarn, textiles and petrochemicals empire which is now India's third largest private-sector corporation. His sons are actively involved in the business.

Bombay's New Rich live in style. They have taken over the clubs where the elite used to gather in the days of the Raj, and many send their children abroad to be educated – though, nowadays, many prefer a university in America rather than Britain. They have elegant homes, but they do not generally go in for the ostentatious display of wealth. You have to go inside their homes to see what money can buy – big rooms (probably with a fine view of the sea), splendid furnishings, impressive art collections, plenty of servants. They may still show respect for the former titles, but being the son of a prince no longer guarantees automatic entry to the ruling circle. He is expected to work for his place in the sun, like everyone else.

6

The Fords and the Kennedys

America's Old Money families may lack titles, and their history may not go back as far as those of Europe and countries like India, but dynasties like the Kennedys, the Rockefellers, du Ponts, Mellons, and Fords are accustomed to being regarded as the equivalent of royals. Donald Trump, one of the *nouveaux riches*, calls their offspring 'members of the Lucky Sperm Club' – people who are bred to be aristocrats and who never have to prove anything to anyone. Some undeniably feel that way, but Trump is wrong to assume that *all* of them do. Many share the Duke of Westminster's view that they have a duty to hand over to the next generation a family estate which is in better shape than the one they were given.

Henry Ford II told me, a few years before his retirement, that he felt a strong responsibility to the Ford Motor Company. 'I wouldn't be happy with myself if I didn't fulfill that responsibility.' It was the kind of remark one felt compelled to take with a large pinch of salt, but his record supported it: he had run the business for three decades with steely determination.

Lee Iacocca, who found out just how determined Henry could be, later tried to portray him as a spoiled rich kid who did not deserve the legacy which fell into his lap. 'Henry,' he said, 'never had to work for anything. Maybe that's the bane of rich kids who inherit their money. They go through life tripping through the tulips wondering what they would have been without daddy.' But Iacocca, who was fired by Henry, can hardly be called an impartial observer. His comments, it seems to me, were largely inspired by

47

envy and resentment. He felt that he was better qualified to run the Ford empire than Henry, and when he was sacked he thought that he could score off his old boss by exploiting the public's sympathy for the underdog who has to struggle for recognition. He went on to become a great success at Chrysler, so his self-confidence was clearly justified. But his remarks were unfair: Henry pushed himself hard and the company saw massive expansion during his long reign.

Henry died of pneumonia in 1987, so the feud is over. The business is no longer run by a family member, but direct descendants of the founder still have about 40 per cent of the shareholder votes and two of the fourth-generation Fords have made it plain that they would like to be in the driving seat. They are Henry's son Edsel II, and Edsel's cousin, William Clay Ford Jr. Both are members of the board and are among the company's senior executives. It is entirely possible, therefore, that one day a member of America's best-known industrial dynasty will, once again, be in charge of the business created by Henry's grandfather.

Neither of them *needs* to work. Edsel is reckoned to have about $87 million. They could easily afford to spend the rest of their lives 'tripping through the tulips'. Edsel and Billy are driven by a different kind of need – the need to be respected for their abilities, their professionalism, their dedication to an enterprise which the Fords have always felt belonged to them even though they have had to let in outside managers and shareholders. It is not simply a matter of pride, although that certainly comes into it. For them, as for so many other children of the rich, it is also a matter of proving that they have *merit*, that they are as good as anyone.

The Young Fords are very much aware that their name and heritage no longer guarantee automatic promotion. They also recognize that many of their colleagues think that they have an unfair advantage. It is the old story: people assume that you are getting special treatment because of who you are, not because of what you can do. Billy says that when he started work at Ford he felt that he had to be the first in and the last out, and volunteer for all the jobs that nobody else wanted, just to prove himself.

Edsel, who is nine years older, was groomed from childhood for a company job. He scraped through high school and college, and did not graduate until he was twenty-five. He is understandably defensive about it. College, he says, was not his forte. 'I am a doer, not a thinker.' He feels that he should be judged on how good a manager he is, not on how well he did at school. He joined the Ford Motor Company in 1974 as a product analyst and later became marketing plans manager. In 1985, he was appointed director of sales and operations at the Lincoln-Mercury Division. Others say he is very competent, but have not yet made up their minds whether he is good enough to become chief executive officer.

When he first went into the business, the press made comparisons between him and Prince Charles. (The two men were both born in the same year, 1948.) Edsel was annoyed. 'The crown prince thing is so stupid,' he said. 'There is no crown prince; I'm not the heir apparent. Ford is not a private company like it was when my dad took it over. The board of directors is responsible for running the company. If I get to the top, it will be because I worked to get there, not because I was born into it.'

Like Henry, he has always had a passion for cars. 'As a little kid,' he recalls, 'I used to collect small plastic replicas and trade them like baseball cards. Later my father would bring home a car every weekend. I used to drive them up and down the driveway long before I had my license.' As a teenager he visited race tracks all over the world and he spent one summer in California with a company-sponsored team. Today he owns a pair of vintage 12-cylinder Ferraris. He is also keen on powerboat racing. Inevitably, this has brought accusations that he is something of a playboy. He indignantly denies it. Other people, he points out, have hobbies of their own and no one ever says that they cannot combine them with being professional managers.

Billy is more studious than Edsel. He graduated from Princeton and earned a master's degree in management from MIT's Sloan School. He did not give the company much thought in college. In his senior year, when all his friends were looking for jobs, he also scheduled interviews with a couple of banks. But then, he says, 'I realized that everything I had came from the Ford Motor Company. And so I thought I owed it to my heritage, so to speak, to give the company my best shot.' His father asked him if he was sure that it was really what he wanted to do. 'You don't have to do it on my account,' he said. 'Life's too short to be miserable. Do what you want. But do it well.'

After joining the business in 1979, he moved through half a

dozen brief assignments and was then given a job in product planning. He did not much care then for the Ford bureaucracy and at one time considered starting a company of his own, perhaps a mail-order business for fly fishermen. But he stayed with Ford and went to Switzerland in 1986, to supervise the sales and deal support organization. He would like to be the boss, but he is not obsessive about it. If it does not work out, he says, he will do something else important, either inside or outside the company.

Both Edsel and Billy are married, with young children. Edsel has named his eldest son, now nine, Henry III – a clear indication of his aim to continue the dynasty. He seems to be more determined to get the top job. His two sisters, Charlotte and Ann, strongly support his campaign for a bigger family say in the way the business is run, but they are not candidates for the top position.

Edsel himself is named after the founder's father, who also fought hard for what he considered to be his birthright. His life was in many ways a sad one – a fact which had a profound influence on his own son, Henry II, who once said that he took on the burden of running the business 'to make it up to my father, to show the world that my father's seed was made of good-enough stuff'.

The first Edsel's problem was the familiar one of how to cope with an autocratic patriarch – a volatile, self-centred, eccentric genius who, although he loved his son, could not bear to give him any real power. The struggle went on until Edsel died at the early age of forty-nine, a rich but unhappy man.

Edsel was born into the Ford Motor Company. As a baby he was taken for a ride in his father's first car. As a teenager he spent much of his time in the family garage, taking apart and reassembling foreign cars. Later he took cars on cross-country road tests. There was never any question of doing anything else. He wanted to go to an Ivy League university, but Henry Ford felt that his own experience proved that higher education was an affectation. He maintained that his son could learn everything that was worth knowing at the Ford Motor plant. Edsel was disappointed, but obeyed. At this stage, he still worshipped his father. 'He is a great man,' he told reporters.

When he turned twenty-one, the 'great man' took him to a Detroit bank and told one of the vice-presidents: 'I have a million in gold deposited here. This is Edsel's birthday and I want him to have it.' It was the kind of gesture which, to most of us, would be a dream come true. A million is useful at any time, but it meant a lot more in those days than it does now. It could have bought *freedom*, and Edsel should probably have taken the money and bolted. But he did not. Henry would have been furious and Edsel did not want to make him furious. Besides, he thought his destiny was settled: he expected to become president of the Ford Motor Company and he looked forward to it. 'I have not worked out a separate business philosophy for myself,' he said. 'It has not been necessary because on all material points I agree absolutely with my father's philosophy. I do not merely accept his beliefs: I feel as strongly about them as he does.'

He got his wish, eventually, but he soon discovered that being president did not mean that he could actually *do* anything. The old man constantly overturned his decisions and humiliated him in front of Ford executives in order to show who was boss. Edsel decided to put up a new administrative building; his father stopped the project. He wanted to build small, inexpensive aeroplanes; Henry said: 'That's no good. Stop it.' When sales of the Model T dropped alarmingly, Edsel commissioned designers to work on a new car. When he told Henry about his plans, the old man said: 'Rub it out.' Ford executives, not surprisingly, decided that Edsel's orders did not count. When he fired a senior manager who had defied him the man promptly went to Henry, who told him that he could stay. And so it went on.

The old man not only denied his son the authority that was supposed to go with the job but also made a point of setting others against him. He said it was to 'toughen up' Edsel, but the real reason was that it helped to keep power in his own hands. The strongest of these rivals was a young man named Harry Bennett, who was about the same age as Edsel when he first came to work for Ford in 1917. He had been a boxing champion in the US Navy, and Henry made him head watchman at the plant. Bennett was an uneducated man, and he knew nothing about the motor industry. But he was tough and soon took charge of a newly formed services department, which looked after security and maintained order among the workforce. When trouble broke out on the labour front it was Bennett, not Edsel, who was asked to deal with the unions. His influence grew rapidly in the years that followed. Ford began to treat him like a surrogate son and Bennett felt strong enough to ignore Edsel, whom he contemptuously described as 'that weakling'.

As Henry got older, his behaviour became even more capricious and, at times, sadistic. Edsel bore the brunt of it. His health started to suffer and he seriously thought of quitting. He had married an attractive woman in 1916 and had four children of his own: why not devote more time to them? But friends urged him to hold on. Henry would not live for ever; it would be foolish to endanger the children's heritage. Edsel reluctantly agreed. But the fights continued and after another showdown with Bennett, which he lost, he finally decided that he had had enough. He would leave. Before he could implement his decision, however, fate struck a cruel blow: Edsel fell ill and when he was rushed to hospital it was discovered that he had cancer of the stomach. He died soon afterwards.

The children had watched all this with growing bewilderment. Their grandfather had been kind to them when they were small – teaching each of them to drive, building a treehouse on his estate, and taking them to the plant with him on Saturday. They knew that something had gone wrong, because he seemed to have grown indifferent to them. But Edsel, determined to be a good father himself, had seldom talked about his problems. His death came as a terrible shock.

Henry II and his brother Benson had joined the company years before, starting on the production line. Neither had been much good at college; Henry went to Yale but left without graduating and Benson dropped out of Princeton. Both had always taken it for granted that, like their father, they would one day take over the running of the business. Henry, the eldest, now decided to take up Edsel's cause and make it his own. He had always been the leader of the younger generation of Fords and he was in many ways very much like his grandfather – complex and cunning, energetic and ambitious.

He strongly believed that the Old Man was to blame for Edsel's death and was fiercely determined to get rid of Bennett. But he was shrewd enough not to make his feelings known at this stage. When he showed up in Edsel's old office, his grandfather ignored him. Bennett was patronizing. Ford had more or less promised him the presidency, and he did not regard the young fellow as a serious threat. Henry went along with him, but quietly prepared for the inevitable showdown. It finally came in 1945, when Bennett seemed about to take command. Edsel's widow, who had inherited some 41 per cent of the company, confronted her father-in-law with an ultimatum: if her son was not put in charge immediately, she would sell all the stock. The old man reluctantly called him to his office and offered him the presidency. Henry said he would accept if he had a completely free hand to make any changes he wanted to make. His grandfather bristled but accepted the terms. Henry immediately drew up a letter of resignation for him to sign, and called a board meeting for the next day. When Ford's letter was read aloud, Bennett stormed out of the room. Henry fired him a few hours later.

It was sweet revenge for Edsel's 28-year-old son, but he quickly discovered that the company was in a mess. It had not made a profit for fifteen years and it was losing money at the rate of $1 million a day. Henry restructured the entire management team. He threw out the Bennett stooges and hired competent outsiders, including Robert McNamara, who was later to become president of Ford and, subsequently, Defense Secretary in John F. Kennedy's administration. His new allies became known as the 'Whiz Kids' and, under his leadership, they achieved a remarkable turn-around. The old man lingered on for another two years; he died at the age of eighty-three.

Henry II was not an easy man to work for. He, too, was inclined to be autocratic and moody. There were many more power struggles in the years that followed, though none that seriously threatened his own position. He treated his brothers badly; Benson and his younger brother Bill both became alcoholics. He also made mistakes. The worst, ironically, was to launch a car which was supposed to honour his father's memory. It was called the Edsel and it was the biggest flop in the company's history; the venture resulted in a net loss of some $350 million. Far from honouring his father's name, he made it a synonym for failure. But the Ford Motor Company recovered and went on to become a vast and successful international organization.

Henry had a rather messy personal life – he was married three times – and his relationship with his own children was far from perfect. Edsel II feels that he could have done more to fuel his rise to the top of the business, but he is not bitter about it. His sister Charlotte lives with her third husband, Edward Downe Jr, who founded a New York publishing company, in a Manhattan penthouse filled with contemporary art. She recently published a new edition of her popular etiquette book, *Charlotte Ford's Guide to Modern Manners*. His other sister, Anne, is also a New Yorker. She is married to Chuck Scarborough, a handsome local television anchor man.

When I interviewed Henry in 1975 he said that he would like Edsel to succeed him some day, but that he was not going to insist on it. He thought the company had grown too big for one man – even he had to concede that, though he intended to go on for a while longer. This also seems to be the view of most of the professionals who are in charge today. Ford is the third largest industrial corporation in the United States, and they feel that the emphasis should be on the team rather than on any individual. But someone has to be chief executive officer and Edsel clearly hopes his turn will come.

One can only speculate about the future of Henry III. Under the terms of Henry II's will, the young boy is due to inherit twice as much as his brothers and cousins. Will he feel equally compelled to take on the formidable task of preserving the dynasty, or will he settle for an easier life?

The same question had to be faced by the scions of an even more famous American family – the Kennedys. Given their tragic history, it would hardly have been surprising if they had all decided that enough was enough. Yet Joe Kennedy, Bobby's son, is actively pursuing a career in politics and John F. Kennedy Jr has become an assistant district attorney, which is generally regarded as a stepping stone to higher public office.

Could there be another President Kennedy one day? The prospect may seem remote, but one never knows. Joe is already a Congressman, and many people hope that he will eventually try to make it to the White House. John has kept a lower profile, but at the 1988 Democratic Convention he appeared before delegates to introduce his uncle, Senator Edward Kennedy, and there is a good deal of speculation about his future. He has his father's charisma, and the Kennedy name still carries a lot of clout.

Twenty-six years have passed since that awful day in Dallas when Lee Harvey Oswald shot the country's thirty-fifth and most glamorous president and put an end to his fairytale 'Camelot'. Like most others who were around at the time, I have an indelible memory of John F. Kennedy Jr, the little boy in a blue coat and short pants, saluting his father's bronze coffin. We had seen pictures of him playing happily on the floor of the Oval Office: now we saw this sad child, clearly still bewildered by the sudden turn of events. He had been looking forward to his third birthday party at Hyannis Port a few days later. During the funeral, he tried to pull away from his mother, saying: 'I want a flag to take home to my daddy.'

Bobby became a surrogate father and lavished attention on him. But his own son, Joe, was given the dynastic burden. 'You are the oldest of all the male grandchildren,' he wrote to him from the Justice Department on the day of Jack's funeral. 'You have a special and particular responsibility now which I know you will fulfill. Remember all the things that Jack started – be kind to others who are less fortunate than we, and love our country.'

John was later sent to a Roman Catholic school, but he was a restless and inattentive pupil and had to be switched to another school. His cousins called him 'Mama's boy' because he would not play football and join in other games.

Bobby was elected to the Senate and in 1968 tried to win his party's nomination for the presidency. His prospects looked good when he, too, was assassinated. His brother Ted promised to 'pick up the fallen standard', but Jackie said she hated America and wanted to get out of the country. 'If they are killing Kennedys, my children are number one targets,' she declared. She subsequently married Aristotle Onassis on his Greek island of Skorpios. John and his sister Caroline went with her, but she later agreed that they should complete their education in the United States. Landing at John F. Kennedy international airport, John frowned at photographers.

Onassis, by all accounts, was a caring and generous stepfather. He took him fishing and gave him hundred-dollar bills to buy bait. But school continued to be difficult: John was bright but more rebellious and troublesome than Caroline. For a time, he regularly saw a psychiatrist. He eventually got into Brown's University where he earned a bachelor's degree in history in 1983.

At one time, he seems to have been attracted to the stage. He appeared in campus productions and was offered a part in a film, as his father. (Jackie objected, so he turned it down.) In the summer of 1985, he starred in six invitation-only performances of *Winners* at the 75-seat Irish Arts Theater in Manhattan. But he told a reporter: 'This is not a professional acting début. It's just a hobby.'

He has also travelled a great deal. The summer before he went to college he attended National Outdoor Leadership School with students from America and Africa, studying mountaineering and environment issues on Mount Kenya. The following summer he met government and student leaders in Zimbabwe, and worked briefly for a mining company in Johannesburg.

After graduating he involved himself in political organizing, advance work, research, and fund-raising. He then took a $20,000 a year job in the city of New York's Office of Building Development. In 1986 he moved to the Development Corporation as acting deputy executive director, conducting negotiations with developers and city agencies. Later that year, he entered law school. Between classes, he worked with the New York governor's HELP programme, the Fresh Air Fund, the Kennedy Library, and the Kennedy Foundation's associate trustees. In 1988, after a series of interviews, he was appointed one of about 400 assistant district attorneys in the office of Manhattan prosecutor Robert Morgenthau. He is said to be keenly interested in criminal law.

At twenty-eight, John lives alone in a two-bedroom apartment in New York. The former 'Mama's boy' has become an active outdoorsman – he skis, rafts, snorkels, hikes, and goes camping. He is a handsome young man whose name has been linked in the gossip columns with well-known young women like Brooke Shields, Madonna, and Princess Stephanie of Monaco. *People* magazine has called him the 'sexiest man alive'.

So far, he has shown little public interest in following in his father's footsteps, despite that début at the Democratic Convention. He has lent his name to good causes, but he doesn't court publicity. He routinely refuses all interview requests. Caroline has been even more reticent; she is married and, apparently, wants no part of any effort to repeat history.

Joe is different. He seems to love the limelight and appears to be very conscious of 'the special and particular responsibility' which Bobby thrust upon him all those years ago.

In 1979, the two boys were at the ceremony to mark the opening of the John F. Kennedy library. John read Stephen Spender's poem 'I Think Continually of Those Who were Truly Great'. Joe got up and gave a speech which he had entitled 'the Unfinished Business of Robert Kennedy'. It began: 'As I stand here and think about my father and what his life was all about ·. . .' He then launched into a passionate denunciation of the power of Big Oil, Big Coal, and Big Money. Everyone there noted the distinction: the president's son valued the memory of the father he had hardly known but the older Joe felt he had a higher obligation. It may have been bravado – who can tell? Since then, however, he has been elected to Congress and has made other speeches on the same theme.

Joe was sixteen and at boarding school when Uncle Ted called to tell him his father had been shot. He flew to Los Angeles, but it was too late: Bobby Kennedy was dead. It was a frightful blow. He worshipped him and he had been looking forward to the presidential campaign.

Bobby had already tried to groom him – he had introduced him to key aides and allowed him to sit in at meetings. He had promised that after he had left school he could join him full time. Now the future was gone.

He was sent to Spain for a few months, to stay with an old friend of the family, but he felt lost. When he went back to school he was moody and showed no interest in studying. He often displayed a violent temper. It took him a long time to pull himself together. He rejected Harvard and enrolled at the Massachusetts Institute of Technology, but he wasn't happy there. Like John, he went to a psychiatrist. He thought that he might do better at the University of California, but that didn't work out too well either. When he told his mother that he had in effect dropped out, she had Ted get San Francisco's Mayor to offer him a job paying $750 a month in the city's Public Heath Department as 'Co-ordinator for Federally Funded Programs'. But he knew he was being used and resigned after three weeks.

Soon after the Library opening, Ted Kennedy announced his candidacy for the Democratic Party's nomination. Joe ran his campaign in Iowa, organizing the state and making speeches in all the small towns. The Kennedy name ensured attentive audiences. But Ted lost Iowa and most of the other primaries. The public, it seems, would not forget what happened at Chappaquidick. He is still in the Senate, but it seems unlikely that he will have another go at the presidency. Joe may have a better chance.

There was a time when members of the family thought that his younger brother, Bobby Jr, was the one most likely to succeed.

He seemed to be the brightest of the children and did well at Harvard; his thesis was turned into a book. He began to make public appearances, speaking on themes like 'Where is the Idealism of Youth now?'

But Bobby Jr had a reckless streak and while still at school he started to experiment with drugs. He was caught and put on a year's probation. Everyone felt that he had learned his lesson, and the clan was delighted when he got married in 1982 and became an assistant district attorney. But he failed his bar exams and not long afterwards he was in trouble with the police again when they searched his belongings and found some heroin. After pleading guilty, Bobby Jr was sentenced to two years probation and ordered to spend time in 'community service'. It effectively ended his presidential aspirations.

A younger brother, David, also had problems with drugs. He became a heroin addict and was sent to various rehabilitation centres. He dropped out of Harvard and bummed around in California, where he took to alcohol as well as drugs and was arrested for drunken driving. 'Politics is crap,' he told anyone who would listen. David died in a lonely hotel room in 1984.

Joe was always the most serious of the Kennedy boys. In the late 1970s he worked for the Community Services Association in Washington and, later, set up the Citizens Energy Commission in Boston. The idea was to create a business that would show, in a politically exemplary way, how to solve the energy crisis. Citizens Energy would buy crude oil from Venezuela, have it processed in the Carribean, sell the gas and other by-products at market prices, and use the profits to bring in heating oil which could be sold throughout Massachusetts to the elderly and the poor at a 40 per cent discount. The scheme was effective and helped his career.

Now thirty-seven, he is married and has two sons of his own, Matthew and Joseph P. Kennedy III. As a Congressman he has considerable influence but he is not yet a serious force in national politics. The really fascinating question is why he should want to be.

It was easy to understand the ambitions of the previous generations. Grandfather Joe had made millions out of shrewd deals and wanted his sons to be a powerful political force. But when he embarked on his determined campaign he had no reason to expect that both Jack and Bobby would be slain by an assassin's bullet. The new generation of Kennedys is all too well aware of what happened and knows the risks involved in trying to win back the presidency. Although Jack and Bobby are said to have been killed by lone gun-men, acting out whatever fantasies possessed them at the time, there is still a widespread feeling that sinister forces, somewhere out there, mean to get any Kennedy who aims too high. Bobby Kennedy was a sworn foe of organized crime: would they allow Joe to tackle his father's 'unfinished business'?

A Kennedy can still count on being flattered and receiving a great deal of support. The glamour is seductive and there is no reason to doubt that Joe has a genuine sense of commitment to public service. But clearly the family also has formidable enemies. One doesn't *have* to be president to play a role in public service.

The other question, of course, is whether someone like Joe could get elected to the White House. The world has changed, and America is not as keen on the Kennedys as it used to be. Even Jack's reputation has been affected by the disclosures about his womanizing and by a closer examination of some of the ways in which he used his presidential powers, notably his secret war against Castro and his involvement in Vietnam. 'Uncle Ted' has never quite managed to live down the events of Chappaquidick. Given today's power of the media, it seems unlikely that the public would be allowed to forget any of these things.

The renowned family unity, too, is not what it was. It played a crucial role in getting Jack elected, but since then it has weakened considerably. It is entirely possible that Joe will make it to the Senate, but the White House may be beyond reach.

Perhaps the most intriguing thing about him is that he seldom misses an opportunity to knock the rich. He is convinced – or says he is – that America is being sold down the river by its own upper class and tries to project the image of an ardent champion of the underprivileged. 'All men *are* created equal, goddamit,' he said in a recent speech. As a politician, he prefers to deal in emotions rather than in intellectual debate. 'If you try to make an academic argument, you fail miserably,' he asserts. 'You've got to go out there and get people angry about what's happening to the greatest nation on earth.'

7

Bugs and Business

Many of Europe's Old Money families have lived with the challenges posed by a famous name for much longer than the Fords or the Kennedys. The Rothschilds, for example, have done so for eight generations.

The Rothschild reputation, established over more than two centuries, is a formidable asset. It opens doors. But some members of the clan have also found it something of a liability. Everyone they meet tends to make two basic assumptions: that they are very rich (and can afford to share their wealth) and that they are experts in finance. Neither is necessarily true. Some of the Rothschilds have only modest means and many have opted out of the banking business. The present Lord Rothschild, for example, is an eminent scientist.

The story of the dynasty is well-known. It has been told so many times that it has become difficult to separate fact from legend. Many of the Rothschild exploits have been exaggerated or have been embroidered by amusing bits of fiction. Generations of Rothschild children have had to cope with questions about their family history. Is it really true that their ancestors outsmarted Napoleon (yes, they did) and that they enabled the British Government to buy the Suez Canal? (Well, they certainly played a major role.) Did the great Nathan Rothschild really make a killing on the London Stock Exchange when a carrier pigeon brought him advance news of the victory of Waterloo? (He made a lot of money, yes, but he got the information through a courier who brought him a Dutch newspaper with a report of Napoleon's defeat and he did not keep the news to himself: he immediately passed it on to the prime minister of the day, Lord Liverpool.)

The present Rothschilds tend to dismiss the legends as nostalgia. They are proud of what their ancestors did, and family traditions are continued in all sorts of ways. Many of them, for example, have the same given names as earlier Rothschilds and some of them are still prominent in the world of finance. N. M. Rothschild is still a private bank. But they recognize that times have changed.

The dynastic constitution was laid down in the eighteenth century by the founder, Mayer Amschel Rothschild, who sent his sons abroad to form a comprehensive international network. All key posts were to be held by members of the family, not by hired hands. They were to work as a team: brilliance might be individual, but accomplishment was joint. They were to eschew all quarrels. Solidarity was what mattered, and it was not to be diluted by outsiders brought into the family by marriage. His will was explicit: his daughters, sons-in-law, and their heirs were to have no part whatsoever in the firm, nor were they to have the right to examine its books, papers, inventory etc. 'I shall never forgive my children,' he declared, 'if they should against my paternal will take it upon themselves to disturb my sons in the peaceful possession of their business.' Anyone who upset the family harmony would be limited to the legal minimum of estate valued far below its real worth.

His son Nathan, founder of the British branch, wrote an almost identical will. He, too, made his sons the sole inheritors of the firm. Anselm, one of Mayer's grandsons, said in his will many years later: 'I charge all my dear children to live constantly in perfect harmony, not to allow family ties to loosen, to avoid all disputes and unpleasantness and legal actions; to exercise forbearance and tolerance to one another and not to let themselves be carried away by angry passions . . . let my children follow the example of their splendid grandparents; for those qualities have always insured the happiness and prosperity of the whole Rothschild family, and may my dear children never become unmindful of this family spirit.'

One can only guess how the Rothschild daughters felt about all this; none of them seems to have been willing to engage in serious battle with their brothers.

Solidarity was considered so important that the Rothschilds went in for inbreeding on a royal scale. Of the family's fifty-nine weddings in the nineteenth century, half were between male and female Rothschilds. Four of Nathan's seven children married Rothschilds. The men said that they simply found their cousins and second cousins more attractive than other women. Perhaps so; at any rate, it helped to keep the money as well as the power in the family.

Mayer's boys established branches in London, Paris, Vienna, and Naples. He stayed behind to look after the original Frankfurt bank, a job later taken over by Amschel, the eldest son. The brothers kept in close and constant touch and their collaboration resulted in many lucrative deals. Nathan did particularly well in London, making bold and clever use of funds sent to him from Germany. In 1822, the Austrian Chancellor was so grateful for a large personal loan that he arranged to have all the brothers and their direct descendants elevated to the rank of baron. They chose an elaborate escutcheon which incorporated a symbol of their unity which the family has kept to this day – five arrows.

The supremacy of the Rothschilds in international banking lasted a hundred years, from the Napoleonic Wars to the beginning of the First World War. They dominated the money markets and financed the schemes of kings, princes, and governments. They built railways in Europe and factories in South America. They developed oil fields in the Sahara and water power in Newfoundland. 'Money,' wrote the German poet Heinrich Heine, 'is the God of our times and Rothschild is his prophet.'

The barons lived in regal splendour. They had palatial residences and magnificent art collections. They won great races and acquired fine vineyards. One, Alfred Rothschild, even had a private symphony orchestra and a private circus so that he could be conductor, or ringmaster, whenever he felt in the mood.

The Rothschild children were treated like princes. You may have heard of the tramp who sees a tiny boy being helped by a butler into an elegant coach and exclaims wistfully: 'So small – and already a Rothschild!' It is one of the many stories told about them over the years.

But nothing lasts for ever. The branches in Vienna, Frankfurt, and Naples vanished a long time ago and so have many of the Rothschild mansions. The Rothschilds are nothing like the force they used to be, or even among the world's richest people. They still enjoy minor privileges like fixing the price of gold, but these

The Prince of Wales and his two sons, William (left) and Harry, all try to shake hands with the
headmistress on Harry's first day at school

Gerald Grosvenor confronts the photographer in the garden of his childhood home in County Fermanagh, Eire

At twenty-one, on the family's estate at Eaton, near Chester. Today he is the richest man in Britain

Above: Henry Ford, autocratic patriarch, with his unhappy son, Edsel

Left: Henry Ford II sails for Europe with his family. He had a messy personal life

Left: Parents' day at Eton in 1929. Britain's best-known school remains deliberately old fashioned

Below: The memorial library at Harvard. The college wants to encourage the newly talented but also feels that it has an obligation to 'old money'

Christina Onassis with her only child, Athina, in the Bois-de-Boulogne, near her Paris home. She died a few months later, leaving her fortune to the little girl

J. Paul Getty III, two years after he was kidnapped in Italy. The kidnappers had cut off his ear

Patty Hearst in 1983. Abducted at the age of nineteen, she became a member of the 'Symbionese Liberation Army' and took part in a bank robbery

Top: Publishing tycoon Robert Maxwell, who says he won't leave a penny to his children

Below, left: Son Ian, *and right,* his brother Kevin, who told the author: 'I have no God-given right to be a billionaire just because Dad is'

are shared with others. The bank has tough competition in the international marketplace.

N. M. Rothschild, the company founded by Nathan, is now a medium-sized London merchant bank. It is part of a group which is registered in Zug, Switzerland, and known as Rothschild Continuation Holdings. Evelyn de Rothschild, the current chairman, says the move was designed to 'bring the family closer together'. The group employs more than 1,500 people in fourteen countries.

The French and British Rothschilds still maintain a close relationship, but some of the old traditions have been broken. In 1960, N. M. Rothschild accepted the first outsider as a partner and in 1970 the bank was reorganized as a limited company. The Rothschilds still own and control it, but the key executive positions are all held by people from outside the family. They make the profits and they are eager to become rich themselves, which causes a problem. The firm has a profit-sharing scheme, based on merit, but it does not give them a chance to build up the kind of capital they could get elsewhere. The Rothschilds naturally want to attract and keep the best talent – but how do you do that when there are so many other enticing opportunities in the financial world?

Even the renowned family unity is not what it was. In 1980 a direct descendant of Mayer, Jacob Rothschild, made headlines when he announced that he was leaving the bank to set up his own financial services company. It was a surprise: Jacob had been widely regarded as the most promising of the younger Rothschilds, a future chairman. He had gained a brilliant first class degree in history at Oxford and had worked briefly at Morgan Stanley in New York before joining the family firm. He had talked enthusiastically about all the things he was going to do at Rothschild. So why was he leaving?

It emerged that he and Evelyn disagreed about the direction that the bank should take. Jacob favoured an aggressive expansion policy: he felt that it had to become much bigger if it wanted to stay in the first division and that it had to hustle for business. Evelyn took a more conservative view. Jacob was dismayed when his own father took Evelyn's side. 'He felt that a father should support his son through thick and thin,' said a friend of both of them. For some years, they were not on speaking terms. The dispute was so bitter that, when Jacob left, an attempt was made to prevent him using the family name in his own business. He fought back and the attempt failed: he became chairman of J. Rothschild Holdings. He is also chairman of Britain's National Gallery and he owns Clifton Nurseries, near his London home. He and his wife Serena, heiress to the Dunn shipping fortune, have a house in Little Venice, a neo-classical mansion in Wiltshire, and a converted farmhouse in Corfu. They have four children, Nathaniel, Hannah, Beth, and Emily. One of them, Beth, is a horticulturalist. None seem to have shown any eagerness to work for the Rothschild family bank.

Jacob, who inherited many millions when an aunt died in 1988, will be a lord when his father dies. The English Rothschild family gained a hereditary peerage in 1885. It took some doing. Queen Victoria was vigorously opposed to the idea when it was first suggested to her. 'To make a Jew a peer,' she said, 'is a step I could not consent to. It would be ill taken and it would do the government great harm.'

The Prime Minister and others pleaded with her. Lord Granville conceded that the notion of a Jew peer was startling, but went on: 'he represents a class whose influence is great by their wealth, their intelligence, their literary connections'. He added that it would be wise to 'attach the financial interest in the City of London to the Crown instead of running the risk of driving it into the extremist camp'.

The Queen would not be moved. She did not relent until sixteen years later. By then, the Rothschilds had helped Britain to buy the Suez Canal and Disraeli had won her heart. By then, too, the Rothschild who had been nominated for the honour was dead. It went to his son, Nathaniel Mayer de Rothschild.

The first Lord Rothschild was an able financier, but his eldest son, Lionel Walter, had absolutely no talent for making money. His Lordship was so infuriated by his ineptitude at the bank, and by his pursuit of other interests, that he disinherited him in favour of his second son, Charles. Before he rewrote his will, however, he settled on Walter a sum which guaranteed him the life to which he was accustomed.

Walter's great passion was the natural history museum he built on the family estate. Eventually the museum held – mounted, arrayed, and captioned in exemplary fashion – more than a quarter of a million birds and over two million insects, including many specimens not found in other collections. He wrote hundreds of scientific papers, financed a number of expeditions, and published a periodical. His flea collection was particularly famous. But, as his Lordship had recognized, bugs and business did not mix. Walter was so hopeless at managing his financial affairs that in 1932 he had to sell his precious birds to the New York Museum of Natural History to stave off bankruptcy.

Brother Charles became a senior partner in the bank, but he too was a gifted natural historian. 'Had I my way England would see little of me,' he wrote wistfully. 'What I would really like is to live in a nice island or settle in Japan and Burma and be a professional bug-hunter.' He frequently took his own children on zoological outings. Like Walter, he became an expert on fleas, and he published several papers on the subject. His collection was later donated to the British Museum.

Charles contracted sleeping sickness in 1916. It was then an incurable disease, and a few years later he committed suicide. His daughter Miriam carried on her father's work: she became co-author of an important book on parasitology, called *Fleas, Flukes and Cuckoos*, and has written several others. Another daughter, Kathleen, went off to America and became a noted patron of jazz musicians. Their brother Victor, the present Lord Rothschild, also preferred science to finance. He became the most eminent of the non-banking Rothschilds – a Cambridge don, a war hero, a fellow of the Royal Society, head of various research establishments, and adviser to a prime minister, Edward Heath. He has several doctorates.

Victor inherited £2,500,000 from his father, plus the family homes. He was a prize fellow at Cambridge and, in his student days, decided that he wanted to follow an academic career. But when he was twenty-one, his mother begged him to enter the bank. 'It came as rather a shock,' he later recalled, 'to learn that my parents, while realizing that I was a scientist, were most anxious for me at least to try the life of a banker in the City of London.' He did, but hated it. After six unhappy months he went back to Cambridge to be a science don. In 1936 he married the attractive daughter of a lawyer and they had three children – two girls and Jacob. But Barbara Rothschild preferred London society to the academic world and they were divorced after the Second World War. He has three children by a second marriage – including a brilliant daughter, Emma, who graduated from Oxford at the unheard-of age of seventeen and then won a scholarship to the Massachusetts Institute of Technology. His son James farms the family property in Suffolk.

The younger generation of Rothschilds clearly does not feel bound by the edicts laid down in the distant past. Sons may go into banking, but it is very much up to them whether they do so or not. Daughters are no longer expected to marry other Rothschilds. Many members of the clan still have a strong wish to sustain and enhance the family's traditions, but they are under no obligation to work as a team or to accumulate fortunes. Old Mayer would not have approved, but no doubt they welcome their freedom.

8

New Money

The New Rich tend to have mixed feelings about the Old Money class. They resent the assumption that it is in any way superior, but at the same time admire some of the attributes which the Old Rich *want* them to admire: their social graces, good taste, self-assurance, and casual attitude to wealth. In Britain, of course, they also tend to be envious of the grand titles which adorn the aristocracy – though our honours system makes it possible for many of them to capture titles of their own.

The disdain of so many Old Money people for the *nouveaux riches* is often returned in full measure. Some of the New Rich get quite worked up when they talk about the Old Rich. They are, they say, 'stuffed shirts'. They are weak, lazy, degenerate. They cannot hold their own in today's highly competitive world. Their social graces, like their accents, are irritatingly pretentious and the casual attitude to wealth hides envy of the skill, vigour, and imagination of those who really 'make things happen' in modern society – the entrepreneurs. The creator of wealth makes a far more important contribution than the one who merely inherits it, lives on the income, and then passes it on.

To some extent, this is a form of defensiveness. But many of the New Rich feel that all these strictures are fully justified. This is because, unlike Old Money, they tend to judge success in life chiefly by one's ability to triumph in the marketplace. As they see it, life is about beating the competition, building supermarkets and office blocks, buying up other companies, and making millions in the process.

Not all the New Rich, it must be said, are quite so passionate about the alleged shortcomings of the Old Rich. For many, they are simply irrelevant; they are people who have opted out of the ceaseless struggle for success and can, therefore, be ignored. But the view that Old Money is weak, lazy, and degenerate tends to be widely shared and, inevitably, influences the attitude of the children of New Money. A man who has worked hard to *be* someone, to 'make it', naturally wants to be admired for *his* achievements and he wants his children, especially his sons, to follow *his* example.

Many self-made men come from poor families and, deep down, are heavily influenced by their own childhood. They know what it is like to be hard up and insecure, and they find it difficult to forget how cruel life can be. They grow up with a fierce determination to improve their lot, to make sure that they will never be poor again. They also persuade themselves that they are doing it because they want their children to 'have all the things I never had'. But the basic motive is a selfish one: they want to banish that feeling of insecurity, that dreadful fear of being at the mercy of events rather than in control of them, and they want to 'show them all' that they have what it takes to be a winner.

You might have thought that, once they have accumulated enough money to guarantee a prosperous existence for life, the New Rich would ease up and enjoy themselves. But for many the battle can never stop. Some find it impossible to shake off the fear that good fortune will not last. Film star Michael Caine, for example, once told me that, although he had made many millions, he still worries that, one day, his accountant will call him and say that it has all gone. So he goes on making more and more films. For others the whole business becomes a thrilling game: they derive immense satisfaction from outsmarting rivals, acquiring their treasured possessions, and having their own judgement vindicated. Money as such ceases to be important; it is merely the yardstick by which the world judges their success. They may give it all away in the end, but they cannot give up the chase.

The children of such men, ironically, often grow up with fears of their own. They feel insecure because their fathers are too busy to show them the kind of love which every child needs, and they are terrified that their own performance will fail to live up to their parents' high expectations. In many cases, fathers set one child against another: they become pawns in the game he enjoys so much. His children, too, must be 'winners'.

They are privileged in one sense: their parents have money. They do not have to worry about rent collectors knocking on the door late at night. That is the public perception, anyway. The reality may be different. Fathers who are still on the way up, who aspire to great wealth but have not quite made it yet, often have another set of financial worries. They borrow heavily to finance their various ventures and they take enormous risks. Most enterprises – and New Money fortunes – are built with OPM, Other People's Money. The gamble may come off, but it is also possible that it may fail. Most self-made men have sleepless nights now and then. They generally try to shield their children from problems of this sort, but they do not always manage to disguise their anxieties.

If there is a crash, the children suffer along with the parents. The sudden loss of wealth that they have come to take for granted, the public exposure of their father's failure, and the *Schadenfreude* of people who were thought to be friends can be an awful shock. The banks come knocking at the door; the family's home may have to be sold; the parents' marriage may fall apart; their fathers may even commit suicide. The poor are usually better at handling setbacks than the New Rich: they are more used to them and the fall is not quite as dramatic. They can always go out and get another job. The rich have tasted success and find it harder to cope with defeat.

Last year, a friend of mine, a Texas oilman, hanged himself one Saturday morning in his garage. During the oil boom, his business had been valued at more than $30 million. He thought the good times would last and borrowed a great deal of money to finance further expansion. When oil prices collapsed, the banks called in the loans and he became frantic. In the end, he felt that suicide was the only way out. His children were puzzled. They had no idea that things were that bad. He had never discussed his problems with them (it might have helped) and they could not understand why he had taken such a drastic step. The family surely could have started a new life somewhere else. That would have been my view, too. Indeed, I had told him just that when he had mentioned his troubles to me a few months earlier. But he clearly concluded that, for him, it was not a feasible option.

That is the tragic side of the coin, an extreme example of what can happen when ambition goes too far. But the New Rich are great optimists, perpetually convinced that they can 'make it', that somehow everything will work out to their advantage. Paul Getty used to say that the best time to buy or invest is when everyone is pessimistic. He regarded recessions as periods of opportunity. He had a favourite dictum: the meek shall inherit the earth, but not the mineral rights. Most of the New Rich would agree with him – and, of course, they often turn out to be right.

As soon as they reach their goal, if not before, they usually acquire all the trappings they associate with Old Money and which they may have roundly condemned in earlier days. Country estates are no longer regarded as pretentious symbols of inherited privilege but as highly desirable proof of their own arrival in the ranks of the rich. Expensive town houses or apartments become a must, so that their wives can give the kind of dinner parties they have seen written up in society magazines like *Town & Country* and *Harpers & Queen*. Inquiries are made about the possibility of joining one or more of the elite gentlemen's clubs, and the children are sent to exclusive schools. If they have made it really big, the New Rich will probably also add some touches of their own – things which Old Money people can no longer afford (and, in many cases, never could), such as yachts, helicopters, and private jets. It is the ultimate victory over the upper class: you do not just try to join it, you *outdo* it.

The Old Rich tend to dismiss all this with a contemptuous shrug. What else can you expect from the *nouveaux riches*? They have never understood that you cannot buy style off the shelf, that you do not become a member of the upper class by writing a cheque. But they are not necessarily hostile: after all, the New Rich are *meant* to follow their lead. New Money must aim to become Old. It will take time, of course, and they may falter along the way, but the very fact that the New Rich are so keen to make a start is confirmation of Old Money's basic superiority. The efforts of some of the New Rich often have the opposite effect of the one intended: Old Money people are amused rather than impressed. They have a good laugh when some new millionaire buys a grand mansion and attempts to turn it into his version of an aristocratic family seat. The result is so often a ghastly mess.

America's robber barons used to ransack the art treasures of

Europe in their scramble to emulate the nobility. Medieval castles were stripped of their carvings and tapestries, and shiploads
of crystal chandeliers, old Tudor chests and bedsteads, Louis
XIV furniture, old armour, statues, porcelain, and paintings by
European masters made their way across the Atlantic. Other
parvenus did the same. William Randolph Hearst, for example,
built himself a ludicrous 'castle' and filled it with items bought on
sundry shopping expeditions. The practice continues – only today
they have to compete with the New Rich from other countries,
including Japan and Europe itself.

In fairness, it must be said that some of them have very
good taste, or at least the good sense to hand the job over to
a professional interior decorator. New Money homes do not *have*
to be a mess. Many are not: there are some fabulous homes in
cities like London and New York that have been created by
New Money people with a genuine sense of style. Their owners
appreciate not only the treasures of the past but also the work of
modern masters: patronage of talent is no longer confined to the
traditional upper class.

Many of the New Rich have also created a way of life which,
although different from that of Old Money, is by no means
inferior. Old Money people do not have a monopoly on civilized
behaviour, and I can well understand the resentment of those who
think that they do. But some of the New Rich *are* impossibly
vulgar.

Their children may not become aware of it until they go to one
of those exclusive schools and begin to see their parents through
the eyes of others. Because the schools still teach Old Money
behaviour they will, inevitably, discover that much of what their
parents say and do is regarded as gauche. Pride in the father's
achievement may turn into embarrassment. They may even feel
compelled to criticize his manners and attitudes, which naturally
tends to produce an angry response: he sent them to an expensive
school to get an education, not to acquire fancy airs. (He does not
understand that learning the social graces is very much part of that
education.)

New Money people tend to be even more annoyed by attempts
to question their ethos, by suggestions that their restless drive for
success may not be as admirable as they think. Their children
are reminded that, without their father's success, they would be

nowhere. He had to struggle to get where the family is today and it ill behoves them to denounce his efforts. 'Look at all I have done for you' is a common reaction. He has not really done it for them but for himself, but that does not prevent him from insisting that they show proper gratitude. More often than not, the teachers are blamed for 'filling their heads with all this nonsense'.

Because so many self-made men see their children as another personal possession, as an extension of themselves, they are dismayed when they appear to be 'going off the rails'. The problem rarely arises when they are very young. Small children tend to be overawed by a dynamic father and are generally eager to please. He is, after all, the one who can gratify their desire for material comforts. Parents have an effective means of control: they can supply or withhold things which the child wants and needs, including pocket money. They can (and usually do) desire systems of rewards and punishments which keep their children in line. This may continue until the children have grown up. It is then, however, that they often become 'difficult', especially if, like Old Money children, they have acquired a trust fund of their own.

One of the great worries of the New Rich is that their children will want to do something entirely different from what they had in mind, that they will try to assert their independence by marching off in a new direction, and in so doing deprive their ambitious parents of the opportunity to create a dynasty based on the family business. The warning signs tend to appear while they are at college: they may indicate a strong interest in history, Greek, or some other academic subject and announce their intention of making a career of it. They argue, reasonably enough, that money is supposed to buy freedom of choice and that they can surely devote themselves to something they *like*. But that is not how their fathers see it. The whole point of spending all that money on their children's education was to equip them for a 'useful' adult life. Who needs history?

Mothers tend to be equally upset if their children choose a career which they consider to be below their hard-won station in society. She has struggled to climb up the social ladder (while father was busy making his millions) and now her sons and daughters are trying to drag the family down again. Someone has to perform tasks like nursing and teaching, but must they be done by *her* children? Their response, in many cases, is to use the methods they have found so effective in dealing with rivals: they make threats or try to bribe their children into submission. It does not always work, but such tactics *can* be quite persuasive.

I am not, let me make it clear, suggesting that *all* the New Rich behave like this. They do not; I know many parents who accept that their children are entitled to do their own thing and who take considerable pride in whatever they manage to achieve, particularly in fields like science and the arts. There is no shame in having a son or daughter who gains fame as a scientist or as a painter. What I *am* suggesting is that such behaviour is fairly common. It often takes years before they throw in the towel.

Many children, of course, do not need to be persuaded: they are more than willing to follow in the footsteps of their parents. They relish the prospect of one day lording it over a big corporation, or of becoming a Society queen. Some cannot wait for their fathers and mothers to step aside, so that they can take over. They may even drop out of college because they consider it a waste of time to continue with a formal education.

The happy fathers may insist that their sons start at the bottom, but progress tends to be swift. It is not unusual for the scions of the New Rich to become managing directors before they are thirty. By then, Dad will have taught them all the stuff they could never have learned at school or college. They may retain the manners they have acquired at Eton, Winchester, or St Midas, but underneath they have become as tough, wily, and ambitious as their mentor. His values are their values. Loyalty is weakness; sportsmanship is dumb; using people is good business; winning is everything. They have become enthusiastic members of the entrepreneurial class.

There is, you may feel, nothing wrong with this. The New Rich are surely right about one thing: society as a whole benefits from the creation of wealth and it is the entrepreneur, not the inheritor, who deserves much of the credit for the material progress it makes. Whether society also benefits from all those clever financial deals is another matter; the point is that entrepreneurial imagination is a considerable force for good as well as evil. The business empires created and run by New Money not only produce goods and services but also provide employment for numerous people. The interests of the New Rich are shared in many ways with others, including Old Money people who live off the dividends they pay. Competition is tough, and requires

73

tough leadership: one may regret that, but it is the harsh reality of our times.

One hopes, nevertheless, that Old Money influences will survive in the scramble. It is commonplace to say that money is a means to an end, not an end in itself. Sadly, many of the New Rich do not agree: they pursue wealth for the sake of it, not because of what it can do for their families and the community. One would like to think that their children, who have had a greater opportunity to mix with Old Money people and their cherished institutions than any generation before them, will show a little more sense. But I would not bet on it.

9

The Showbiz Kids

Many fortunes have been made, and continue to be made, in the world of show business. We live in an age of mass entertainment, and performers who hit the jackpot, especially in America, can earn millions in a relatively short time. Singers, actors, sports stars, television personalities and writers of popular fiction have all joined the ranks of the New Rich. So have others in the industry – producers, directors, agents, promoters.

In some cases, the millions are made by entertainers who are still in their teens or barely out of them. The Beatles are a classic example.

Early fame and fortune can be a heady mix, which many young people find harder to handle than they care to admit. Look at Elvis Presley, a talented singer who became an international celebrity in the 1950s and came to a tragic end, destroyed by success and self-indulgence.

Parents usually try to help, but they have to be careful: their well-intentioned efforts may be resented and can lead to a long period of estrangement. Junior no longer wants to be treated as a child: he is a *star*. People ask for his autograph; girls swoon; the press prints flattering profiles; hangers-on tell him he is unique; the money keeps rolling in. The last thing he needs is a parental attempt to bring him down to earth. He has left all that behind, hasn't he? What do parents know about the world in which he has made such an impact? He wants applause, not a lecture.

The Beatles went through this exciting but difficult period, and there were times when it all proved too much. They split up at the height of their success, which was probably a good thing. John Lennon was later shot by a madman in New York, but the others seem to have managed to enjoy their fortunes. Paul McCartney made more than $200 million and royalties still bring him a substantial income. During his pot-smoking days he was jailed for nine days in Tokyo, but all that is over. He is semi-retired from pop and has done his best to ensure that his own three children lead a normal life. They have been educated at state schools.

In earlier days, entertainers usually had to serve a lengthy apprenticeship, which kept them in touch with everyday realities. Julie Andrews, for example, first learned her trade, at an age when other nice girls were playing with their dolls' houses, performing twice nightly in front of tough music-hall customers. Today, young people can achieve stardom almost overnight.

Some, of course, vanish within a few months and find that their parents are useful after all. Flatterers are fickle friends, but mothers can usually be relied upon to provide genuine solace.

Performers with staying power become household names and the process of accumulating wealth goes on for many years. Bob Hope, who has been delivering one-liners for as long as any of us care to remember, is reckoned to be worth at least $250 million. Lucille Ball made more than $75 million because people loved Lucy. Frank Sinatra, Julio Iglesias, Dean Martin, and Tom Jones have all become extremely rich by appealing to the romantic longings of young people *and* their parents. Many film stars are multi-millionaires, including Michael Caine, Roger Moore, Clint Eastwood, Charlton Heston, and Paul Newman. Elizabeth Taylor, who starred in her first film at the age of twelve, has made (and spent) several fortunes. Composer Andrew Lloyd-Webber has become one of the richest men in Britain by writing the music for a whole string of successful shows.

Sooner or later (usually sooner) most of these high-fliers create families of their own. We tend not to hear much about their children, for very good reasons. One is that publicity may attract the attention of kidnappers. Another is that stars hate to be upstaged by anyone, including members of their own families. But the main reason is that many showbiz people tend to lead rather messy personal lives, which they naturally prefer not to advertise. Their children often have a hard time.

On the face of it, the children of the rich and famous would seem to have it made. They are brought up in a luxurious environment. Their fathers or mothers are admired by millions, and they meet all kinds of fascinating people. Many are spoiled rotten. But there is another side, which the public only gets to see when, from time to time, we learn that the son or daughter of a prominent showbiz personality has been hauled into court for using drugs or for some other misdemeanour. I would not wish to suggest that it happens to all of them – that would be far from the truth. What I am suggesting is that it tends to happen more often than in other walks of life.

The entertainment world is a highly competitive business, in which people will do just about anything to get to the top. For every actor, actress, pop musician or TV personality who achieves even modest success there are thousands who get nowhere. Week after week, young people leave their small-town homes and head for cities like Los Angeles, America's fantasy capital. Their parents may object, but there is generally little they can do. They wait anxiously for news from their precious offspring. Sometimes it is good; more often it is not. Los Angeles has a glamorous image but the reality is quite different: it is a tough town, populated by people with inflated egos who, far from welcoming newcomers, seem hell-bent on making their lives a misery. The place reeks of ambitious insecurity.

Many give up and, sensibly, decide to pursue other careers. Some become addicted to drugs and alcohol. Those who succeed usually have another kind of worry: how to make sure that they *stay* at the top. One expensive flop can spell disaster. Even the big names cannot be sure that the money will keep rolling in; months may go by without another offer. It can be very unnerving.

Most performers are like children: they need constant attention, constant reassurance that they are still loved and wanted. They find it difficult to cope with rejection. If they have a run of bad luck, their families are inevitably affected. Bored and frustrated, they tend to lash out at those who are closest – their marriage partners or their own children.

Many try to overcome their feeling of insecurity by embarking on an affair. It is common enough in showbiz: the bedroom antics described in the novels of Hollywood writers like Jackie Collins may seem like lurid fiction but many of her implausible scenarios are based on fact.

Affairs may lead to divorce and subsequent remarriage. Many famous stars have been married several times, and have had children by different partners. We generally forgive them – divorce is not such a big thing these days – but we do not have to live with the consequences. The children do. They find themselves shuttled from one home to another, often in the years when they most need a stable background. They try to come to terms with conflicting loyalties, and do their best to please both parents, which may be an impossible task.

Michael Reagan, the eldest son of former President Ronald Reagan, has written a moving account of his childhood, which he said turned into a 'living nightmare'. Most Americans were surprised to hear it: their president hardly seemed the kind of man who would be a cruel father.

Adopted at birth (Ronald Reagan was then a Hollywood star and married to actress Jane Wyman) he was pampered to begin with. But his parents were divorced when he was only three, and soon after he learned for the first time that he was not their natural son. His older sister Maureen (who was a natural daughter of the Reagans) mentioned it during a quarrel. He did not know what it meant and asked Jane Wyman to explain. She told him that his parents had not been able to give him a nice home, and that they had put him up for adoption because they wanted the best for him. 'Your father and I,' she assured the little boy, 'chose you because you were just what we wanted.' It mollified him for a while, but he found it hard to shake off the conviction that his birth mother had given him away because she did not love him and he was bad.

Michael adored Ronald Reagan and Jane Wyman, but the divorce and their busy work schedule meant that he could see each of them for only a couple of days a month. 'I never really found out who they were, and I don't think they ever really knew me,' he later wrote in his autobiography, *On the Outside Looking in*. He was sent to boarding school and envied other children because they could go home and were able to go on family holidays with their parents.

When Ronald Reagan married another actress, Nancy Davis, he hoped that they would have him move in with them. But neither he nor his sister was invited to the wedding and they remained at boarding school. Nancy and Jane heartily detested each other, which made things even more difficult when the children spent time with one parent or the other. Michael was so miserable that he contemplated suicide. Jane took him to a child psychiatrist, who said that he needed a family environment and that it would be better all round if he went to live with his father and Nancy. He was fourteen and delighted when, this time, they agreed to take him. But by then they had two children of their own, and again he felt unwanted, an outsider. He never dared to call Nancy 'Mom'. Eventually he went off to another boarding school.

Michael stayed in touch with the Reagans during the years that followed and was an occasional visitor to the White House. He married and had children who, one hopes, had a happier time than he did.

Michael's case is unusual because of the circumstances in which he came by his parents. But his experience is by no means unusual in the turbulent world of showbiz. Another fascinating story is that of John Wayne, star of numerous movies and, for most people, as much a symbol of stability as Ronald Reagan. Married three times, he had seven children – four by his first wife, Josephine, and three by his third wife, Pilar.

John Wayne was born in a small town in Iowa, where his father was a pharmacist. His original name was Marion Michael Morrison. He hated it and was glad when, at the start of his movie career, a producer suggested that he should change it to John Wayne. His family and friends always called him Duke.

Duke's childhood was marred by the poverty of his parents and their constant fights. He ran away several times, travelling for many miles before someone found the small boy and made sure that he returned home. When he was eight, his father was diagnosed as having tuberculosis and the family moved to California, where they struggled to make a living as farmers. Wayne later recalled that there were many days when he was desperately hungry. It no doubt helps to explain why he worked so hard even after he became immensely successful: he wanted to make absolutely certain that nothing like it could ever happen again, either to him or to his children.

Duke's parents later moved to Glendale, where his father got a job in a pharmacy. The eleven-year-old boy augmented the family income by delivering newspapers. He went to a local school and was a good student. His mother expressed the hope that he would become a lawyer, but instead he went to work as a propman in California's burgeoning film business. He then became an actor and was lucky enough to get his first starring role at the age of twenty-two. He got married and four children arrived in quick succession – Michael, Tony, Patrick and Melinda. But the marriage broke down after ten years and, on a trip to Mexico, he met the woman who was to become his next wife, a voluptuous girl called Chata. It turned out to be a disastrous choice and they, too, were eventually divorced. He then married Pilar, a Peruvian movie actress. She did her best to make friends of the children and for a time all seemed well. But trouble developed when her own children arrived: the four oldest deeply resented having to share their father's life and affection with them.

Duke refused to be drawn into the conflict (his own childhood experiences had been bad enough) and he devoted more and more of his time to making movies. The older children saw little of him, which increased their resentment. Pilar and the younger children sometimes accompanied him to the remote locations he favoured, and they even appeared in some of the films. But at the age of fifty-seven he was struck down by lung cancer, and although he recovered and went on making movies, his mood changed.

As Pilar later recalled, he was often unreasonably angry. Some of his towering rages reduced everyone around him to tears. The children could not understand what was wrong with their father, who had always been so kind to them. Pilar kept urging him to retire, but he adamantly refused to consider it: indeed, he insisted on working harder than ever. She eventually decided that she could take no more, and after twenty-five years of marriage they agreed to separate. Her children had to start the usual routine of shuttling to and from each parent's home.

John Wayne died six years later, at the age of seventy-two. His eldest son, Michael, took charge of the funeral arrangements and was the executor of his will. Wayne left $7 million. All the children were provided for, but Pilar was specifically excluded from the estate and she was not allowed to collect some personal possessions from the home they had once shared. Michael, she told the press, even objected to her using the name 'Mrs John Wayne', although she was his legal widow. He no doubt had his reasons, but it is sad that they could not settle their differences.

Charlie Chaplin was another star whose personal life left much to be desired. In his film persona as the Little Tramp he was known and loved around the world. But Charlie the man was a complex character who got embroiled in three unhappy marriages, many affairs, a paternity suit and an immorality charge. He had a fixation for young girls which caused him many problems. He eventually married Oona O'Neill, daughter of American playwright Eugene O'Neill. The Little Tramp was fifty-four; she was only seventeen, a year younger than his first son. None of his previous marriages had lasted more than a few years. But Oona remained steadfastly at his side for the last thirty-four years of his life, bore him eight children and created a happy home for the family in Switzerland.

Michael, the most outspoken of the Chaplin children, once said: 'To be the son of a great man can be a disadvantage; it is like living next to a huge monument. One spends one's life circling round it, either to remain in the shade, or to avoid its shadows.' Charlie always said that he did not want any of his children to go into showbusiness, but most of them at least dabbled in it and one, Geraldine, became a star in her own right.

There are countless other examples of Hollywood relationships which resemble the kind of thing we are accustomed to watching on TV soap operas like *Dynasty*. I have singled out a few because they seemed to me particularly interesting. They are certainly not the worst.

Many showbiz children have problems even if their parents stay happily married to each other. It is difficult enough to be the son or daughter of a successful businessman; it can be more difficult still if one's mother or father is a superstar. Having a famous name can be a liability rather than an asset. At school, other children tend to assume that you are getting special privileges and resent it; if your father happens to be a movie tough guy, they may also want to find out how tough *you* are. Then comes the difficult choice: do you try to follow your parents into showbiz or opt for an entirely different career? The temptation to have a go is there. You have the background and the connections. But you have also had ample opportunity to learn what you are up against, and you know that the public will inevitably make comparisons. How do you follow a superstar?

Some have accepted the challenge and have done well. Michael Douglas, son of Kirk, has won fame in his own right with movies like *Wall Street* and *Fatal Attraction*. He likes to tell how his father saw a woman in a department store pointing at him and telling her son excitedly: 'Look, there's Michael Douglas's father!'

There are others: Liza Minelli (daughter of Judy Garland), Jason Connery, Lloyd Bridges, Nancy Sinatra, Geraldine Chaplin, Jamie Lee Curtis. Most of them landed their first film role on the strength of their name.

Hollywood publicists know how to make the most of it. But it is not enough. Errol Flynn's son, Sean, faltered after an indifferent start. He found it hard to live up to his father's swashbuckling image and, despite his good looks, never made it as an actor. He went to Africa to hunt big game and lived the playboy life on the Riviera, but he wanted his life to have some significance and he became a news photographer on the Vietnam battle front. He disappeared in Cambodia at the age of twenty-nine.

Jane Fonda, whose mother committed suicide when she was twelve, also felt the need to escape from being Henry's daughter. 'It's difficult to have a very famous parent who is perfect in the eyes of the world, because you are trying to live up to an image,' she said. 'I needed to go out from under that and for me that meant leaving the country and seeing what it was like for me in a different culture.' She married French film director Roger Vadim and later became a controversial campaigner for various causes, notably America's withdrawal from Vietnam. She has since made successful movies and has also become a star of the keep-fit industry.

Some showbiz kids have settled for a role behind a movie camera. Michael Wayne, for example, became a producer during his father's lifetime. (One of his films starred John Wayne, with Michael's brother Patrick playing his son and Pilar's child, Ethan, his grandson. It is hard to think of a more ironic piece of casting.) But many more have opted for a less demanding way of life. A few have even changed their names to avoid being compared with their father or mother. One cannot really blame them.

10

Double Trump

The real estate business may be less glamorous than showbiz, but it has made many people very rich. It has also brought fame to flamboyant characters like New York's Donald Trump, who gets as much media attention these days as a Hollywood star. He has been featured on numerous magazine covers and has even played himself in a TV series. His name is emblazoned on buildings in Manhattan, Atlantic City, and Florida. He has written a best-selling book, *The Art of the Deal*. His lifestyle is lavish – he has luxurious homes, a private jet, a helicopter, and a magnificent yacht which he bought from Adnan Khashoggi. He is an authentic New Money hero, a real-life soap character.

His father, Fred Trump, made millions in real estate before him. But Donald has done infinitely better: he is a *billionaire*. 'He amazes me,' Trump Senior has been quoted as saying. 'He's gone way beyond me, absolutely.'

Fred had already accumulated a tidy fortune by the time Donald, the second of his five children, was born in 1946. His story provides a classic example of the poor boy who made good. His own father, a Swedish immigrant, died when Fred was only eleven. The boy supplemented his mother's income by doing odd jobs – everything from delivering groceries to shining shoes. He took night classes in carpentry, because he felt that if he learned a trade he could always make a living. But he had greater ambitions, and after leaving high school he decided to have a go at construction. He built a modest one-family house in Queens, one of the New York boroughs, and used the profit to build more. It was a struggle, but it brought him the success he longed for. He eventually put up and ran some 24,000 apartments in Queens and Brooklyn.

The children were raised in a large family home, but Donald says that they never thought of themselves as rich kids – they were taught to know the value of the dollar and to appreciate the importance of hard work. 'Life's a competition,' Fred said in an interview published in 1980. 'I brought my kids up in a competitive environment.'

The first born was a girl, Maryanne. She was bright, but it never occurred to Fred that women might be interested in a business career. (Maryanne later became a federal judge.) His hopes, in those early days, centred on his eldest son, Fred Junior. He would be tough and hard-working and he would take his natural place in the family enterprise. He would be just like his old man. At least that was the plan. As so often happens, Junior had other ideas. He worked with his domineering father for a while, but his heart was not in real estate and he had little feel for it. They clashed constantly and Junior went off to pursue what he loved best – flying aeroplanes. He moved to Florida and became a pilot for TWA. But that did not work out either (he grew too fond of the bottle) and he got a job on charter boats. He eventually returned home and Fred made another attempt to involve him in the business. It was in vain. Junior went through the motions, but his drinking got worse and he suffered from acute depression. He died in 1980, at the age of forty-three.

Donald, eight years younger, had a much more assertive personality and stood up to his father. As a child, he resented the fact that Junior was being groomed as the heir. He wanted that role for himself, and he competed with his older brother in the most determined ways. Junior reluctantly accompanied Fred on his tours of building sites; Donald did so enthusiastically.

At school, his exuberance and competitive drive often got him into trouble. When he was thirteen, Fred sent him to the New York Military Academy to 'straighten him out'. Donald later said that the Academy taught him how to channel his aggression into achievement. He became one of its best baseball players and in his senior years was made a captain of cadets.

After his graduation, he toyed with the idea of attending film school at the University of California. He was attracted by the glamour of the movie industry and admired people like Sam Goldwyn and Louis B. Mayer. In the end, though, he decided that real estate was a much better business. By this time, it had become apparent that Junior was not the son Fred had hoped for, so his father was delighted by the news. But he insisted that Donald should get a college degree before joining the company.

Donald applied to the Wharton School of Finance at the University of Pennsylvania and he got in. He showed up for classes and did what was required of him, but he found academic life boring and, while still at college, bought and renovated several properties. He also talked his father into joining him in his first big deal – buying a 1,200-unit apartment development in Cincinnati called Swifton Village. He had found out about it while studying lists of federally financed housing projects in foreclosure. The Village had 800 vacant apartments, the developers had gone bankrupt, and the Government had foreclosed. The Trumps were able to get it for $6 million, which was half as much as it had cost to build just two years earlier. They were also able to obtain a mortgage for what they paid, plus about $100,000, which they put toward fixing the place up. In other words, they got the project without putting down any money of their own.

Donald faced the formidable task of getting the place rented, and rented to good tenants who would stay there. He tackled it with his usual enthusiasm. He devoted all the time he could to making the complex more attractive, getting rid of the bad tenants, and persuading the right people to move in. Within a year, he had 100 per cent occupancy. But the area itself was deteriorating and Donald decided that he had better get out while he could. The Trumps sold the village to a real estate investment trust at a profit of $6 million. It was an impressive start to what would turn out to be a spectacular career.

Donald managed to get his degree and immediately joined his father's company on a full-time basis. His share of the profits from the Swifton Village deal had been modest: when he left college he had a net worth of around $200,000, most of which was tied up in buildings in Queens and Brooklyn. But he had gained valuable first-hand experience and he was eager to show that he could make a lot more. There was no longer any doubt about his status: Fred Junior had walked away from the battlefield and Donald had become the obvious successor. But he did not want to be known simply as Fred's son, and he was not content with building rent-controlled and rent-stabilized housing in the outer boroughs. He wanted to try something grander, more exciting. To him, that meant making it big in Manhattan.

Fred did not share his lofty vision. He was keen to expand, but he felt more comfortable doing it on familiar turf. He agreed, however, to give Donald free rein. If he wanted to enter the high stakes of major-league real estate, Fred would not stand in his way.

Donald rented a small apartment on the Upper East Side. He still went to Brooklyn every day, to work in the family business, but he spent as much time as possible in Manhattan – walking the streets, getting to know properties, meeting influential people. He quickly discovered that making his mark was not going to be easy. Prices were discouragingly high.

Then, in 1973, things began to go badly wrong for the city of New York. Its debts rose to such an alarming level that many people feared it would go bust. There was a serious crisis of confidence. Hardly anyone wanted to know about new real estate development. Trump shared the concern, but he had always been an optimist: he thought that Manhattan was the greatest place in the world. He was sure that all would be well in the long run. The crisis might spell trouble for others, but for him it presented a great opportunity.

He had long been fascinated by the huge abandoned railyard along the Hudson River. It belonged to Penn Central, which was financially destitute. He went to see the man in charge of selling off its assets and secured an exclusive option to buy two parcels of the waterfront land. He did not have to put up any cash; Penn Central even agreed to pay his development costs, in return for a promise of future profits. 'Those properties,' the liquidator was later quoted as saying, 'were nothing but a black hole of undefinable risk. We interviewed all kinds of people who were interested in them, none of whom had what seemed like the kind of drive and backing and imagination that would be necessary. Until this young guy Trump came along. He's almost a throwback to the 19th century as a promoter. He's larger than life.'

The 'young guy' soon had another idea: would Penn Central also agree to sell him the dilapidated Commodore Hotel, next to Grand Central Station? It had been losing money for years and was in a shocking state, but the location was good and he thought he could do something with it. His father thought he was crazy and so did a lot of other people. As Fred recalled later: 'I told him that buying the Commodore at a time when even the Chrysler building was in receivership was like fighting for a seat on the Titanic.'

Donald was twenty-seven years old, had never built anything in Manhattan, and knew nothing about hotels. It took remarkable nerve to take on such big commitments. Looking back, he concedes that everything could have gone horribly wrong – but, hell, you couldn't make an impact without taking a chance.

Penn Central wanted $10 million for the Commodore, and they asked him to put down a non-refundable $250,000 for an exclusive option. It was still a substantial sum of money for him then, and he stalled for as long as he could. He eventually found a partner – Hyatt – and managed not only to raise the finance but also to get a special tax abatement from the city. The deal went through and Donald announced that he would totally rebuild the hotel: he would make it one of the most glamorous places in Manhattan.

It all sounds very simple now, but the project took four years to complete and there were many anxious moments. The situation in New York got worse before it got better. People urged him to settle for refurbishing the Commodore rather than spending millions and millions on creating a brand-new edifice. But Donald was adamant – and, in the end, his judgement turned out to have been absolutely right. The Grand Hyatt opened for business in September 1980 and was an instant hit. It established him as a man who could get things done and it enabled him to go on to his next venture – Trump Tower.

The vast, glitzy Trump Tower is, today, one of New York's best-known buildings. It is hard to believe that ten years ago it existed only in Donald's imagination. Fred had been astonished by the boldness of his son's earlier concepts: the Hyatt project and his plan to build a convention centre on the railyard site. (It took some doing, but in 1978 the city chose it over others that had been considered.) He was *dazzled* when Donald told him what he proposed to do on Fifth Avenue. He would, he said, tear down the eleven-story Bonwit Teller building and erect, in its place, a sixty-eight-storey skyscraper (later reduced to fifty-eight storeys) of bronze-coloured glass with a stunning atrium, elegant boutiques, spacious offices, and luxury condominium apartments.

'I love real estate because there's something about creating something that's visible,' he said. 'There's an artistic merit.' Critics were to dispute that when the Tower was finished, but meanwhile he pursued his objective with patience and cunning.

The owners of the Bonwit building were prepared to sell, but they only had a twenty-nine-year lease on the underlying land. So Trump went to the company that owned the land, Equitable Life Assurance, and persuaded the directors to enter into a fifty-fifty partnership. He then asked Tiffany, which was directly adjacent to Bonwit Teller, if he could buy the 'air rights' above its famous store. He needed these rights in order to put up the much larger building he had in mind. He eventually got them for $5 million. The next step was to get planning permission and to raise the money for the actual construction. The Chase Manhattan Bank agreed to provide the finance and he set to work; the budget for the whole job was over $200 million.

Donald has made other big deals since. He owns gambling casinos in Atlantic City and he has bought New York's Plaza Hotel for $400 million. ('For me,' he said when he announced the Plaza acquisition, 'this is like owning the Mona Lisa. It's not just an investment, it's a work of art.') But it was the audacious Tower venture which really made his name, and which demonstrated convincingly that he was in a very different class from his father. It made him at least $100 million, and he has managed to buy out his 50 per cent partner, Equitable Life Assurance. He has an office and a stunning apartment in the building. *Fortune* magazine reckons he has a net worth of between $1.5 billion and $2.1 billion. It is more than he will ever need – but that, as he says, is not the point. It gives him the clout to make more deals, and to turn his other visions into reality.

His critics, and there are plenty, say Trump is brash, vain, ostentatious, opportunistic, a hustler, a parvenu. *Time* magazine has called him 'a symbol of an acquisitive and mercenary age'. He puts it down to envy, and there is no doubt an element of truth in that. His numerous admirers claim that what annoys the critics most is that he so obviously *enjoys* his success. They see him as a shining example of what can be done if one tries hard enough; it keeps their own dreams alive. Associates say that he has a keen eye for cash flow and asset values, and that he is a brilliant negotiator. The press may emphasis the showmanship, with his eager encouragement, but there is a shrewd businessman behind that glamorous façade. His diligent self-promotion may look like an outrageous ego trip, but it has practical value. It attracts wealthy buyers and it lures gamblers to his casinos. There is undeniably a Trump mystique.

Donald himself says, simply, that he loves making deals – the bigger the better. 'That's how I get my kicks.' He is obsessive about work, like his father before him. 'I enjoy working, it's been good for me. My personality could never change. If I were working in a small town shovelling coal, I'd still be the same personality.'

Sharing his life – and work – is his wife, Ivana. Raised in Czechoslovakia, she was a championship skier in the Czech Olympic team before moving to Canada, where she got a job as a model. They met at the Montreal Summer Olympics and were married ten months later. He promptly put his bride right to work, supervising the interior decor of all his projects. He later put her in charge of one of his Atlantic City casinos and she now looks after the Plaza Hotel, for what Trump has described as 'a salary of $1 a year and all the dresses she wants'. He proudly says that she is as competitive as he is. They have three young children. According to Ivana, they are being taught 'traditional values'. Donald hopes that his eldest son, inevitably named Donald Trump Junior, will follow him into the real estate business. The boy has already shown some interest – but will history repeat itself? Donald has all too vivid memories of what happened to his elder brother; his death at an early age was a terrible shock. (The younger brother, Robert, is a quiet, gentle character who works for the company as a vice-president.) Donald is determined to ensure that his own son will have a happier time. It will be fascinating to see how he handles *that* challenge in the years ahead.

11

Fortissimo

London, too, has its share of New Money heroes. One of the most successful is the remarkable Charles Forte, who first arrived in Britain at the age of five, unable to speak a word of English, and later built up a vast hotel and catering empire from a most unlikely base – a Regent Street milk bar. He has now handed the reins to his only son, Rocco, who is determined to make it bigger still.

I have known Charles since his early days as an entrepreneur, and I have long admired not only the skilful way in which he has made his visions come true but also the manner in which father and son have handled what might so easily have been a turbulent relationship. It is one of the happier stories in this book.

Charles Forte was born in a poor mountain village in Italy. His own father (Rocco is named after him) had tried his luck in America, where he was given a job in a factory in Pittsburgh, but he did not take to the New World and returned to the village. Charles says that if the family had stayed there he might have ended up tending goats instead of becoming an international hotelier, a multi-millionaire, and a British lord. But his father was an ambitious man. One of his cousins had gone to Scotland, where he had opened a small shop, and Rocco decided to join him there. He worked hard and soon had a business of his own, a café in Alloa. He sent for his family and Charles journeyed to Scotland with his mother.

It was a bewildering experience for the small boy. He went to a kindergarten and learned to speak English – though with a marked Scottish accent, which he still partly retains despite his many years in the south. He then attended a nearby school, but he was not much of a scholar and he did not enjoy the experience. His father felt that he would do better in Italy and he went to a boarding school in Rome. He loved the city and might well have made it his permanent home, but the Fortes were doing well in Britain and his father was anxious to have him back. The business had expanded considerably – he now had several cafés and a wholesale chocolate and cigarette business. Two of the cousins had started what was to become a string of cafés and ice-cream parlours around the English coast. Charles, then seventeen, decided that his future lay in his father's adopted country – and, having made up his mind, he resolved to become 'the most successful Forte of all'.

Clearly, this could not be accomplished overnight. Rocco insisted that his son should study book-keeping and account-ancy, which he did, and later got him a job with one of his cousins in Weston-super-Mare. He stayed for eighteen months and learned how to run a café. By then his father had decided to leave Scotland and concentrate on the south; he opened a large café in Bournemouth and invited Charles to join him. During the next few years he acquired several other seaside cafés. As a junior partner, Charles was expected to help with everything – he would even wash the dishes. By the time he was twenty-two, he was manager of the family establishment in Brighton. He greatly admired his enterprising father and, in later years, made sure that his own son also learned the trade by starting at the bottom and working his way up. But he still wanted to be 'the greatest Forte of all' and he felt that it could only be done by launching his own business.

One day he read in a London evening paper that an Australian had opened a milk bar in Fleet Street. It was an intriguing idea and he went to have a look at it. The Australian seemed to be doing well, and Charles suggested that they should form a partnership. He had only about £400 in savings, but he reckoned that he could raise more from his father and other relatives. He was turned down, so he walked the streets of London looking for premises that might be suitable for a milk bar venture. He eventually found one in Regent Street and managed to get a lease. His father did not think much of the concept, but reluctantly agreed to put in £1,000 in cash. Charles went to a firm of catering equipment manufacturers and persuaded the senior partner to let him have the necessary equipment on credit. He also talked several other investors into backing him. When he opened his bar, he had a 60 per cent share of the enterprise.

For a time, it seemed that his father's scepticism had been justified. There was no shortage of customers, but he was not making a profit. Something was wrong. Charles realized that until he could find the right balance between income on the one hand, and costs on the other, the sums would not add up. He worked out the essential ratios which would guarantee the profits, and says that the system is still the basis of the vast Trusthouse Forte business. 'It has been refined into more statistics, into graphs, and so on. But if that simple system had not been there from the beginning, I would have stayed in two shops, turning up morning, noon, and night and asking: How are we doing? Have we taken any money today? Can I pay the rent tomorrow?'

When the Second World War began, Charles was interned because of his Italian birth. His real expansionary phase did not begin until it was over. It was then that he embarked on the series of bold take-over moves which were to make him a major force in the hotel and catering business. It took great courage, and he was often short of cash. But he was blessed with enormous energy and he had that essential quality: unlimited self-confidence. He thought big and never took 'no' for an answer.

I first met him when I was the young City Editor of the *Evening Standard*, the paper that had published the item about the Fleet Street milk bar. He struck me as unmistakably Italian: spontaneous, voluble, emotional, gregarious. One could easily see him as the successful owner of a *trattoria*. But there was obviously more to him than that. He had already surprised the financial world by having a go at complacent companies which, he reckoned, could do much better if he were in charge. He had also discovered a crucial fact: that the people who manage banks, insurance companies, and other institutions are always interested in solid assets and ready to listen to entrepreneurs who know how to make them more profitable. Charles Forte was not a wheeler-dealer, in for the quick killing, but he understood the game and had an impressive grasp of essentials. He was not a member of the Establishment – indeed, he was regarded as a foreigner – but his enthusiasm was infectious and he had a good record. He promised much and delivered more.

A crucial stage was reached in 1970, when his company embarked on merger talks with Trust Houses. This resulted in a dramatic and much-publicized struggle, which he won. He went on to build a worldwide organization with more than eight hundred hotels and four hundred restaurants. In his excellent autobiography, published in 1986, he says that he owes everything to his father. This seems unduly modest: Charles had a good apprenticeship, but his great accomplishments were very much his own.

The key to it all, I think, was an extraordinary mix of professionalism and audacity. He has always had a keen eye for detail, combined with grand visions. Walking through a kitchen with him, as I have done on several occasions, is an enlightening experience – nothing, but nothing, escapes him. His staff respect him for it; they know that, if need be, he could do every job himself and do it well. He has been very loyal to colleagues who have worked with him for a long time. But he is also tough, demanding, impatient, temperamental. He has mellowed now that he is in his eighties, and no longer plays as active a role as in the past. But in his prime he was often a difficult man to work for, and not an easy man to have as a father.

His son was born in 1945. He also has five daughters. One, Olga, works for the company: she is in charge of design and decor. But Rocco was always the heir apparent. Charles says that he never pressed him to join the business but was delighted when he decided to do so.

First, of course, there was the matter of his education. Charles sent him to an English public school and went to see him every other weekend. During the school holidays, Rocco earned extra pocket money by working in some of his father's establishments – waiting at table, washing up, and tackling other menial tasks. Charles wanted him to go to university, so he went to Oxford and got a degree in modern languages. (He also became a fencing blue.) He then spent three years getting his articles as a chartered accountant. Rocco might be a 'rich kid' but he was expected to work as hard as his father did. When he joined the company he had to make his way through every division. It was a long and arduous apprenticeship.

He was eventually given various management assignments. One that he particularly enjoyed was running the Sporting Club in Cannes. He had a large measure of independence, met interesting people, and made a profit. 'I sent him there as a punishment,' Charles recalls, 'but he had a great time.'

As Rocco climbed up the corporate ladder there were the usual envious charges of nepotism. He says they never worried him. 'At the end of the day you are judged on your own ability. I think I have shown that I can do the job. If I hadn't joined the company I would have gone into some other business and worked hard to make a success of it.'

His personality is more subdued than that of his father. He is level-headed, well-mannered and better at hiding his feelings. But, as colleagues know, he can be just as tough and determined. Inevitably, the two have clashed from time to time. 'I am a strong-willed character,' Rocco says, 'and so is he. It's hardly surprising that we should occasionally have a difference of opinion. I have felt frustrated at times because I didn't have the authority when I wanted it, but he has given me more and more – a lot of people wouldn't have done that.'

Both recognized a long time ago that they needed each other. Charles wanted his son to succeed him; Rocco relished the prospect of running a large business. 'I am very ambitious,' he says. 'I love the excitement of making things happen. To see the results of one's actions can be very rewarding. In an organization of this size the fascination is endless. My father built up the company; my job is to ensure that it continues to grow. I would like to make it ten times the size it is now. There is a lot of scope for expanding our international operations.'

Trusthouse Forte has performed well since he became chief executive in 1983 (profits have grown substantially) and his father proudly says that 'the business is in safe hands'. The family still has about 10 per cent of the shares and Charles hopes that Rocco will be at the helm for a long time to come. 'We are not just managers,' he says. 'We have a proprietorial interest in the company that has always been with us. When we leave a room, we turn the light out. When we see something that needs painting, we want to see it painted, because we own part of this, we have grown into it, we are part of the whole thing and everything is important to us.' Rocco agrees, but he knows that much depends on how the financial world judges his stewardship.

He is extremely wealthy and could easily afford to lead a life of leisure. Clearly, though, he has no wish to do so. In his bachelor days he escorted a series of attractive women and developed a passion for fast cars, which led gossip columnists to describe him as a playboy. He indignantly denies it; he had fun, yes, but he also worked long hours. In 1986 he married Aliai Ricci, the pretty young daughter of an Italian friend of the family. They now have a child of their own, Lydia.

Charles has always been very keen on keeping fit; so is Rocco. Each year he takes part in that formidable test of endurance, the London Marathon. He knows that he has no chance of winning the event, but that does not deter him. 'I do it,' he says, 'because I enjoy the challenge. The Marathon calls for a big effort. I am content if I can improve on my time.' He also shares his father's fondness for shooting, fishing and golf. He would like to have his own grouse moor; perhaps he will one day get round to buying it. Meanwhile, he has his sights on a target which has proved annoyingly elusive: the Savoy Hotel group. The Fortes made a bid for it in 1981 and ended up owning about 70 per cent of the company, but because of the Savoy's peculiar voting structure they control less than half the votes. Few things would give father and son greater pleasure than being able to walk into one of the group's famous hotels – they include Claridge's and the Connaught – and being welcomed as the undisputed owners.

12

Not a Penny

Another remarkable London entrepreneur, Robert Maxwell, made news in 1988 when he said that he would not leave a penny to his children. It had long been assumed that he had created his vast fortune for their benefit as well as his own, and there was no reason to suppose that he had fallen out with them: on the contrary, the family seemed to be very close.

Maxwell, once a Labour Member of Parliament, explained that he was opposed in principle to inherited wealth. 'It can stifle initiative in a later generation,' he said. The fortune, held by a foundation he set up in Liechtenstein many years ago, would therefore go to charity.

One of his sons, Ian, said after the announcement: 'I and all of my sisters and brothers have always known that the wealth my father helped to create would be returned for the benefit of science and medicine. We are all delighted and welcome it.' Another son, Kevin, has since told me: 'I am grateful for his decision. I do not believe that a child has an inalienable right to inherit. I am very comfortable that I have to fend for myself and may do well through my own endeavours. I have no God-given right to be a billionaire just because Dad is.' He added: 'I went to school with children of wealthy parents, and I saw how much unhappiness can be caused if one has a lot of money at an early age. Some of them had drug problems. I am also glad that money isn't an issue in our family: if it were, we might so easily end up quarrelling.'

Many people find it hard to believe that Dad really means it. They think that, when he dies, the Maxwell family will run the foundation for its own benefit as well as that of various charities. Kevin denies it.

Robert Maxwell had a traumatic childhood. He was the third of nine children of dirt-poor Hasidic Jews who lived in a primitive village in Ruthenia, then part of Czechoslovakia. His father, a labourer, was often unemployed and Robert's abiding memory of those days is that he was perpetually hungry. During the Second World War, he lost his parents and four siblings in Auschwitz; he escaped by joining the Czech underground. He was caught and sentenced to death, but managed to get away. He then joined the French Foreign Legion, together with other Czech volunteers. He came to Britain at the age of seventeen, wearing a French uniform and not knowing a word of English. He later became a British army officer and was awarded the Military Cross for bravery.

It is an extraordinary story, and there is no doubt that it has had a deep and lasting effect on him. He is passionately opposed to war in any shape or form. 'I would hate to see my children go through the same experience,' he says.

Fortunately, they have not had to. They have had a relatively comfortable life, though with a father like him it has not been easy. He has always been a workaholic with great ambitions – a restless, mercurial, highly competitive, and very demanding man, never satisfied with his achievements, no matter how impressive they may seem to others. In his excellent biography, Joe Haines quotes a former employee as saying: 'He is an attractive monster with a touch of genius.' It strikes me as an apt description. I have known Maxwell for a long time and for the past two years I have been one of his senior executives. He has considerable charm, which he knows how to use to good effect, and a wide range of talents, including an extraordinary gift for languages. He can drill to the core of any issue, and his enthusiasm is infectious. He makes things *happen*, which is why I went to work for him. But he *can* be a monster. His moods change with lightning speed and his rages are awesome. He is constantly ordering, pushing, scolding, and hectoring.

Maxwell often appears to be quite unaware of the effect this has on others. He can be kind and considerate, and sometimes seems genuinely surprised when people tell him that they want to quit. How can they desert him? He admits that his behaviour can be exasperating, but he is building a great communications empire and you cannot do that without being tough, can you? Yes, he is impatient. He wants results and he wants them now. Yes, he expects a lot. But, he points out, he sets a good example: no one works harder than he does. Yes, he sometimes loses his temper. But people often do foolish things and he is not the kind of man who suffers fools gladly.

All true. The problem is that not everyone has his stamina, dedication, and sense of mission. Not everyone lives to work. Not everyone has the ability to build an empire. Maxwell knows he is unique, but he thinks others should be just like him – which is impossible. Late one Friday night, not long ago, he was flying home from Paris. He looked at his son Ian, stretched out in the lounge, exhausted. 'This generation, they flake out,' he said with a sigh. 'Hey, Dad,' Ian protested, 'I've put in a fourteen-hour day.' Maxwell frowned and said: 'That's what I mean.'

He started his business after the war. It was a stroke of genius to recognize the enormous potential in the international exchange of scientific information. He borrowed money and launched science journals which he made required reading throughout the world. Today his company, Pergamon, has several hundred and is hugely profitable. He has since come to play a more glamorous role as a press baron, but it was this basic concept – so simple and yet so grand – which laid the foundation for his empire.

Most people would have been content with it; not Maxwell. He also wanted to be a newspaper proprietor, so he bought the Mirror Group. Now he wants to have one of the world's ten leading communications groups. He is well on the way to achieving it, following his acquisition of the Macmillan group in the United States. His fertile mind produces a constant stream of new ideas. Ask him why he is doing it and he invariably replies: 'I want to be of service.' Question his seemingly inexhaustible appetite for work and he says: 'I like to keep busy.'

He has been loyally supported for forty-five years by his charming wife, Betty, who comes from a wealthy French family and who has given him nine children. Their first-born son, Michael, died after a car accident when he was only twenty-one. They also lost a daughter, Karine, when she was still a little girl. She had acute leukaemia. All the surviving seven children had to prove themselves academically before embarking on a career. All but one have worked for him at one time or another. Philip is a scientist with a job at Pergamon's office in Oxford. Christine runs a subsidiary called Sci-Tech Publishing Services Inc. in California. Ghislaine is in charge of Maxwell's Corporate Gifts, one of the many companies in the group. Ian and Kevin are joint managing directors of Maxwell Communications. He drives them harder than anyone else.

Ian and Kevin both have dual British-French citizenship and are bilingual. They did well at university and could easily have found employment elsewhere. But they admire their father and are constantly striving to please him.

Ian graduated from Balliol with a BA honours degree in French and history and joined the business immediately afterwards. Robert told him that he was in favour of nepotism, provided that those who benefited from it had the ability to do the job. Being a Maxwell was an advantage, but it also imposed obligations. He could not let the side down. In 1980, at the age of twenty-four, Ian was made managing director of Pergamon subsidiaries in France and Germany. All seemed to be going nicely – until he was abruptly fired when he failed to pick up Robert at Orly airport because he preferred to meet a girl instead of keeping an appointment with his father.

Ian later recalled his dismay in a contribution which he, along with the other children, made to a special book compiled for Robert's sixtieth birthday. 'I called you at the Paris apartment from a roadside phone outside Mâcon at 11 p.m. to make my apologies – only to be told that this was a gross dereliction of responsibility, that I was putting love before duty and that I was duly relieved of the managing directorships of both our French and German offices. I don't know if you can imagine what it was like hearing this bombshell that night, stuck in a phone booth, running out of money some 300 miles south of Paris. I thought the world had caved in – and I'd just been ignominiously jettisoned earlier in the day by my then girlfriend to boot!'

Father and son made it up a couple of months later at the Mark Hopkins Hotel in San Francisco. 'You are not a man to hold grudges or to belabour a point,' Ian wrote in the birthday book. 'I often think you unnecessarily use a howitzer to shoot a chicken, but when the smoke has cleared the chicken often discovers that you were only firing blanks.'

He added: 'You know, of course, that you are an impossible

act to follow, but you are a marvellous example to try to emulate in so many ways.'

Ian became Vice-President, Marketing, of Pergamon Press in New York. He has also been chairman of one of the football clubs owned by the Maxwells. In recent years he has spent much of his time looking after the group's interests in France. He is a director of TFI, the main French television service. But Robert makes a habit of dispatching Ian and Kevin to any part of the world at any time to follow up contacts, make speeches and presentations, and negotiate deals. They have also accompanied him on his numerous trips, often at such short notice that they have barely had time to pack more than their passports.

Travelling with Robert Maxwell is a memorable experience. He has a helicopter pad on the top of his office, so that he can reach Heathrow in a matter of minutes. There his private jet waits for him. He has no patience with formalities like customs and passport control: he expects VIP treatment and gets it. In the plane, he makes constant phone calls or holds a meeting with executives. On arrival, he rushes to his appointment, makes whatever deal he has in mind, and quite frequently gets back to his London office on the same day. Or he may suddenly decide to go somewhere else – to Moscow, perhaps, or to Frankfurt. He has so many things on the go that you never quite know what he will do next. When he has to be in New York, he often takes Concorde (an aircraft made for people like him) and has another company helicopter to whisk him away from the airport to the Manhattan offices of Macmillan.

Ian has learned to take all this whirlwind activity in his stride. Like other executives, he even puts up with being telephoned at 2 a.m. because he knows that, for his father, there are no time zones.

Kevin, who is two and a half years younger, also has an Oxford degree. He joined Pergamon after leaving university, but left in 1984 after a domestic disagreement with his father. Robert objected to his marriage. Kevin had met Pandora Warnford-Davies at Oxford and had lived with her from the age of twenty while they were still undergraduates. At twenty-five, he decided that they should get married and she accepted his proposal. Robert was against it. What was the rush? There were so many other important things to do. Kevin stood his ground. He pointed out that Robert himself had been only twenty-one at the time of his marriage. Anyway, he said, he was old enough to make his own decisions about life and he had every intention of going ahead. Robert turned up at the wedding, but Kevin nonetheless went to work for another company.

He stayed away for just under a year. His father found that he missed him and invited him to return at a much higher salary. Kevin gave it careful thought. He had enjoyed his spell of independence, but he also missed his father and the exciting world he had created. Robert was difficult – no doubt about that. Even as a child Kevin had found him a hard taskmaster: the school report was always a fraught occasion because he would not tolerate second best. Kevin knew what lay ahead of him; so did Pandora. But he was still young and he decided to give it another try.

The next few years were to be every bit as frantic as he had expected. With Ian in Paris, he was most closely involved in his father's daunting work schedule. He turned up early every morning, long before the rest of the staff, for parental lessons in business affairs. The rest of the day was spent in a seemingly endless round of meetings. He often had to remain in the office until late at night, negotiating the details of one of Robert's many acquisitions. He went to Moscow, Beijing, Tokyo, Geneva, Frankfurt. He stood in for his father when Robert had agreed to address some conference but decided that he could not, after all, spare the time. It was heady stuff for someone still in his twenties, but as a friend and colleague I occasionally felt sorry for him. I could lead a reasonable personal life; he could not.

Robert still insisted on making most of the decisions and would not hesitate to reverse any decision made by his son, which undermined his authority with the executives who reported to him. But Kevin realized that he still had a lot to learn, and he had great respect for his father's business acumen. Fortunately, he was also better at hiding his emotions. When they disagreed, they did so in private.

Kevin is in many ways like his father, though much less volatile. He has the same ability to grasp the essentials of any situation and he has become a skilful negotiator. Most people speak highly of him. He is never pretentious or arrogant, and although he can be very tough he denies that he has a ruthless streak. 'Ruthlessness,' he says, 'is not an attribute I would like to cultivate. It's not necessary.' He sees himself as a manager who manages his assets well; if it involves sacking people, that is part and parcel of the responsibility.

In his own contribution to the birthday book, he thanked his father for being a good teacher. He added: 'Above all, you have given me the sense of excitement of having dozens of balls in the air and the thrill of seeing some of them land right.' He has since moved to New York to look after the day-to-day running of Macmillan, which Robert acquired in 1988 for a staggering $2.7 billion. He and Pandora have three young children and live in a country house twenty minutes from the city. He commutes to the office every day, and still makes frequent trips across the Atlantic. He is widely regarded as the heir apparent.

Kevin says that he and his father now have an 'incredibly close' relationship. 'I have never felt in his shadow, only that he is a tremendous help. I stand up to him all the time but not for its own sake. We are very much a partnership. Sometimes he wins, sometimes I win.' He recognises that many people still think he only has his important job because he is a Maxwell. 'I don't let it bother me,' he says. 'I know that I have to prove that I can do it, and I intend to do just that.'

13

The Snatch Racket

One of the great fears of the rich is that their children will be kidnapped for ransom. The risk is a price one pays for being successful and famous, which is a major reason why so many wealthy people hate publicity. It may be good for the ego, but it can have all kinds of unfortunate consequences.

Kidnapping is as old as history, though the word itself goes back only to the seventeenth century – it was first used to describe the 'trade of decoying and spiriting away young children to ship them to foreign plantations'. Julius Caesar was kidnapped by pirates in 78 BC; they collected a ransom but after he was set free he pursued them and saw to it that they were executed. Richard 1, Coeur de Lion, was kidnapped on his way home from the crusades in 1192 and held captive for more than a year. In medieval England the abduction of wealthy heiresses was commonplace. When a suitor was rejected he simply took. The Government eventually imposed stiff penalties for such behaviour and in 1707 it was made punishable by hanging. By the late eighteenth century it had largely died out.

In America, the early 1930s saw what newspapers described as an 'epidemic' of the crime – the 'snatch racket'. The most famous case was the kidnapping of the Lindbergh baby which produced such a public furore that it helped to build up a new law enforcement agency, the FBI, and gave its name to a new law, the Lindbergh Law.

The famous aviator lived with his family in a remote New Jersey farmhouse four miles from the nearest road. Charles Junior was put to bed at his usual time by his nurse. When, later that evening, she went to check that he was asleep the cot was empty. There was a ransom note on the window sill. When the news was made public, it caused a sensation. Lindbergh was a national hero: how could anyone do this to him? More than 100,000 people offered their help – including Al Capone, who was serving an eleven-year jail sentence and who confidently asserted that, if released, he would get the baby back. Ships and planes were brought in to help in the search. It was in vain: seventy-two days after the kidnapping, the body of Charles Junior was found in a small hollow about a mile from the Lindbergh home.

As more kidnappings followed, death penalty bills were introduced in several states. In June 1932, a Federal Kidnapping Bill was passed and the young director of the FBI, J. Edgar Hoover, was put in charge of 'a nationwide warfare against racketeers, kidnappers, and other criminals'. Hoover declared that he knew of 'no more heinous crime than kidnapping' and his agents went to work. They had considerable success. A 35-year-old German carpenter, Bruno Hauptmann, was charged with the Lindbergh kidnapping and went to the electric chair under New Jersey Law. (The Federal Bill did not, initially, include the death penalty, but after a six-year-old girl was abducted on her way home from school, and chained to a stake in the desert, President Roosevelt signed an amendment.) By 1938, the epidemic was over.

There have been many other cases on both sides of the Atlantic in more recent decades. Two that particularly caught the public eye, in the early 1970s, were the kidnapping of Patty Hearst in California and of Paul Getty III in Rome. Around that time, too, Greek authorities arrested two gangs – one Greek, one West German – on charges of plotting to seize John F. Kennedy Jr and hold him to ransom.

In Italy, which had become notorious for this kind of thing, another hazard emerged: the possibility of being mistaken for someone else. British businessman Rolf Schild was kidnapped while on holiday in Sardinia; the gang, unfamiliar with English, apparently thought he was a member of the Rothschild clan. A more obvious risk is that kidnappers, taking their information from press estimates which are often exaggerated, may overestimate the amounts of money which the family of a victim can raise. An Italian friend of mine is an economics professor who, some years ago, was appointed head of a bank. His name frequently appeared in the newspapers and a gang of kidnappers assumed, wrongly, that any man who was head of a bank must be extremely wealthy. They abducted his young grandson and demanded an enormous ransom. My friend was frantic. He loved the child but simply did not have the cash. He sold his house; so did the boy's parents. It was not nearly enough. He borrowed as much as he could, but the kidnappers were still not satisfied. He eventually managed to convince them that they had squeezed him dry. The child was released, unharmed. On the day the little boy came home he solemnly said to my friend: 'Grandfather, I'm not going back to school. I'm going to start work so I can pay you back.'

One predictable outcome of all this activity, and the publicity given to it, was a sharp increase in the amount spent on personal security. People hired bodyguards (including female agents who could pose as their children's nursemaids or governesses), bought Dobermann pinschers, and installed expensive alarm systems. There was also a rush to take out a ransom insurance: Lloyd's of London had been offering this kind of policy for years, but now a number of American firms did likewise. Many prominent people, who had once made strenuous efforts to get their names into the newspapers, hired public relations men to keep their names *out* of them.

Security has remained a thriving industry. Most millionaires recognize that nothing guarantees complete success: if a gang wants to kidnap someone, they will. Kidnappers have tended to become increasingly professional. They may spend months – and considerable sums of money – preparing their move. But the rich feel they must do *something* to protect themselves against this menace.

One of the first and often most difficult decisions that relatives have to make is whether to call in the police. The kidnappers' instructions are always explicit: keep quiet or else. The family has to consider the risks. For the police it is just another job; there is no emotional commitment. An incompetent or over-zealous officer may make a mess of it. It is tempting, especially if one is rich, to conduct secret negotiations, hand over the ransom, and get the victim back without any fuss.

In Italy, there was an outcry when a magistrate announced that henceforth he would block all the assets belonging to the family of someone who had been kidnapped, so that there would be no money to pay the ransom. For a while the move seemed quite effective, but then it was found that people simply stopped going to the police. When the authorities did get to hear of a case, they found families totally unco-operative. Ransom money continued to be paid; families who had their assets blocked borrowed it from wealthy friends. The magistrate abandoned his hard line.

It is natural that people should want to save the lives of those they love. But the issues are not always as clear-cut as they seem. Consider what happened in the two famous cases mentioned earlier – the kidnappings of Patty Hearst and Paul Getty III.

'Don't let me be killed'

In July 1973, a few days after sixteen-year-old Paul Getty III had apparently gone missing in Rome, a letter arrived by special delivery at the apartment he shared with his German girlfriend, Martine. It was addressed to his mother, Gail, and was in Paul's handwriting.

> Dear Mummy,
> Since Monday, I have fallen into the hands of kidnappers. Don't let me be killed. Arrange things so that police don't intervene. You must absolutely not take the thing as a joke.
> Try and get in contact with the kidnappers in the manner and the way they tell you to.
> Don't let the police know about the negotiations if you don't want me to be killed.
> I want to live and to be free again. Arrange things so that police don't know I have written to this address.
> Don't publicise my kidnapping.
> This is all you have to know. If you delay, it is very dangerous for me. I love you.
>
> Paul

Martine hurried round to Gail's apartment on the Via dei Monti Parioli with the letter, but Paul's mother was out so she took it to the police. They were sceptical. True, there had been a number of kidnappings in recent months and, as the grandson and namesake of 'the richest man in the world', Paul was an obvious target. But they suspected that it might be a hoax – arranged by Paul himself.

He was already well known to them. A rootless and troublesome young man, he had been spending most of his time with the hippies in the Piazza Navona and at night could often be found drunk in dubious clubs and discothèques. He loved to drive his Harley-Davidson motor-cycle at dangerous speeds through the crowded and narrow streets around the Vatican. He had once been arrested during a communist demonstration and accused of throwing a Molotov cocktail into the *carabinieri* barracks. The charges had been dropped, but the arrest had made headlines and the press had dubbed him 'the golden hippie' and 'the darling of the Rome hippie colony'. The police knew he was penniless; he and an Italian friend earned what they could by painting and selling their work on the Spanish Steps.

Their suspicion increased when the first demand for money came on the following day. The kidnappers telephoned and asked for 300 million lire (then about 300 thousand pounds.) The police felt that the modest ransom demand was the work of amateurs and turned up evidence that Paul had been socializing with known criminals. They also told the press that, when she was closely questioned, Martine had revealed that he had talked about arranging his own kidnapping 'to raise money'. The Rome daily newspaper, *Il Messagero*, carried the headline: 'Kidnap or joke?'

Paul's mother, however, was convinced that her son was in danger. She called the reporters in and told them that she was willing to pay a ransom for his safe release. 'I hope to know, to have proof,' she said, 'that my son is well. I hope that it will all end as quickly as possible. We don't know how the next contact will be made. The important thing is that they be convinced we are willing to deal.'

She immediately sought help from her ex-husband (she and Paul's father had been divorced in 1965) and from the boy's grandfather. The old man, reputed to be worth billions, refused to have anything to do with the affair. He issued a brief, prepared statement in answer to all press inquiries: 'Although I see my grandson infrequently and I am not particularly close to him, I love him nonetheless. However, I don't believe in paying kidnappers. I have fourteen other grandchildren and if I pay one penny now, then I will have fourteen kidnapped grand-children.'

Getty had been charmed by the boy when he was very young, but he thoroughly disapproved of what the 'bright, red-headed little rascal' had become. Paul III had antagonized him not only by his behaviour but also by his open expressions of contempt for all that the rich stood for. 'I am a refugee from a Rolls-Royce,' he had written. 'I am an escapee from the credit card. I can eat one meal a day. And life is a banquet. The rich are the poor people of this earth. They are a suffering minority whose malnutrition is of the spirit. Pity the rich. In terms of living they are beggars.'

Like the police, the older Getty also had doubts whether the kidnapping was genuine. But his view that paying the ransom would only encourage more kidnappings was sincerely held. His refusal made headlines round the world and was widely seen as yet another example of the billionaire's legendary meanness.

On 24 July the kidnappers, or those posing as kidnappers, increased their demand to a staggering 10 billion lire – some 15 million pounds. In a telephone call to Gail's lawyer, they said: 'We want to be paid in very small notes. You will be told later where the exchange will be done. Let us know on radio or TV if you agree to the terms.'

That evening, the lawyer called a press conference and said the ransom was unreasonable and the kidnappers should ask for less. Four days later there was another telephone call: 'What do you mean you can't pay that much? You want to find the boy dead somewhere?'

'There isn't that much money in the whole world.'

'How much can you pay?'

'The most kidnappers in Italy ever got was 300 million lire.'

'That is a joke. We have spent that much on expenses.'

'I'll talk to the boy's mother, but I know she doesn't have any money.'

'Tell her to get it from London.'

A week later, the kidnappers seemed ready to settle for 300 million lire. Gail's lawyer offered them about a fifth of that amount – a hundred thousand dollars. Three weeks passed and the demand was up again, this time to 3 billion lire. The lawyer repeated his earlier offer.

'For a hundred thousand dollars,' said the angry voice on the telephone, 'we'll send you a photo of the boy missing an arm or a leg.'

The police saw the wavering demands as further evidence that the kidnapping was a hoax. Even the lawyer was beginning to have doubts. But there was at least a possibility that the whole business was all too real, and the family sent an emissary to Rome to investigate and, if necessary, to act as an intermediary.

By this time, Paul had been missing for more than a month. Later, much later, it was to become clear that the kidnapping had indeed been real and that he had undergone a frightful ordeal – grabbed by a group of men, driven blindfolded to the bleak mountains of Calabria, chained to a stake under a makeshift shelter, and watched day and night by armed guards wearing masks. Meanwhile, he was able to listen to news bulletins on a small transistor which they had given him and he was understandably dismayed when he heard people being interviewed in Rome declaring their firm belief that he had not been kidnapped at all. In the weeks that followed he was moved to different locations, and the guards began threatening to cut off one of his fingers unless his grandfather paid the ransom soon. 'We'll send them a piece each month,' one of them warned him, 'until he pays. We'll cut you into little pieces for a whole year.'

On 10 November, an express package posted twenty days before in Naples arrived at the Rome offices of *Il Messagero*. Inside it, sealed in a plastic bag, was a human ear with a tuft of blood-encrusted reddish hair and a written note: 'We are the kidnappers of Paul Getty. We keep our promises and send the ear. Now find out whether it belongs to Paul. Unless you pay the ransom within ten days, we shall send you the other ear. And then other pieces of his anatomy.'

The paper contacted Gail, who immediately identified the ear as Paul's. A forensic expert also confirmed that it had been cut from a living human being and that 'comparisons indicate it belonged to Paul Getty'. But to make sure there was no misunderstanding another Rome daily, *I Tempo*, was invited to send a reporter to a location on the Rome–Naples highway. There he found an envelope containing Polaroid pictures of Paul standing in front of a cave. His right ear was missing. In the envelope was a note threatening to cut off his foot next.

The world was horrified, and the older Getty at last recognized that something had to be done. As he subsequently recalled in his autobiography: 'with that [the amputation] it became apparent that there was no hope of outwaiting – or outbluffing – the kidnappers. Criminals who would savagely mutilate a victim would not hesitate to kill him.' Publicly, though, he continued to insist that he would not pay any ransom. 'My position is still the same,' he said. 'I must consider the safety and welfare of all my grandchildren and the rest of the family. What has happened to my grandson Paul is heartbreaking and I pray that he will be safely returned. But I know that for me to become involved in any ransom could make things worse. It is a lonely decision, but I know it is the right one.' Privately, he told his son, Paul's father, that the ransom should be paid by him because there was no knowing what the kidnappers would demand if they felt that 'the richest man in the world' was ready to give in. It was decided that they would offer a ransom of one million dollars. As Paul II did not have that kind of money, his father agreed to lend him $850,000 at 4 per cent interest, on the understanding that it would be repaid in full by an annual deduction of $7^{1}/_{2}$ per cent of the funds which Paul II received from the Sarah C. Getty Trust. A formal agreement was drawn up.

On 17 November lawyers acting for J. Paul Getty II issued a statement in London: 'Mr Getty has offered to pay a ransom to the kidnappers. The amount is the maximum that the father is able to raise for the return of the boy. Acting upon the advice of those familiar with such cases, he has required that the boy be released simultaneously with the payment of the ransom, since this is the only way in which the safety of the boy can be assured.'

Gail wrote an open letter pleading with the kidnappers to accept the ransom and release her son:

We have talked at length, you and I. Always I have felt that you were surprised because the grandfather and father have not been moved by the future of young Paul. You have not believed me. Yet this is the truth. I have interceded with the grandfather and the father. The grandfather has remained firm. But the father has agreed to pay a ransom of one million dollars (more than that he cannot give you). I beg of you – accept the money that has been offered to you. In this supreme moment of my life as a mother, decisive only for the life of my son,

I feel only pity. Pity for my little Paul, so alone, his adorable face mutilated. Pity for you, who do not know what is good in life.

The kidnappers, however, insisted that one million was not enough. In the end, the old man relented: out of the $3.2 million demanded he would contribute $2.2 million and lend the rest to his son. The money was put into an Italian bank and then withdrawn in small notes, every one of which was recorded on microfilm. A Getty associate took the money to the destination nominated by the kidnappers, on the highway to Calabria. Police agents in disguise trailed him and were able to get the registration number of the kidnappers' car, which subsequently led to their identification.

Paul was driven from the hideout to the same highway, blindfolded, and set free. When the local police found him, the seventeen-year-old boy told his rescuers: 'I am Paul Getty. Give me a cigarette. Look, they cut off my ear.'

In London, his father made a brief statement to the press. 'I intend,' he said, 'to devote the rest of my energies to teaching the Italians the meaning of the word "vendetta". I suggest those associated with the kidnapping would be well advised to sleep always with one eye open.' A spokesman for the old man said it was his eighty-first birthday and the boy's release was 'the finest present he could have'.

The Italian police eventually tracked down the kidnappers, who turned out to be members of a Mafia-style gang. Paul identified one of the ringleaders at their trial, and some of them were given jail sentences. Only $17,000 was ever recovered. During the trial, the prosecutor said there was 'no doubt that the hypothesis that Getty faked his kidnapping was false'. Martine, the girlfriend, denied ever telling the police that Paul talked about arranging his own kidnapping to extort money. (She later married him and they had a child, Paul Getty IV.)

The old man, inevitably, was much criticized for his handling of the affair. How could a billionaire be so callous? He might have been suspicious about the circumstances, but the money was small change to him. If he truly loved his grandson, as he claimed, he surely should have acted at once.

With hindsight, the long delay certainly seems hard to understand and his decision to make his son repay the loan looks extraordinarily mean. But Getty's basic point was valid enough: there was every reason to fear that, if the kidnappers had gained an easy victory, others might well have been encouraged to go after his other grandchildren.

The Urban Guerrilla

The Getty dilemma still troubles many wealthy people with large families. They also recall, with uneasiness, another case that hit the headlines in the mid-1970s: the kidnapping of Patty Hearst. It raised a question which is as relevant today as it was then: how vulnerable are the children of the rich to brainwashing by determined kidnappers?

Patty Hearst, granddaughter of publishing millionaire William Randolph Hearst, was nineteen when she was abducted while having a shower at the apartment she shared with the man she was about to marry, Steven Webb, near the campus of the University of California in Berkeley. A white woman and two black men broke in, knocked Steven out with a bottle, and carried her off naked and struggling. They later announced that they were members of the self-styled Symbionese Liberation Army. When, a few months earlier, they had killed the schools' superintendent for Oakland, a man called Marcus Foster, they had warned that their next stop was going to be the kidnapping of a 'prominent person'. They chose Patty. She would be released, they said, in exchange for a food distribution programme to the poor of San Francisco.

For the next six weeks she was kept in a closet, blindfolded, and subjected to periodic indoctrination by her captors. She was bullied, ranted at, lied to, and threatened with immediate execution if the police should try to free her.

Miss Hearst became a true media event. At the direction of her kidnappers, she sent taped messages to the outside world urging that her father and the state government meet the demands for her release. The first cassettes were subdued, reassuring. The tone changed: soon she was hectoring her father over what seemed to her his callous reluctance to speed up the food distribution. When the first food delivery programmes ended in ugly riots, a cassette arrived full of abuse and rancour. 'I have been hearing reports about the food programme. So far it sounds like you and your advisers have managed to turn it into a real disaster . . . it sounds like most of the food is of low quality. No one received any beef or lamb, and it certainly doesn't sound like the kind of food our family is eating.' She berated her mother for wearing a black dress on television, saying: 'That doesn't help at all.'

Thirteen weeks after the kidnapping Randolph Hearst managed to settle the details of the ransom: $4 million in trust placed in San Francisco's Wells Fargo Bank, together with a legally binding agreement to release $2 million worth of food if Patty were released within a month, and a further $2 million nine months later. Mrs Hearst put aside her black dress and the family prepared to greet their daughter home. Instead, they received an astonishing new tape. Patty's voice sounded cool and crisp. 'Mom, Dad, I would like to comment on your efforts to supposedly secure my safety . . . You were playing games – stalling for time – time which the FBI was using in their attempts to assassinate me and the SLA elements which guarded me . . . I have been given the choice of, one, being released in a safe area or, two, joining the forces of the Symbionese Liberation Army and fighting for my freedom and the freedom of all oppressed people. I have chosen to stay and fight.'

On Easter Monday, a few weeks later, the SLA, having run out of funds, held up the Hibernia Bank in San Francisco. They got away with $10,000, wounding two passers-by. When the FBI released the photographs taken by the bank's camera there was no doubt at all in anyone's mind that the girl in the black wig in the middle of the lobby, brandishing a gun, was Patty Hearst. A 'Wanted' poster went up for her arrest, with the words 'Considered Armed and Dangerous'.

For the next eighteen months, she remained with the SLA as a loyal participant in the group's addle-brained mission. The police stormed the SLA hideout in a black neighbourhood of Los Angeles, and everyone in the house was killed, but Patty was absent at the time. She was eventually captured and, despite protesting that she had been coerced to join in by her captors, she was sent to jail for bank robbery and other felonies. After serving twenty-two months she was pardoned by President Carter and returned to the family about whom she had said: 'I would never choose to live the rest of my life surrounded by pigs like the Hearsts.' She later married her bodyguard.

Psychiatrists say that it is not unusual for victims of kidnappings to develop a friendly relationship with their captors. The first stage of the ordeal is generally disbelief and anger, often accompanied by threats of what the law will do to them when (not if) they are caught. This is followed by fear of what may happen if they cannot be traced, or the ransom is not paid, or the kidnappers become desperate enough to kill. Threats of imminent execution or mutilation can keep a hostage in a constant state of panic.

At this point he or she may decide to try another approach altogether. The emphasis switches to humouring the captors, to go along with whatever strategy they propose. Letters are written, tape messages are recorded, and the victim may agree to make a video film. The script is, of course, written by the kidnappers and invariably includes strong emotional pleas.

If weeks go by without a result – as happened in the case of Patty Hearst – there is usually a keen sense of betrayal. Has the victim been forgotten? Doesn't anybody *care*?

Now the resentment is turned against the family rather than the captors, who readily agree that the parents or other relatives are being unreasonable. Why don't they *do* something?

Even Aldo Moro, the former Italian prime minister who was kidnapped by the Red Brigade, wrote letters to the leaders of the Christian Democrat Party that became, day by day, more accusatory and forlorn. Imagine, then, the feelings of a nineteen-year-old girl who knew that her parents could easily meet the demands and who had to wait many lonely weeks for action.

As the outside world turns into 'them', the victim becomes increasingly eager to please the captors. They have a common cause: both want to solve the problem. Survival lies in collaboration. It may grow into friendship of a sort – a phenomenon which has been called the 'Stockholm syndrome', following a well-publicized case in Sweden. In 1973, an escaped Swedish convict, Jan-Erik Olsen, walked into one of Stockholm's largest banks, produced a submachine-gun, and took some hostages, two of them young girls. During the six days of their captivity, these prisoners developed a curious affection for Olsen and a fellow-convict who had joined him. When they were released, and the gunmen were led away by police, one of the girls called out to Olsen's accomplice: 'Clark, I'll see you again.' Long afterwards she continued to feel close to the two men; Olsen, too, told police that he could not have killed his hostages because he had got to know them too well.

But it is one thing to be friendly and quite another to take an active part in the captors' criminal activities *after* the family has agreed to pay the ransom. That is what made the Hearst case so incredible.

Patty may have lost all sense of direction and identity during the weeks she was kept in solitary confinement, but she admitted later that she was never unaware of what she was doing. Her relationship with the kidnappers went well beyond what she may have felt was necessary to survive. That is what persuaded the court to uphold her conviction – and what frightens wealthy parents.

What they find hard to understand is that young people from their kind of sheltered background can, apparently, be converted to radical causes by a bunch of ruthless fanatics. Why on earth should an attractive nineteen-year-old like Patty have wanted to rob a bank to support a ridiculous organization calling itself the Symbionese Liberation Army? How *could* she have turned into an 'urban guerrilla'?

They forget – or, more likely, have never discovered in the first place – that many of these fanatics are intelligent and educated people who sincerely believe in what they say. They talk persuasively about Marx or Lenin, Mao or Che Guevara. They eloquently denounce the rich and insist that only drastic measures can bring justice to the world.

Few go to extremes like kidnapping their potential allies, but one should certainly not underrate the appeal of such fervour to impressionable young men and women. Patty Hearst was clearly fascinated by the SLA's plan to distribute food to the poor. The California of the 1970s was full of people who wanted to change the world. It still is. Mercifully, they do not all feel the compulsion to become 'urban guerrillas' and rob banks.

14

Family Feuds

The threat to family unity does not always come from outside; often, the members of a wealthy clan fall out without any help from others. When they do, it can lead to bitter feuds which sometimes go on for many years.

Family fights are not confined to the rich, and it would be wrong to give the impression that they are more prone to squabbling than anyone else. Feuds are the exception rather than the rule. They usually centre round two fascinating subjects – power and money – and because they so often turn into protracted legal battles they tend to attract a lot of attention. Like everyone else, the rich would much prefer to keep their disputes private. But this is difficult to do when the fight involves millions and the courts get involved. The press and television love to see wealthy people get into scraps with their 'own kind' and can always be relied upon to give them maximum publicity.

Rivalry, envy, and plain bloodymindedness all play a part in these conflicts. The rich can afford to pursue even the most frivolous litigation, and the legal profession has a vested interest in encouraging them to do so.

The risk of dissent grows as the family expands. The founder generally manages to maintain at least a semblance of unity while he is alive. His children may be engaged in a power struggle behind the scenes, but he is usually in a position to assert his authority. The danger becomes much greater when he departs for that Great Boardroom in the Sky, leaving behind him a will which, in trying to be fair to everyone, causes all kinds of trouble. Cousins and other relatives may get involved in the struggle, along with his own children. The sheer number of second or third generation members can split a family apart. It becomes too large, too diverse in interests, and too scattered geographically to maintain common interests. The family members who do not work at the company become critical of those who do, and seek either to take over or to sell out.

Second marriages, divorce settlements, and the birth of new children can all lead to serious disputes. In many cases, corporate predators, along with lawyers, try to exploit the divisions. Individual family members are offered tempting sums of cash to part with their shares, which may be used as a springboard for a bid that is unwelcome to the sons or cousins who are active in the business. Naturally, they tend to see such deals as an act of betrayal. Trusts and other devices can help to keep an enterprise in family hands, but the defection of one or more shareholders has forced the sale of many family-owned enterprises and caused permanent bitterness between relatives.

To many people, these nasty quarrels seem further proof of the selfishness and greed of the rich. The interests of loyal employees are seldom considered, nor is the public interest. They fight because they have no sense of commitment to anyone but themselves. But sometimes the issues are much more complex than it may appear: the participants in the struggle are passionately committed to the business and determined to defend their rights.

The Gucci War

The name 'Gucci' is associated throughout the world with elegance and style. Most people were, therefore, astonished by the extraordinary story that hit the headlines in September 1986: Aldo Gucci, the 82-year-old patriarch of the famous clan, had been sent to jail. Even more extraordinary was the fact that the man primarily responsible for his public humiliation was one of his three sons, Paolo Gucci. It was the bitter outcome to a family quarrel that the press had gleefully dubbed 'The Gucci War'.

In the dock of the Manhattan courtrooms, Aldo was in tears as Judge Vincent L. Broderick sentenced him to prison for a year and a day. His career had been one of the great success stories of the times, yet here he was, at an age when he could reasonably have expected to enjoy a luxurious retirement, being treated like a common criminal. Judge Broderick made it clear that the punishment would have been even more severe but for Aldo's age and his obvious repentance. Millions of dollars had been 'diverted' to accounts outside the country. Taxes of seven million had been evaded. This kind of behaviour, said the judge, was simply not acceptable in the United States.

During the much-publicized trial, Aldo had admitted that 'fraudulent devices' were used to get the money out. But he had pleaded not guilty to the charges of tax evasion: this, he insisted, had been done without his knowledge by an accountant of the firm, who had since died. He had offered to repay the entire sum, plus interest.

When he heard the verdict, Aldo refrained from condemning Paolo and other members of the family who had brought the crime to the attention of the authorities. 'Some of my sons,' he said, 'have done their duty and others have had the satisfaction of a revenge. God will be their judge.' It is not hard to imagine, though, how he must have felt. Italian families are not supposed to wash their dirty linen in public. Cheating the state was a common enough practice, but usually one could rely on family members to keep quiet about it. He had made his children rich, and he had been betrayed. How *could* Paolo have done this to him?

Paolo's 'defence' was that his father and others had treated him badly. He had been unjustly fired from the family business, even though he was a director and a shareholder, and then had been prevented from marketing his own products under his own name. At a heated board meeting, he had been physically assaulted by some of the Guccis. It was an outrage. His only recourse had been to sue them for breach of contract, infliction of severe emotional stress, and assault and battery. He had not intended to reveal evidence of illegal transactions and he had certainly not envisaged that his father would go to jail. He had hoped that the mere threat of court action would force the old man to accept that Paolo had at least the right to trade under his own name. But Aldo had remained adamant. It was *his* fault that the authorities had learned about the family's transgressions.

Paolo had a point: his father surely ought to have foreseen the consequences. But he clearly could not bring himself to make peace with his unhappy son. Paolo was furious and his lawyers made the most of the case, which included the argument that he had been sacked because he had questioned the board's 'conspiratorial and malicious conduct' in running the company. To back this, damaging papers were introduced into the lawsuit and, inevitably, the Internal Revenue Service got wind of them. From then on, the affair was out of the family's hands.

To understand Aldo Gucci's dangerously stubborn attitude one has to consider several factors. He was a domineering personality who expected obedience from his children even when they had reached middle age (Paolo was fifty-one when all this happened). He, Aldo, had made Gucci into a household name and he felt that he had the right to insist on maintaining control over what he regarded as his personal fiefdom. Last, but not least, he had to cope with formidable pressure put upon him by other members of the family who resented Paolo's independent spirit. Paolo's ideas and actions were in conflict with his own vision of the future and, having dismissed him from the board, he could not allow him to exploit the Gucci name.

Ironically, Aldo himself had often fought with his own father, the equally strong-willed founder of the business. The difference was that they had usually managed to patch up their quarrels and had kept them out of the public eye.

The house of Gucci has humble origins. Gabriello Gucci, Aldo's grandfather, was a partner in his brother-in-law's straw hat factory in Italy. He was a poor businessman and the company became a workers' co-operative. His teenage son, Guccio, ran away to sea and ended up in London, where he talked himself into a job as a dishwasher at the Savoy Hotel. He learned English and was promoted to waiter. This gave him the opportunity to study the ways of the rich. Daily, he saw guests arriving with piles of expensive luggage, embossed with crests and initials, and invariably made of leather. It was a material he was familiar with and when he returned to Florence, after three years, he joined a local firm which specialized in high-class leather goods. He married a local girl and children quickly followed. Aldo was the eldest, and when Guccio opened his own shop in 1923 Aldo and his younger brother, Vasco, went to work for him. (Rodolfo, the youngest, decided to become an actor and appeared in some of the early silent films.)

Aldo, it soon emerged, not only had a good head for business but also displayed the greatest enthusiasm for his father's venture. It was Guccio who came up with the famous palindromic 'GG', but Aldo commissioned the design, had it embossed in metal, and fixed it in a prominent spot.

Then, as now, Florence was popular with tourists and they clearly liked what the Guccis had to sell. Aldo married one of the customers, a nineteen-year-old Englishwoman who had been a lady's maid to a Rumanian princess, and she bore him three sons in quick succession. He was already getting impatient with his father, who he felt was much too cautious. Aldo thought the family should open shops in other cities, including some abroad. Most of their customers were foreigners: why not make it possible for them to continue buying Gucci products when they got home? Guccio disagreed: they were doing well enough in Florence. Eventually, though, Aldo managed to persuade him to open a store on the elegant Via Condotti in Rome. It was a hit, but a year later the Second World War put a brake on his expansion plans.

He resumed his efforts as soon as it was over. There should, he said, be Gucci branches in foreign cities like Paris, London and New York. As before, Guccio was against it. He felt that his son's ideas were too risky, especially his proposal to open a shop in America. But Aldo persisted. Paris and London got their Gucci shops and by 1952 he was in New York, opening a branch just off Fifth Avenue.

He made it clear to Paolo that he and his brothers were expected to join the firm, but Paolo at first resisted. He did not care for the notion of spending his life as a shopkeeper. He applied for a job with BOAC, the British airline, but turned up late for the appointment and by the time he got there the post was filled. Aldo told him not to be stupid: his future was with the Gucci business.

Guccio Gucci died in 1953. Aldo, Vasco, and Rodolfo each inherited an equal number of shares, but Aldo assumed full control. His hands were now free and he devoted all his formidable energy to expanding the company, crossing the Atlantic with increasing regularity. Gucci stores were opened in Chicago, Philadelphia, San Francisco, Beverly Hills, and Palm Beach.

Paolo remained in Italy, where he showed an impressive creative flair. He also demonstrated an early readiness to stand up to his father, particularly in fields like production, design, and marketing. He felt that the firm's methods were inefficient and old-fashioned. When he was made a member of the board he started to press vigorously for the implementation of his ideas. One was that selected merchandisers should be offered the right to sell the Gucci products in return for an annual licence fee to the company for doing so. Aldo, Vasco and Rodolfo rejected it.

Vasco died of cancer in 1975, but Rodolfo had given up his acting career and had begun to play a prominent role in the business. He was openly hostile towards his pushy nephew, who in turn criticized him for being, as he saw it, too conservative. When Paolo proposed that the company should set up a chain of cheaper shops, like Benetton, he was told that such a move would violate Gucci's traditional policies and was out of the question. A series of other incidents followed and Aldo, trying to act as a peacemaker, asked Paolo to come and work for him in New York. He made him vice-president and marketing director, in full charge of production and marketing, but Paolo was soon complaining that he was not allowed to do anything. Aldo, too, seemed determined to keep him on a tight rein. Rodolfo continued his sniping, and after one quarrel he fired Paolo from the parent company in Italy. The scene was set for the battle that was to do so much damage to the Gucci name.

Paolo decided that, after twenty-six years, he was entitled to compensation and when his uncle refused he took the company to court in Florence. His father was livid at this first display of dissent in public and wrote him a letter confirming that the board had dismissed him from his job, in the United States as well as in Italy. Aldo and Rodolfo were even more angry when they heard of his plans to market his own lines under the name Paolo Gucci. Lawyers were retained, and restraining suits taken out. In every market where Paolo Gucci goods appeared, Gucci's agents worked to prevent their sale.

Rodolfo, having defeated his nephew, kept up the pressure with his brother's agreement. But Aldo was getting worried about Rodolfo's growing power and they, too, began to quarrel. Aldo decided to call a meeting of stockholders to establish who was in charge, and since Paolo still had shares in the company he was asked – amazingly – to help out. Paolo said he would only agree to that if he were allowed to use his name on his own products. His father said he could not make that concession.

Then came a new development: the company suggested that if Paolo would drop all charges and give up his trademark the whole Gucci empire would be reorganized. A newly created line of merchandise, to include the items Paolo was producing or licensing under his 'PG' logo, would give him the scope to design and expand his ideas around the world. He would be back in the fold. Paolo signed an agreement and, in March 1982, attended the new company's first board meeting. It was a disaster. Paolo was left in no doubt that he would not be allowed to impose his radical ideas, notably the proposal that Gucci should sell lower-priced lines to a younger, less affluent public. They also remained adamantly opposed to the concept of licensing. Nothing, it seemed to him, had really changed.

The arguments continued during the next few months, and then Paolo was fired again. But he attended another board meeting, at which, he later claimed, he was physically assaulted when he asked questions about the company's financial affairs and produced a tape recorder so that he could record the replies. The truce was over: henceforth, the war would be waged in the courts. The final outcome was not only Aldo's disgrace but also the family's loss of control of the company.

Looked at dispassionately, it seems astonishing that the Gucci family could have been so self-destructive. The business was enormously successful, and there was enough money for everyone. As the man who had made it all happen – as he saw it – Aldo clearly had reason to expect his children to be grateful and loyal. But Aldo himself had often fought his father over the direction of the business and he had eventually got his way; was it so wrong of his son Paolo to want to follow his example?

The difference, of course, was that Aldo only had to do battle with Guccio, while Paolo took on the whole clan. He also did something Aldo would never have done – he went to court against his own family. They *should* have been able to settle their disputes without lawyers.

But the Gucci war raised another interesting question, which in the end turned out to be a central issue in the fight. Did Paolo have the right to use his own name for his products? He certainly thought so, and he argued that the symbol 'PG' could not possibly be confused with 'GG'. The family, on the other hand, felt that he was simply trying to exploit the worldwide Gucci reputation, that it would cause endless confusion, and that it amounted to unfair competition.

It could obviously be argued that, if Paolo felt that his ideas were so much better, he should have come up with an entirely different label. His father and grandfather had proved that it was possible to turn the name of a shop in Florence into a famous international trademark; why couldn't he think up another Italian name and do the same? If the thought ever occurred to Paolo, he did nothing about it. He had been born a Gucci and he was going to succeed as a Gucci – if not in the family firm, then outside it. I have no doubt that the scions of many other wealthy families would agree that he had a valid point.

It might all have been so very different if only Paolo had stuck to his original resolve not to become a shopkeeper – if he had got that job with BOAC. How Aldo must have regretted, in later years, that he had told him he was 'stupid' to think of another career!

Sally's Stand

The Gucci saga was a classic example of a struggle between a forceful father and a son with a mind of his own. It happens much more often than is generally realized, though it rarely has such dramatic results. But it is not always the sons who go into battle – sometimes the daughters, too, can surprise everyone with their determination.

Women still tend to play a minor role in family enterprises, or more likely none at all. But now and then one of them makes a stand. It may not have any serious or lasting consequences, but it *can* shake a business empire – and family – to its foundations. This is what happened when Sally Bingham decided to embark on a feminist crusade against the 'sexist males' in her family. The fight with her brother made almost daily headlines in newspapers across America and she was featured on magazine covers. The outcome, however, saddened many people: her revolt felled a great communications dynasty with a strong tradition of public service and commitment to liberal causes.

The Binghams were Old Money, one of the leading families of Kentucky. They lived in a large Georgian mansion east of Louisville, which they had named Melcombe after a country estate in Dorset, England, where Binghams had lived since the twelfth century. When the prominent and powerful visited Louisville, they called at or stayed in Melcombe.

In the 1930s, Sally's grandfather, Robert Worth Bingham, had been President Roosevelt's ambassador to Great Britain. An anglophile, like other Binghams before him, he had been a frequent guest of the King and Queen at Windsor Castle.

The family fortune was based on the ownership of two newspapers, the *Courier-Journal* and *Louisville Times*, which Robert had bought with money he had inherited on the sudden and somewhat suspect death of his second wife in 1918, less than a year after their marriage.

Nothing troubled the smooth first-generation transfer of the estate from Robert to his son Barry. It was Barry who took on responsibility for the business. His siblings were not rivalrous. They allowed themselves to be bought out and happily departed for Britain. His brother Robert lived for much of his adult life in Scotland, and his sister Henrietta was, for some years, a fringe member of the 'Bloomsbury group', a literary and social clique known for its snobbishness.

Under Barry's shrewd leadership, the newspapers became prosperous and influential. He ran them autocratically in the style of his father. His liberal position put him in frequent conflict with conservative Kentuckians. He vigorously supported a variety of causes, notably the civil rights movement of the 1960s. The papers also took other major controversial stands in the sixties and seventies, including opposition to the Vietnam War. Over the years Barry added other interests: a television station, an AM and an FM radio station, and a printing company.

In the third generation, however, terrible things happened. Within two years, two of his children were killed in violent, careless accidents. Jonathan, the youngest boy, was electrocuted while trying to feed some lights directly off a power line. Worth, the eldest son and heir presumptive, died on Nantucket when the surfboard he was carrying across the back seat of his Volkswagen was struck by a passing car; it snapped forward, breaking his neck. His place in the line of succession was taken by Barry Junior, the second son. But no sooner had Barry Junior been elevated to the publisher's chair on his father's retirement in 1971 than he was struck down with Hodgkin's disease. He survived, but the family was in disarray and sorrow.

Junior did his best to deliver what was expected of him. He had been to Harvard, rowed on the crew, and joined the Marine Corps. As publisher, he added three more Pulitzer prizes to the five the papers had won in his father's time.

There were two sisters – Sally and Eleanor. Both were absent for most of the sixties and seventies. Eleanor, the youngest, attended various colleges, including New York University and the University of Sussex in England. During those same years, she worked as a volunteer at a camp for migrant workers' children on Long Island, and on a kibbutz in Israel. She then ran a boutique in London and later returned to America, where she began a career of documentary film-making, working out of New York. She married and had two children.

Sally graduated from Radcliffe in 1959, and then went to live in the East, first in Boston and afterwards in New York. She had shown talent as a writer. While still at college, she had won the national first prize for a short story in the annual *Atlantic Monthly* creative writing contest. She was also the first woman to win the Dana Reed Prize, an award given for the best undergraduate writing to appear in a Harvard University publication. By the time she was twenty-one, she had a three-book contract with Houghton-Mifflin, which resulted in the publication of a novel and two collections of stories. She also wrote four plays.

In 1977, she decided to go home again. Twice married, twice divorced, she was the mother of three sons. She said later that she was 'demoralized' and wanted to be 'a little safer for a while'. About the same time, Eleanor also returned to Louisville, after some ten years' absence.

Barry Senior, their ageing but still powerful father, decided that, to knit the family interests, they needed to be involved in the business. He made them voting members of the boards of the family companies. He also appointed three other women to the boards – his wife, Mary; Worth's widow, Joan; and Junior's wife, Edith.

Barry Junior reluctantly supported the appointments, which he was powerless to prevent. But he was hostile to them. He resented the fact that all these women could criticize his decisions without having to bear the burden of decision-making. But he agreed to put up with it, provided they did not seek to interfere in day-to-day management.

This seems to have been acceptable to Eleanor and most of the others. It was *not* acceptable to Sally. She wanted a bigger say. At board meetings, though, it was made plain to her that running the companies was 'man's work'. Barry, she later complained, took no notice of anything she said. He treated the meetings as a pure formality, then did what he wanted.

It was not good enough. Sally started to talk openly about the 'rampant sexism of the Bingham males' and insisted on being heard. 'We rich women,' she declared, 'are uniquely handicapped in defending our rights, which may seem to belong to us only because of the charitable instincts of fathers and brothers. These rights are not rights but favors.' She was talking about rights to power, not just power over her trust-fund wealth, which she already had.

Specifically, she wanted to be book editor of the papers, as her mother had been. Barry Junior objected to giving her that 'right' (or 'favor') on the grounds that the papers already had a book editor, someone who had been awarded the post on her merits, not her birth. Sally only got the job after asking her father to intercede.

It may seem absurd that Junior should have resisted a demand which, given her position, was not unreasonable. Sally was as well qualified for the job as he had been for the role of publisher when his father had given it to him. He, too, had been helped by birth. But, of course, there was more to it than that: Junior felt that it would be the thin end of the wedge, the start of a process of constant interference in the running of what he regarded as his personal domain. He was also angry that Sally had made her views public: the Binghams just did not do that kind of thing.

The breaking point came in 1980, when Junior insisted that each board member should sign a 'buy-back' agreement which stipulated that should they receive an outside offer to sell their stock the Bingham companies would have sixty days to match the offer. This was an entirely legitimate and somewhat standard procedure against take-overs, and it is rather surprising that it was not done earlier. Everyone agreed to sign except Sally. She told him that since he did not trust her, a piece of paper would not make it any better.

During the next three years, their relationship remained tense and acrimonious. Then, in 1983, Junior gave his father an ultimatum: either the women family members left the boards of the companies or he would resign. The women, he said, were making no contribution. They had to go to make room for experienced professionals.

Again, Sally was the only one who refused to leave. If the women were making no contribution, she said, it was because they were not allowed to. She told an interviewer: 'The sexism, then as now, was really obvious. The attitude of the management never changed from the day I arrived on the board. At the board meetings we'd have to listen to bra jokes – jokes about the size of women's breasts. It was like going back to the fifties. There were so many women at the lower levels unhappy and the affirmative action plan had run aground. Although Barry employed some women in management positions, essentially women were there as window dressing. He certainly couldn't handle women at his level. At meetings, everything was wonderful, but do not ask to see figures.'

Her mother sided with Junior, accusing Sally of trying to destroy her brother. 'But,' Sally told the *New York Times*, 'I wasn't about to back down. They made me feel guilty, they shunned me, but finally at the age of forty-seven I was able to stand my ground.'

Her father recognized that the move, ostensibly directed at all the women, was really aimed at her. He said as much to Junior, who offered a compromise: he would turn over management of the companies to a group of non-family professional managers. Barry Senior dismissed the idea at once; the companies, he said, might as well be sold if the Binghams were not going to run them. Ultimately, though, he also ruled in favour of his son; the women would have to go. Sally remained defiant, but was voted off the boards at a shareholders' meeting in March 1984. She then shook the family by publicly announcing that she would sell her 15 per cent share stake to outside bidders. Her sister Eleanor, who had been complaisant until now, also told Junior that she was not interested in staying in any company with him at the head and her dependent on dividends.

His response was to make them both an offer. He would buy

Sally's shares and exchange Eleanor's stake in the newspapers for his shares in the television company. There was one condition: Eleanor had to persuade Sally to sell at the family price, which he set at $26.3 million. Sally, however, had been given an independent appraisal by a New York firm of investment bankers which put the value of her shares at more than $80 million. She eventually said that she would come down to $32 million. But Junior would not budge from his figure, and Sally would not change hers. The battle was deadlocked.

All this was too much for Barry Senior, who was still the majority stockholder. Reluctantly he decided that the best way to achieve peace among his children was to sell all the companies. Junior protested, but his father was adamant. A public announcement was made the following day.

The Bingham empire was sold, piecemeal, for a total of around $450 million. The senior Binghams were to take about $106 million. Junior and his family were to get $45.6 million. Sally and Eleanor were each to receive about $55 million. In addition, about $84 million was to go into a generation-skipping trust fund established by the founder, to be dispersed to his surviving grandchildren – Barry Junior, Sally and Eleanor – on the death of their parents.

It was more than any of them could ever hope to spend, and considerably more than Junior had offered Sally, who said she would use her cash to set up a foundation for Kentucky women in the arts. Junior, though, could not contain his anger. In a press statement, he called his father's action 'irrational' and a 'betrayal'.

Sally denied that she had tried to destroy her brother's 'stewardship' of the family domain. She admired the papers editorially, she said, and she had harboured no subversive designs on her family's control. She had simply stood on her rights to liquidate her share of the estate – at the right price.

Immediate non-family comment on the dissolution was generally more restrained than Junior's in the matter of blame. There was a good deal of sympathy for Barry Senior, who it was felt had been put in a difficult position by the protracted squabbling between his children and who could be forgiven for being heartily sick of it. People also found it puzzling that, when the chips were down, Junior had refused to raise his figure. The family, after all, could well have afforded to do so. If he had handed over the $32 million demanded by Sally, he would have been free of any threat of interference and would have been able to go on running the company in his own way.

Feminists naturally applauded Sally. For once, the 'sexist males' had got their come-uppance. It was a blow for the cause. It could certainly be interpreted that way, though the result could hardly have been what they wanted: their champion did not succeed in her bid for a share of genuine power and two crusading newspapers, renowned for their liberal traditions, fell into the hands of others.

But one also cannot help feeling a little sorry for Junior. He had, after all, been running the papers for years before Sally decided to come back and make her stand. His father had entrusted him with the task, and he had made a success of it. Sally knew nothing about running newspapers or television and radio stations. He had been willing to buy her out – yet here he was, immensely rich but without the job he loved.

Looking back, the seeds of the trouble were undoubtedly sown when Barry Senior appointed the women to the boards of the companies. He meant well, as all fathers do, and did not anticipate that one of his daughters would try to make much more out of it than he had intended. Junior was foolish not to agree at once that Sally should have the job she wanted – book editor – and unwise to be so sensitive about the questions she asked, quite legitimately, at board meetings. If he had treated her with more respect instead of openly showing his resentment, the course of events might have taken a different turn. But that, of course, is true of most family feuds: the flames start small and, if not carefully handled, turn into a roaring fire.

15

For Love or Money

Another hazard for the rich is that their children may fall under the spell of a fortune hunter. It can happen to members of either sex, but generally parents feel more protective towards their daughters because they are thought to be more vulnerable. It is not necessarily so: young women tend to have a sixth sense about gold-diggers while many young men are amazingly naive.

There have always been people who take the view that the quickest way to a fortune is to marry one. In many families it is regarded as a duty. Sons and daughters are encouraged to go after suitable partners, not merely to ensure their own future comfort but for the sake of the whole tribe. Much time and effort is devoted to preparing them for the task. They are taught the social graces and equipped with everything needed for an elegant seduction: stylish clothes, a substantial expense account, and time off for the hunt. They are shown how to impress not only the prospective victim but, equally important, his or her parents. Mothers, they are told, set great store by social acceptability and will always laugh at jokes about the lower orders. Fathers prefer to talk about business and sport. Never, under any circumstances, let either of them think that you have any time for socialism and other radical ideas.

For many years it was fashionable for members of Europe's nobility to go after young American heiresses. Their families were usually impressed by titles, even if they were of dubious authenticity. Barbara Hutton got three opportunities to put the word 'princess' in front of her name, and one chance each for the titles 'countess' and 'baroness'. These labels are no longer as important as they once were, but they still help – not only in America but also in Europe itself. Mothers everywhere are incorrigible snobs and so are their daughters, despite women's lib. The *nouveaux riches*, especially, cling stubbornly to the notion that a title not only makes a man superior but also ensures that he will behave with decorum. So they warmly embrace the endless stream of conniving, penniless knights, counts, and princes.

Another useful ploy, these days, is to call yourself a banker. It can mean almost anything (some of the biggest scoundrels of the postwar years have been bankers) but you will almost certainly be regarded as the kind of shrewd, respectable, well-connected gentleman whom families love to add to their family trees. Daddy may invite you to join his board of directors, but he is unlikely to ask you to dirty your hands with such mundane tasks as making or selling his products.

Most rich parents usually advise their offspring to 'stick to their own kind'. But the definition of 'own kind' is much broader than it used to be. Generally it means, today, people from prosperous backgrounds who share similar tastes and attitudes.

Old families are by no means averse to the idea of linking up with new wealth in order to replenish their family fortunes, though they prefer to have some assurance that the new wealth will last and that the new members of the clan are not going to be socially embarrassing. At the same time, the *nouveaux riches* welcome marriages with the scions of socially prominent families because they expedite the acceptance of family members into the upper class. To some extent, it is simply an exchange of wealth for status. The *nouveaux riches* want to be upper-class; Old Money is willing to help them in return for the financial clout they can provide. In Britain, Mrs Thatcher's 'entrepreneurial revolution' has not really changed this situation: it has simply allowed more people to take part in the game.

But for the self-made tycoon, marriage to the offspring of another tycoon may be even more desirable. Kings and rulers used to form alliances by marrying off their sons and daughters to other rulers and their children; the modern business tycoon seeks to protect and expand his empire by forming similar alliances with others of his kind.

What they all have in common is the fear that their sons or

daughters may run off with someone who is entirely 'unsuitable'. A brilliant academic who has acquired some stature will do, even if he is poor, provided he does not harbour radical views. He is unlikely to be a fortune hunter. But there is a long list of people who are not acceptable. For heiresses the most common misalliances seem to occur with chauffeurs, horse trainers and stable hands, ski instructors and tennis coaches. Heirs tend to get involved with actresses, models, airline stewardesses, and their own secretaries.

Parents themselves, of course, are not immune to the charms of such people. Indeed, self-made tycoons are notoriously susceptible. They tend to marry early, often choosing dull but supportive wives who bring up their children and applaud their ambition but who, after some years, become an awful bore. The moment of danger arrives when he has reached the top of whatever hill he has sought to climb. He can afford to relax, to turn his attention to the other good things in life. It is at this point that he is liable to fall heavily for a glamorous young woman. She openly admires his success (which is gratifying), refrains from criticism (which is comforting), and revives his interest in sex. Friends comment on her beauty and he basks in the prestige of his new conquest. Because he is vain and knows next to nothing about the wiles of women, he finds it easy to believe that she is interested in his finer qualities and prowess in bed rather than in his money. And because he can afford a divorce (though it may hurt financially) he may well discard the companion who has supported him loyally for so long.

Women, too, may leave husbands they have grown tired of, though they usually like to make sure that they are still going to be well provided for. If they have money of their own, they can be just as ruthless as men. Heiresses like Barbara Hutton, Doris Duke, and Christina Onassis fell for a succession of fortune hunters at an age when they should have known better.

But parents do not want to see their children do the same. Aristotle Onassis felt free to conduct an open affair with Maria Callas, divorce his wife, and then marry Jackie Kennedy (who certainly showed a keen interest in his money), but he was furious when his daughter married a California real estate agent. He wanted the heir to another Greek shipping fortune as his son-in-law, so he threatened to disinherit her. He was delighted when they parted nine months later.

In most cases, of course, parents claim that they have their children's interests at heart – and often they turn out to have been right. If money is the motive for a marriage, rather than love, it can lead to a lot of misery. But it is plainly ridiculous to assume that marriage between, say, an heiress and a tennis coach must inevitably be based on financial considerations and that love is automatically excluded. For every Barbara and Christina there are a dozen lesser-known but almost as wealthy women who have married opportunists and who have lived happily ever after. There are also many examples of rich young people who have followed their parents' advice and who have lived unhappily ever since. Marrying one's 'own kind' is not always a recipe for bliss.

Today, the children of the rich have far more opportunities to mingle with other social classes – at university, at work, in clubs, and so on. They are, therefore, much more likely to fall for someone who is *not* rich. They have also become more assertive. They do not necessarily accept that they have an obligation to look after the whole clan or that their parents have the right to choose their partners for them. Even the royals occasionally step out of line. Britain's royal family was distinctly unenthusiastic when Princess Margaret, the Queen's sister, decided to marry a photographer. But she went ahead all the same. (Prince Charles, the heir to the throne, displayed a greater sense of duty. He married a young lady who worked in a children's nursery, but her father was an aristocrat and she was deemed to be an eminently suitable choice.)

In some cases, a son or daughter may even be prepared to forfeit all claims to the family fortune rather than give up the romance. If the marriage still takes place, it at least proves that they are wanted for themselves, not for their money. Such a step is rarely necessary. Many parents nowadays accept that, if their children are prepared to go that far, it is better to come to terms with the idea rather than lose them. Quite often, they do not really have a choice because the children have already gained financial independence.

In order to avoid taxes, many of the rich have transferred much of their wealth to their children by means of lifetime transfers. They now tend to receive most of their inheritances in the form of gifts from parents and grandparents who are still alive. They become income beneficiaries of trusts established for them. The result is a subtle change in the nature of family relations, which becomes less subtle when a clash develops. As one wealthy mother once lamented: 'It's hard with children who are on the same economic level. They simply don't have to listen.'

These trust arrangements can also be an effective deterrent to fortune hunters. Sons and daughters may get control of the capital once they have reached adult status, but it all depends on the terms of the trust: they *may* simply remain income beneficiaries throughout their lifetime. This, of course, can still be an attractive proposition, but it means that great fortunes are not always what they seem to be. Meanwhile, there is a very real risk, for the male of the fortune-hunting species, that Daddy will see him not as an agreeable companion for his daughter, born to practise the art of living, but as the son he never had. Once the honeymoon is over, he may find himself installed in the executive suite, in which case he will be expected to work as hard as his new father-in-law, with two or three days off a year. The prospect may appeal to ambitious young men who dream of one day taking over the whole show, but it is hardly an enticing thought for people who are in search of a life of ease and plenty.

A further deterrent is the growing popularity of pre-nuptial contracts. Under these, a marriage partner may be required to relinquish all claims to the other partner's wealth in advance of the wedding. Pre-nuptial contracts first came to prominence in California, where much-married film stars felt the need to protect themselves against the very real possibility that, in the event of a divorce, they would lose a substantial part of their assets. The partner could hardly refuse to sign it, because such a refusal would be a clear indication that money, not love, was the primary motive. In recent years, the practice has spread. It is actively encouraged by parents who see it as another useful way of ensuring that the fortunes they have built up over the years are not put at risk by 'reckless' marriages.

Perhaps the biggest problem for the avid fortune-hunter is that many of the children of the rich have become increasingly reluctant to marry at all. Why bother when it is so easy to find a succession of attractive lovers or mistresses? The possession of wealth, or even just the income from it, virtually guarantees the attention of people who will do everything they can to please. They can be discarded when they become boring or too pressing; there will always be someone else who is only too willing to take

ve: Charles Forte reading
side stories to his children

ht: With his son Rocco who
runs the vast hotel and
ring empire

Superstar John Wayne with one of his daughters. Married three times, he had seven children

above: Drawing lessons from the master — four-year-old Paloma and six-year-old Claude with their world famous father, Pablo Picasso, then seventy-one

right: A happy Paloma Picasso launching a new perfume in Paris. She has gained a considerable reputation of her own in the fashion business

New York's flamboyant Donald Trump — an authentic 'new money' hero, a real-life soap character

Michael Douglas, son of Kirk,
with the Oscar he won for his
brilliant performance in *Wall
Street*

Kirk Douglas in 1961, with his
sons, Eric and Peter

Paolo Gucci with some of the products that bear the world-famous family name

Robert Kennedy Jr on holiday in Paris at the age of fifteen. He later experimented with drugs and was arrested. The judge ordered him to spend time in 'community service'

John F. Kennedy Jr, son of President Kennedy, playing with some of his toys in the White House. He is now an assistant district-attorney

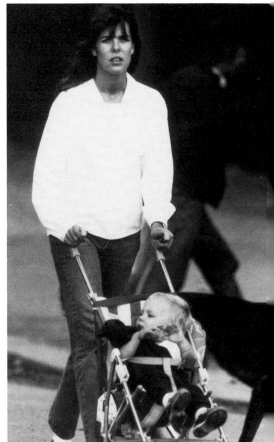

Above: Prince Albert and Princess
Caroline of Monaco as children.
Albert, the heir to the throne, later
went to college in the United States

Right: Princess Caroline, once the
darling of the gossip columns, now has
three children and says she loves being
a mother

their place. Society no longer frowns on these alliances as it once did, and many parents would rather see their offspring indulging themselves in this way than marrying 'unsuitable' partners.

There is no doubt that the various obstacles have put off some of the less determined gold-diggers. One young heiress, Isabel de Rosnay, says they are a vanishing breed. 'Poor things,' she told a reporter. 'They may spend months enmeshing a defenceless heiress and then discover that the girl's money has been taken by the government or is locked in a trust fund, which is almost as bad. So the boys have gone off to find lusher pastures. I don't know what. Oil, perhaps. But I miss them.' The lady was obviously basing her comments on personal experience, but there is ample evidence that the breed has *not* vanished. Indeed, with so many new fortunes being made all the time, the species is probably more numerous than ever. They have simply learned to become more patient and persistent.

The public's attitude to them is somewhat ambivalent. Men who pursue heiresses are either dismissed as gigolos or praised as smart operators who recognize that there is an easier road to wealth than work. Women tend to be more readily forgiven, because it is still widely felt that they should, if possible, try to capture someone with money. But even they are by no means safe from criticism; Jackie Kennedy, for example, had to endure much spiteful comment when she married Onassis.

Parents, who generally reckon they can spot a fortune hunter at once, tend to go to considerable lengths to ensure that their offspring meet the 'right people' – ideally someone who comes from an equally wealthy background. Mothers, especially, are experts at arranging meetings with those they regard as suitable and at shielding their children from 'unsuitable' characters. Employees who are perceived to be too friendly run the risk of dismissal. Young men and women from the 'right families' are asked to dinners and cocktail parties, or may be invited to spend weekends in the country or on Daddy's yacht.

If there appears to be a genuine threat of a serious romance with an 'unsuitable' partner, the son or daughter may be sent away to 'cool off' or, if that proves to be difficult to arrange, may be asked to accompany the parents on a trip to some faraway place, the theory being that exposure to new experiences will induce second thoughts. It does not always work, but they feel compelled to try.

The trouble, of course, is that he or she may meet someone else who is even more unsuitable. The sun can do strange things to people – and in places like Florida or California there are new dangers: good-looking beach-boys, scuba instructors, singers and guitar-players, and (in the case of impressionable young men) nubile girls in seductive bikinis.

It is the fervent hope of every parent that everything will turn out for the best – the 'best' meaning that their offspring will choose someone they thoroughly approve of. If and when that happens they give lavish parties (to make sure that the couple feel publicly committed) and even more lavish weddings. No expense is spared. Their hopes then start to focus on the next generation – the grandchildren they expect to see before long. As grandparents they will be just as determined to exercise whatever influence they can, and they will naturally use their money to bring about the desired results.

Among the rich, as we have seen, the mating game is full of complexities. The same, of course, can also be true of those who are less fortunate, but the rich reckon they have more at stake – which is why they make such strenuous efforts to ensure they come out as winners.

16

Poor Little Rich Girls?

One might have thought that, with women so much more assertive than they have been in the past, the daughters of the rich would, by now, have come to play a far bigger role in the enterprises created by their fathers. But it is still the exception rather than the rule. It is much more common for daughters to concentrate on bringing up a family or to develop some interest outside business. They may sit on the boards of companies, but it is comparatively rare for them to play a major part. Sons tend to get the top jobs – even if, as often happens, they turn out to be less intelligent than their sisters.

When women do achieve prominence in business affairs they usually do so quite independently. This has long been the case. Elizabeth Arden and Helena Rubinstein, the two great rivals in the cosmetics industry for so many years, both created their own future. So did Coco Chanel, who was orphaned at an early age and brought up by nuns. Laura Ashley and Anita Roddick, founder of the Body Shop, succeeded with the help of their husbands. They, and others, have proved that, given the right opportunities and encouragement, women are just as capable of running a business as men.

Occasionally a daughter *does* get the chance to have a go. A much-publicized example is Christie Hefner, who took over as chief operating officer of her father's Playboy empire in 1982 and was made chairman of the board in 1988. Serious and tough, she worked in middle management until Hefner decided that she was someone he could trust to do the job. It is not easy – the Playboy business has been going through hard times – and Christie has had to deal with a lot of sniping, especially from feminists who regard the magazine as the ultimate in male chauvinism. But no one can accuse her of not trying. Most fathers are so accustomed to viewing business as a male-orientated affair they do not even consider putting their daughters in charge. The female offspring of empire builders are expected to marry and produce more heirs; they are not expected to stage boardroom coups and build even bigger empires.

If a founder has no sons, he will usually try to persuade his daughter – or daughters – to marry someone who seems capable of taking over. Naturally he will seek to influence the choice. The prime consideration, in many cases, is not whether the candidate will make her happy but whether he has the qualities needed in a competent successor. This leaves her vulnerable to the attentions of opportunists who will readily embark on a loveless marriage for the sake of their careers. The prospect of rapid promotion and a share in the family wealth is a powerful lure.

Mothers are seldom much help in pushing the idea that daughters are perfectly capable of doing the job themselves. Brought up to go along with the male view that a woman's place is in the home, not in the office, they find it hard to see why their darlings should wish to be different. It seems much more important that, like them, they should strive to become a 'social asset'. Raising a family of their own, they insist, is a demanding enough task. Any time left over is best devoted to charitable work and other useful roles rather than to business. 'Look at your father!' they say. 'He is so obsessed by the company that he doesn't have time for anything else. You don't really want to be like *him*, do you?'

Usually, they do not. They have seen what it has done to their fathers and, very often, to the marriage of their parents, and they do not care to repeat it. They know that, if they do join the company, they are liable to have an even harder time with colleagues than their brothers because they are both privileged rivals *and* women. If they get married, eventually, the husband is likely to apply additional pressure. It is so much easier to accept the way things are.

If they do feel the need to get a job, if only to assert their independence, they tend to look for something outside the family business. Professions like the law and publishing are popular with many of the children of the rich. Increasingly, they also go into politics. The family money can be of considerable help – it provides support during the lean years – but sometimes all financial assistance is rejected. They are determined to make it on their own.

It is easy to criticize the old-fashioned attitude of fathers, and one hopes that it will change in time. But it would be wrong to assert that every daughter longs to be a tycoon. Many are quite happy with the role mapped out by their parents. They do not want to pursue even greater riches; they prefer to spend what they already have. They are content with exercising influence behind the scenes, providing a comfortable home life, achieving social status, and steering their own children in the right direction.

Much has been written, over the years, about 'poor little rich girls' – a label first attached to heiresses like Barbara Hutton. This has, inevitably, led many people to believe that to be a rich man's daughter is a recipe for disaster. It is not necessarily so. But it is natural that we should be fascinated by the stories of women who, although born to greater wealth than the rest of us could ever dream of, have nevertheless made a mess of their lives.

Sad Christina

One of the most prominent examples of recent years is that of Christina Onassis, who died in 1988 at the early age of thirty-seven. Her famous father was, in many ways, typical of the kind of parent who thinks that sons, not daughters, should run the family business. He was shattered when his only son, Alexander, died in a plane crash at the age of twenty-four and he could never quite bring himself to accept that Christina might be an adequate substitute.

Christina was born in New York City on 11 December 1950. Aristotle Onassis was by then an established tycoon, and her mother, the former Athina Livanos, was the daughter of another Greek maritime magnate. She launched her first ship two and a half years later, though her tiny hands were barely able to push the bottle of champagne towards the bow of the vessel. She was pampered from birth: her dolls were dressed by Dior and if she wanted to ride a pony all she had to do was to call for the pure-bred

Mongolians that had been the gift of the King of Saudi Arabia. She was brought up in New York, Paris and London, and on the luxurious yacht which her father named after her. Because the older Alexander was considered to be the business heir, her education was designed to groom her for society. She went to various colleges, including a finishing school in Switzerland, and became fluent in five languages. But her father's business activities, and her mother's social life, left them little time for the children. They travelled around the world, sometimes for months, and occasionally sent postcards from different places — a welcome but scarcely adequate expression of parental affection.

Plump and clumsy, Christina was not a pretty child. She was profoundly shy and for a time refused to speak to anyone. Her mother consulted child psychologists in Zurich, who told her that it was an attention-getting silence associated with insecure, over-protected children.

When she was nine, her father fell in love with Maria Callas, the diva, whom Christina found terrifying. She was devastated when, a year later, her mother got an uncontested divorce on the grounds of mental cruelty. Christina always blamed Callas for breaking up her parents' marriage and never forgave her.

Soon afterwards, Tina Onassis married the Marquess of Blandford (now the Duke of Marlborough) and Ari dumped Callas to marry Jackie Kennedy. Again Christina found only rivalry in her father's choice of woman. Like her brother, she put on a brave face and attended the wedding, but she made it clear that she was 'appalled' at the marriage. The widow of the American president could not provide Christina with the love she so desperately craved and after her father's death she would have nothing more to do with her stepmother.

Three years later it was her parents' turn to be appalled when Christina married, at the age of twenty and in Las Vegas, a middle-aged estate agent called Joseph Bolker, who was the divorced father of four daughters. Bolker, by all accounts, was not in love with her and had been reluctant to marry the eager young girl. Onassis, who had not been informed in advance, was furious when he heard what Christina had done. He threatened to disinherit her and put on all kinds of other pressures. Nine months after the wedding the ill-fated union was over. By this time her mother had divorced Lord Blandford and married Stavros Niarchos, Onassis's chief business rival. The children saw this marriage as a terrible betrayal and were thereafter estranged from their mother.

Alexander's plane crash occurred in January 1973. His relationship with his father had not been an easy one. Onassis had treated him like an office junior and had been unwilling to yield an inch of authority or to give him credit for anything. He had made him feel inadequate and Alexander had often been bitter in his comments about the old man. 'I have to be free of him,' he had once told a friend. 'It's the only way I'm going to survive. I can't take this grotesque man's domination for much longer.'

Ari was full of remorse when he died. His grief was so extreme that at first he refused to bury Alexander; he talked about having the body 'deep frozen', organically preserved until medical science was sufficiently advanced to restore his life. But he eventually came to accept the inevitable, and tried to take more of an interest in his daughter's destiny. He took her along to conferences and business lunches, meeting people at all levels, although she seldom spoke. (Asked why, she told one of his associates: 'My father told me I had to listen to every word, to observe, and to keep my mouth shut until I knew what I was talking about.')

As a Greek, he did not find the notion of a woman in business attractive; as a shipowner he was sceptical of her chances in a business dominated entirely by men. But after a time he conceded that 'it seems just possible that she might some day prove herself capable of running the company'.

The lukewarm compliment did little for her morale. In August of that year she was admitted to the public wards of Middlesex Hospital in London, under the name of C. Danai, suffering from a massive overdose of sleeping pills. Astonishingly, the drama was kept secret from the press.

She recovered, but then her mother died in Paris and Onassis's own health visibly began to deteriorate. His marriage to Jackie was also on the rocks. When he realized that he was going to die he extracted a promise from Christina that she would marry Peter Goulandris, the heir to the world's third-largest shipping dynasty. He thought it would make a great alliance – not only because it would create the largest tanker fleet of all but because he felt that Goulandris was a man who would know how to protect the business that he, Onassis, had built. They went through the traditional Greek 'giving the word of marriage' ceremony and afterwards visited Ari's bedside to tell him the news and receive his blessing. A few days later he was dead.

His estate was estimated to be worth between $400 million and $1,000 million. In his will he left a majority stake of 52.5 per cent in his interest to a foundation in memory of Alexander and 47.5 per cent to Christina. She also received a 75 per cent interest in the island of Skorpios, his yacht, and an income of $250,000 a year.

Christina took her father's death badly. She suffered from bouts of depression and insomnia, and felt lonely. The promise to marry Goulandris was forgotten; instead, she married Alexander Andreadis, the son of another Greek shipowner. They were divorced eleven months later on the grounds of 'incompatibility'. In prepared statements read in court by their lawyers, Christina claimed that Andreadis was 'despotic, foul-mouthed, blindly jealous and yet a womanizer, fanatically self-centred'. He countered that she had 'a peculiar and dictatorial character and didn't really care about me'.

Onassis had not given her control of his empire. She was president of the foundation, but he had laid down that it should be run jointly with thirteen of his old friends and associates. Christina wielded no extraordinary power beyond those of the other members. She had only one vote unless there was a tie, in which case she had two votes.

Nevertheless, she had inherited the other half of his fortune and she made an effort to assert her authority. The will said that the foundation would award prizes in various fields, including art, religion, and education, based on the Nobel system; she announced that it would be devoted essentially to social welfare projects in Greece. When it became apparent that her father had ordered too many supertankers, she led a board decision to cancel the new ship orders.

Over the next few years they pared the shipping fleet down to about thirty-five tankers, freighters and other vessels by selling some and scrapping others. They bought real estate instead, in the United States, Europe, and Latin America. Christina also gave Jackie a lump sum of $25 million, to settle any claims she might have had, and ordered that the name Kennedy never be mentioned in her presence again.

In 1976, against the advice of other members of the board, she chartered five 27,000-ton bulk carriers to Sofracht, the State-owned Russian shippers, and through that deal met Sergei Kauzov, a Communist Party member and a functionary of the chartering agency. Two years later, amid rumours of KGB plots to take over the Onassis fleet, she married him and they set up home in a small apartment in Moscow. Again, though, the marriage did not last and they were divorced in 1980. The Russian collected a 78,000-ton tanker as part of his settlement.

Christina was faced with the challenge of 'remaking my life'. She continued to take an active interest in the business but spent more and more time on personal matters. She had a string of attentive escorts and kept a private Learjet fuelled and permanently available at Le Bourget to fly friends to wherever she needed them. Her weight became an increasingly worrying problem, chiefly because of her addiction to Coca-Cola and junk food. She was hurt when gossip columnists used cruel descriptions like 'Thunderthighs' and 'The Greek Tanker,' and embarked on one of her many crash diets.

In 1984 she fell in love with Thierry Roussel, son of a once wealthy industrialist and considered one of the most eligible bachelors in France. They started to go out and, perhaps for a joke, Roussel told her: 'I'll marry you if you lose 15 kilos.' The wedding took place in March 1984, with a lavish reception at Maxim's restaurant in Paris. But, unknown to Christina, Thierry had been living for ten years with a Swedish beauty, Gaby Landhage, and was still very much in love with her. A friend was quoted as saying: 'Christina told him that she loved him and would give him all the money he could ever imagine. She said he would become one of the richest men in the world. He explained to Gaby that it would be better for his business affairs if he was to marry Christina and she agreed. He told her that nothing would separate him from her – and marriage certainly did not.'

Although marriage to Thierry was far from idyllic, he provided Christina with the child she had hoped for. But seven months later Gaby, too, had a child by him, a son born in Malmo, Sweden. When Christina found out about his double life she was shattered but determined to hold on to him, whatever the cost. She even struck up a friendship with Gaby. It did not work: Christina and Thierry were divorced in 1987.

By now, the management of the Onassis empire was left mostly to the other board members. Christina spent every moment she could with her daughter, heaping on her all the attention she had lacked from her own mother and father. 'For the first time in her life,' said a friend, 'she can have the love of someone who is not paid to be with her, like a servant, or who may have got to know her for her money, like a lover or a husband.'

Ironically, though, they were far apart when Christina died in November 1988 – mother in Buenos Aires, daughter at their home in Europe. Christina had gone to see friends in Argentina, where her father had begun his rise to fame and fortune (he held an Argentine passport to the day of his death) and had talked about buying an apartment there. She called her daughter four or five times a day and spoke as frequently to Thierry. But she also went to parties and, it seems, she had embarked on yet another romantic involvement, this time with a local businessman, Jorge Tchomlekdjoglou.

When she did not appear for a breakfast appointment after one of the parties, a friend went to her room. Christina was dead. Inevitably, rumours began to swirl around. Pills had been found on the floor, and there was immediate speculation that she had committed suicide. But it is now thought that she died naturally. There had been too many pills; too many drastic weight changes; too many periods of stress.

In her will, made out only six weeks before her death, Christina left all her fortune in trust 'for my beloved daughter Athina'. It was estimated to be between $500 million and $1,000 million. The Onassis group said that the trust would be managed jointly with Thierry Roussel, who is Athina's legal custodian, in law, until she comes of age.

Predictably, the world's newspapers felt compelled to offer the new three-year-old 'billionairess' all kinds of unsolicited advice. Some felt that she had little hope of happiness. 'History,' declared the London *Sunday Times*, 'suggests that the cast of Athina's life is already set as one of luxurious misery.' A *Sunday Telegraph* columnist said: 'Little Athina will not only require firm family surroundings and lots of warmth and love. She will also need a moral formation which teaches that you do not achieve happiness by seeking it, but as a by-product of doing something useful and good.'

Christina was widely described as having been spoiled and selfish; she had, one newspaper felt, 'pursued pleasure without a sense of responsibility towards society at large'. It seemed an unduly harsh judgement: had they forgotten her efforts, on behalf of the foundation, to promote social welfare projects in Greece?

But there was clearly a substantial element of truth in the accusation. Christina *was* spoiled, self-centred, and temperamental. Her great wealth allowed her to be. Her first husband, Joseph Bolker, was once quoted as saying: 'All Christina ever wanted was a simple home and a baby.' I find that hard to believe. She *could* have had just that, but she was obviously not prepared to make the sacrifices it would have entailed. She enjoyed her status and was all too conscious of the power of money. She told interviewers what they wanted to hear: that her most fervent wish was to 'meet a man who loves me for myself and not for my money'. If that was really the case, she could have dropped out, changed her name, sold the Learjet. The truth is that she relished the attention of men who, she knew, were attracted by her glamorous name and her much-publicized fortune. She was extremely conscious of the fact that she was no beauty, and she tried to buy what she could not have had if she had been the girl-next-door. Her father had done the same – and she was very much her father's daughter. It was not entirely the fault of her various husbands that their marriages failed so quickly, nor was it entirely the fault of the women in Ari's life that they could not get on with Christina, or she with them.

It *might* all have turned out differently if her father had made her feel more secure as a child. But he was not that kind of man. He was obsessed with the idea of financial and social success; his children were of secondary importance. He loved her, in his own way, but he made it plain that *his* life was more important than hers. She never had a real chance to emulate his business career: how do you follow an act like Aristotle Onassis? Alexander, had he lived, probably would not have fared any better. But she did leave about the same fortune as the one she had inherited, so she was not totally devoid of talent.

Barbara

Christina Onassis often talked about her unhappy childhood, and clearly it deeply influenced her behaviour. Unhappy childhoods do not always lead to misery in adult life: indeed, research by social scientists shows that they can help to create high achievers. It is decidedly premature to make assumptions about the future of Christina's daughter, Athina. But there is no doubt that a troubled childhood can profoundly affect the lives of people who seem to have everything going for them. This is especially true of women who are not brought up with any specific aim.

Much has been written about the turbulent life of the original 'poor little rich girl', Woolworth heiress Barbara Hutton. We have been told about her reckless extravagance, her whims, her seven husbands, and her numerous lovers. Little has been said about her early years, though they clearly shaped her character, leaving her insecure and restless, and like Christina constantly searching for love but unable to sustain any close relationships.

Her mother, Edna, was one of the daughters of Frank Winfield Woolworth, the founder of the famous chain of stores. At twenty-four she married a handsome stockbroker, Franklyn Laws Hutton, and Barbara was born in 1912. She was their only child. Hutton was a compulsive womanizer, frequently absent from home, and when Barbara was four her mother died, apparently from a lethal dose of strychnine poisoning.

The little girl was put into her grandfather's care. He was sixty-four, ailing and melancholic, and her grandmother was mentally unstable. They lived in a grand but gloomy mansion, Winfield House. Barbara had a playroom where she spent much of her time. She had a rocking horse and a dolls' house with tiny bearskin rugs, crystal chandeliers, and Chippendale furniture scaled down to size. Her grandfather often slipped into the room to talk to her, but she missed the parental affection that every child needs.

Woolworth died in 1919 and his wife five years later. Barbara inherited a trust fund of $28 million, worth many times as much in today's currency. But she found herself moved from one home and caretaker to another. She went to live with her father's older sister, who led a hectic social life and had little time for her niece, and they later joined Barbara's father in San Francisco. But they stayed in separate houses and she saw him rarely. When she did, he constantly chided her. On one occasion he said that he had never wanted a child in the first place – a cruel remark which, apparently, she never forgot.

Barbara was a wistful, shy, and lonely girl who often retreated into a world of fantasy. Her grandfather had always called her 'princess' and she was delighted when her aunt's chauffeur made a point of addressing her as 'Your Royal Highness'. She wrote poetry, some of which was scathing about the world of big business.

When she went to school, she found it difficult to make friends because of her money. Other children taunted her because of it; they were either intimidated or envious. She once asked her aunt if she could give all her money away, and was upset when she was told that it could not be done.

Barbara was eleven when her aunt married again and moved with her husband to New Jersey. She was sent to the then fashionable Santa Barbara School for Girls, where no one ever came to see her, not even at Christmas. She later went to New York, where her father had remarried, and did her best to develop a relationship with her new stepmother. Franklyn Hutton decided to buy a pair of adjoining duplex apartments on Fifth Avenue, and, to cover the cost of Barbara's new home, filed a petition with the Surrogate Court. In it he said: 'My daughter, for her safety and welfare in later years, must be brought up surrounded by the luxury and comfort to which her income entitles her, so that upon attaining the age of twenty-one, at which time her fortune is to be turned over to her unrestricted control, she will have no desire or reason to embark upon a scale of expenditure in living to which she has not been accustomed in her formative years.'

It seemed an odd explanation, but the Court obliged and the teenage girl moved into the apartment, complete with Louis XIV furniture and a string of retainers. The 'luxury and comfort' should have made her content, but she still longed for friends and continued to feel inadequate. C. David Heyman, a biographer who later gained access to her notebooks, said he recorded at the time her fear that 'I shall be an old maid. Nobody can ever love me. For my money but not for me. I am doomed. I will always be alone.'

She had another opportunity to make friends when she went to a school in Farmington, Connecticut. Again, though, she seems to have found it a problem. It is hard to believe that the fault lay entirely with her classmates; by all accounts, the 'princess' was not easy to get along with. She was, by then, much too conscious of her status.

Her relationship with her father also remained difficult. As before, he either paid little attention to her or criticized everything she did. He probably would not have bothered with her at all if she had not been so enormously rich. Barbara was certainly aware of the money factor. When she was taken to hospital for an emergency appendectomy, she wrote a one-page will and gave it to a classmate. She wanted to be sure that if something happened, her father would not get a penny of her fortune. The will was not valid, and she recovered anyway, but the gesture says much about her feelings at the time.

He took an interest, though, when she started to date a variety of young men. He strongly opposed these attachments and was dismayed when she announced, in 1933, that she intended to marry Alexis Mdivani, who claimed to be a Russian prince. There were doubts about the authenticity of the title, but she was much taken with the prospect of becoming a real princess. Because she was still under age, her father's permission was needed. He refused to give it, but eventually relented after Mdivani agreed to sign a pre-nuptial agreement that would protect his daughter's financial interests.

Barbara Hutton and Alexis Mdivani were married in Paris that year and lived like royalty in Europe. They later returned to New York, to celebrate her twenty-first birthday and collect a third of the vast Woolworth estate, which had grown to be worth more than $50 million. Her father had played a key role in nearly doubling her original inheritance and she – more mellow towards him by now – gave him $5 million as a reward.

The marriage lasted only two years. Barbara had met someone else in London, Count Reventlow, and fallen in love with him. She decided to seek a divorce in Reno. In her petition she said: 'When I got married I had no conception of love. A strong desire for independence from my family was the main reason I married Prince Mdivani. I realised it was a mistake even before the wedding, but things had gone too far to stop. Yet in reality I was more prepared for marriage than my husband. The Prince was totally unaware of the burdens and responsibilities that such a bond entailed and I am now convinced that he married me only for my money.'

She married Reventlow within twenty-four hours of getting her divorce. Her father was not at the wedding. The following year the couple had a son – hailed by *The Times* of London as 'the world's richest baby'.

One would have thought that, after her own childhood misery, she would have taken great care to ensure that the boy – named Lance – had a happy and secure life. But it was not to be. She spent time with him only when it suited her, which was not often. Within a few years she had grown tired of the count, as she had earlier grown tired of her prince, and the couple separated. The little boy was caught up in an acrimonious battle over custody. In the end, it was agreed that while the child was still of a 'tender age' he would spend the greater part of each year with his mother, and that when he reached 'school age' he would divide his holidays evenly between both parents. Reventlow retained jurisdiction over the boy's education.

Barbara did her utmost to turn him against Reventlow and eventually succeeded in persuading her son that his father hated him. Reventlow never saw him again. In 1972 Lance was killed in a plane crash.

Barbara entered into other ill-fated marriages, including one to Cary Grant. Her father died in 1940 and she flew to his bedside. In his will, he left her nothing except 'a loving father's blessing for her future happiness'. Her reaction was to sue his estate for $530,000, plus 5 per cent accrued interest, to recover monies lent to him over the years. His widow repaid the debt in full.

Papa Picasso's Girl

Happily, not every story about rich girls is a sad one. Many, as noted earlier, manage to cope with the problem of following a prominent, highly successful father. One such story is that of Paloma Picasso.

'When I was very young,' she says, 'I drew without any inhibitions or sense of anguish. But when I hit my teens, people were asking if I was going to be a painter like Papa. It became extremely awkward for me even to take drawing lessons at school.'

One can well understand her dilemma. Pablo Picasso was a celebrated artist, and it is widely assumed that genius is transferable – though there is little evidence to support this glib theory. Her efforts, therefore, were bound to be judged much more severely than those of other children.

149

Her father refused to help. Although he enjoyed having his daughter sketch by him silently as he worked, he never made any attempt to direct her. 'He wanted no pupils and was convinced that art could not be taught,' she says.

Her mother, Françoise Gilot, took the same view. She, too, was a painter but she was concerned that neither Paloma nor her brother Claude should follow in their parents' footsteps: she even locked them out of her *atelier*. It was probably a wise decision. The children did not appear to have any particular talent for painting and, if they had been encouraged to emulate their parents, they would, inevitably, have had to endure endless comparisons.

Paloma has since gained a considerable reputation of her own in the international fashion business. She started with a series of small-time commissions and, in 1981, got her first big break when Tiffany's invited her to design a collection of jewellery. Her products now include perfume and lipstick and she promotes them relentlessly. The Picasso name has undoubtedly helped.

For some time, though, she found it hard to come to terms with being a Picasso. She bitterly resented the fact that people thought she would not have got anywhere as Paloma Gilot – her mother's surname, which she bore for the first eleven years of her life. 'I finally realized,' she says, 'that until I accepted the fact that I *was* a Picasso – as well as the likelihood that some people will always attribute my successes to the name – I would never be able to accomplish anything of worth.'

Some of the great man's other children – he had four – did not cope so well. His first son, Pablo, had a miserable life. (He died at fifty-four, of cirrhosis of the liver brought on by drug and alcohol abuse.) As a child, he had been spoiled by Picasso, who in the early years took pride and pleasure in being a father. He played with him on the beach, devised amusing games, bought him expensive toys, hired an English governess to look after him, and painted delightful portraits of Pablo in fancy dress: as Pierrot, as Harlequin holding a wand and a bunch of flowers, or wearing the gold-braided suit of a toreador.

But then Picasso fell passionately in love with another woman, Marie-Thérèse Walter. They had a daughter, Maya, and in due course he divorced Pablo's mother. He never got round to marrying Marie-Thérèse, but he was enchanted by his little girl. The first child was hurt and bewildered. Maya later went through the same experience when Picasso took up with Françoise Gilot and they had a son, Claude, followed by Paloma. He did not marry Françoise either, and she left him, but she tried to be kind to the older children.

It cannot have been easy. Pablo, not surprisingly, became a problem. At sixteen, he robbed a jewellery store in Switzerland, where he was living at the time, and nearly went to prison. Picasso managed to prevent it by telling the police that he was mentally ill and putting him into a clinic. There were other incidents, including an occasion when he and a friend picked up a couple of girls at a bar in Juan-les-Pins, took them back to the small hotel where they were staying, and early in the morning – by then thoroughly drunk – tried to throw them out of the window. The police were called, and again Picasso had to intervene. Fortunately, the police commissioner was a friend of his, so Pablo got off lightly. Picasso, of course, was furious, calling him a 'worthless creature' and 'the most disgusting son in the world'.

Pablo continued to see his father and at one time worked for him as a chauffeur. But he never seriously developed a career of his own. His world revolved round cars, motor-cycles, alcohol, and drugs. He gave Picasso his first grandchild and named it Pablo, but Picasso had absolutely no interest in grandchildren and it did nothing to strengthen the bond between them. Pablito, as the grandson was called, came to a tragic end. On the morning of the old man's funeral, which he was not allowed to attend, he drank a container of potassium chloride bleach and died three months later, in July 1973.

Maya, who had remained with her mother, first learned of the existence of Claude and Paloma at the age of thirteen. 'When she first saw them she wanted to kill them,' Françoise Gilot later recalled. But once she got over the shock, she enjoyed their company and was grateful for the opportunity to remain close to her father. But he refused to give her his name (her birth certificate had simply said 'father unknown') and, after she moved to Spain in 1953, she never saw him again, even though she returned to France and married in Marseille. She had children of her own, but he never met them.

When Maya heard that Picasso was seriously ill, in 1969, she arrived with them at the electronic gate which guarded his house in Mougins, but was refused admission. The same thing happened when he was dying a few years later. Like Pablito, Claude, and Paloma, she was not even permitted to go to the funeral. They had to content themselves with a distant view of the ceremony from the mountain above, visiting the cemetery afterwards to place the flowers they had brought. In 1977, her mother hanged herself in the garage of her house in Juan-les-Pins.

Like the others before him, Claude was fussed over as a child – he looked very much like Picasso – and then neglected. When Françoise decided to marry someone else, he and Paloma spent their summer holidays with their father, but this came to an end after Françoise had taken legal action to gain some basic rights for her children, starting with the right to use their father's name. She won. Soon afterwards Picasso married Jacqueline Roque, who resented their presence and eventually succeeded in banishing them from their home. During the Christmas holidays in 1963 Picasso told Claude and Paloma that this was the last time they could visit him.

When he fell ill in 1979, Claude arrived with his young American wife, three months after his wedding in New York, but got the same answer as Maya. His father was 'too busy' to see him.

Françoise's legal battle to legitimize her children, which went on for some time, was strongly resented by Picasso. 'They have my name. Isn't that enough?' he told a court reporter.

He died without leaving a will or instructions as to how he wished his great wealth to be divided. A year later Claude and Paloma, and soon after, Maya, were recognized as legal heirs. The estate was valued at $260 million. Jacqueline inherited the largest portion, almost three-tenths of the total estate. Pablo's children got two-tenths, and the others each inherited one-tenth. Jacqueline, like Marie-Thérèse, eventually committed suicide.

Picasso's numerous admirers have conceded that he was selfish and difficult, but they maintain that his genius excuses everything – including the way he behaved towards his children. He was utterly dedicated to his work and irritated by anything that got in the way. He hated responsibility and the demands that family life made on him. During the court battle with Françoise, he told his lawyer that his works were 'much more his children than the human beings that claimed to be his children'. One can imagine the effect that cruel remark had on them.

His own father had treated him with more consideration. A

painter himself, he gave young Pablo much help and encouragement. Not that he really needed it: Picasso was a child prodigy
who could draw before he could speak and whose earliest work
was widely admired. He did not think much of his teachers
or art schools – hence, no doubt, his later remark to Paloma
that 'art cannot be taught'. He probably felt that any effort on
his part would be a waste of valuable time. His own work
seemed so infinitely more important – which, of course, it was.
His turbulent love life was an additional barrier to a close and
sustained relationship with the children.

Artistic genius often leads to behaviour that is offensive and
puzzling in somebody who is otherwise so intelligent. Genius is
an awkward business. Fantasy plays a large part, not only fantasy
in the sense of playing games with reality, but also depression,
schizophrenia, alcoholism, suicide, messy affairs. An artist who
is capable of creating great masterpieces cannot, or should not, be
judged in the same way as a businessman who is merely creating
material wealth. Picasso *ought* to have taken a little more interest in
his children's future and there was certainly no need for the many
gratuitous snubs. The sad fate of young Pablito, burdened with a
wretched father and a grandfather who totally and publicly rejected
him, must give anyone pause for thought. What, one wonders,
would Picasso have made of it?

Genius does not excuse *everything* – the line must be drawn
somewhere. But, at the same time, it would be unfair to blame
Picasso for all the things that went wrong. The women were
equally responsible. He was a demanding companion, but they
could have used their influence to ensure that he and his children
maintained a reasonable relationship. Jacqueline Roque never even
seems to have tried.

Paloma, the youngest, has seldom criticized 'Papa' in public.
She talks with enthusiasm about his 'marvellous work'. It took
a court case to get his name and it was the law, not her father,
who gave her a share of his enormous fortune. It must have
been hard to come to terms with his rejection, but she leads a
happy adult life. Married to an Argentine playwright, she has
homes in Paris, New York, and Buenos Aires. She says that
she likes to make things that are useful, that have a specific
purpose.

Picasso once said of Paloma that she was destined to become

'the perfect woman . . . passive and submissive'. It may have been his idea of female perfection, but he could not have been more mistaken. She may not be a genius, but no one would ever call her passive or submissive – or, for that matter, a failure.

17

Lost Dynasty

Occasionally, the son of an outstandingly successful entrepreneur will go on to do better still. It is the exception rather than the rule. Many more come to terms with the fact that they are unlikely to outdo the founder of the corporate dynasty. They try to help him as much as they can while he remains in charge and may take care of the business after he has gone. Some walk away, with great relief, as soon as the tyrant is in his grave. Others become chairman of the board but leave the actual running of the company to professional managers.

There is a nice story about a New Rich tycoon who, at a dinner party one night, declared that truly brilliant, successful men never have brilliant, successful children. One of the other guests listened to this for half an hour or so, and then said to him: 'You know, this is an awful thing to say about your father.'

The thought that their children will never be quite in their league is not as displeasing to fathers as you may think. Indeed, many find it comforting. They like to regard themselves as unique; a son who upstages his father detracts from his glory. He wants them to do well, but not *too* well. Many are willing enough to oblige, but some become grimly determined to perform even greater deeds. In theory, it should not be all that difficult. They have been taught by masters of the game, and they have a solid foundation to build on. They have money and connections. They do not have to struggle as their fathers did. But this can also be a disincentive: there is not the same compelling *need* to make waves.

I have always been fascinated by people who, although they

could have afforded to take life easy, have built vast new business empires. Why bother? I once had a long talk with one man who did it: J. Paul Getty, then one of the best-known of the New Rich. (The press called him 'the richest man in the world'.) Among the subjects we discussed were his feelings about his father, his own desire to build a Getty dynasty, and his disappointment that things had not worked out as he had hoped and planned.

Paul Getty admired his father and was very fond of him. George Getty Sr was a highly successful attorney and an equally successful oilman. He made an impressive fortune in the Oklahoma oilfields and founded a business, the Minnehoma Oil Company. He often took Paul on visits to exploration sites and he was delighted when his only son showed keen interest. Paul later wrote that it was not the prospect of riches that excited him, but 'the challenge and the adventure in field operations, in the hunt for oil'. He asked his father for permission to spend his summer vacations from school working in the field and was told: 'It's all right with me – if you are willing to start at the bottom.' It meant that he would be employed as a roustabout – an oilfield labourer whose job it was to perform the heaviest (and usually the dirtiest) work on a drilling site. He was paid the roustabout's going rate, $3 a day for a twelve-hour tour, and his father warned him that he could not expect preferential treatment because he was the boss's son. He would have to hold his own with the other men, take his share of the orders, and do his share of the work. Paul accepted these conditions, 'if for no other reason than that, having asked for the job in the first place, I risked losing some of my father's respect if I refused or quibbled'. During the next three years his time was divided between college terms in California and summer vacations working on the site.

Getty Senior naturally hoped that, one day, he would take over the family business. But Paul was not yet ready to settle down. Indeed, he was not at all sure that he wanted to be an oilman for the rest of his life. His ambitions alternated between a desire to become a writer and a wish to enter the Diplomatic Service. His father wisely said nothing about these ideas. Paul persuaded him to finance a trip to the Far East, which he wanted to make 'so that I can broaden my experience of the world'. He toured Japan and China for two months, and developed an interest in art. He spent more time in the oilfields on his return, but then decided that he wanted to go to Oxford University in England to study economics and political science. Again his father agreed to support him, though he seriously doubted whether Paul intended to buckle down to study. His fears were well founded: Paul soon started to roam around the Continent in a second-hand Mercedes-Benz. He constantly wired his father with requests for more cash.

By now, Getty Senior was getting more than a little annoyed with his son's free-wheeling lifestyle. He wrote to tell him that he was seizing the 15,000 shares in the Minnehoma Oil Company which had previously been put in his name. It was Paul's turn to be angry: he accused his father of cheating him out of his birthright. In June 1914, though, the older Gettys visited Europe and their son showed them round. They returned to the United States together and Getty Senior made one last effort to persuade Paul to go into the oil business.

The way he went about it holds a valuable lesson for other New Rich fathers who find themselves in a similar position. He did not rant and rave. He patiently listened to what his son had to say and then presented what he frankly admitted was 'his side of the case' in a reasonable manner. He had always entertained the hope, he said, that Minnehoma would be a family business. It was a company worth millions of dollars, he was nearly sixty and would soon be thinking of retiring; Paul was his only child and the logical choice to carry on the business that he had built. 'You are only twenty-one,' he said. 'You can easily afford a year-long detour before trying for the Diplomatic Service. Would you be willing to consider it?'

Paul said he might, depending on the nature of the detour. 'Try your hand as an independent operator in the fields,' his father urged. 'If the experiment doesn't work out or you are unhappy when the year is over, you can do whatever you wish. You will have my blessing.' He said he would provide him with $100 a month for living expenses while Paul scouted the Oklahoma oilfields for low-cost leases and provide the capital for exploratory drilling. If he found oil, any profits would be shared – 70 per cent to Getty Senior, 30 per cent to Paul.

It was a shrewd move. Paul was not being asked to join the firm (he would almost certainly have refused) but was being offered a chance to do his own thing, with his father's help. He took the bait and started to look around for leases. Long months went by without results, and he was frequently on the verge of giving up. The detour-year was nearly at an end and he had nothing to show for his efforts. Eventually, though, he managed to pick up a lease for $500 and began drilling. He was lucky: the well came in for 700 barrels a day initial production. A rapid succession of profitable lease attractions and additional oil strikes followed. By mid-1916, Paul had become a millionaire in his own right. He was still only twenty-three.

His father had every reason to hope that he would now be ready to join him. Again, though, Paul did the unexpected. He announced that, since there was really no need for him to make more money, he might as well devote his time to enjoying it. He would retire. Getty Senior was appalled, and pleaded with him to reconsider, but Paul's mind was made up, and there was nothing he could do about it.

For the next two years Paul took what he later described as 'a total immersion course in practical application of the pleasure principle'. He went to parties and nightclubs, and played with a series of attractive girls. But the lure of oil proved stronger than he thought. Other men were making fortunes while he was indulging himself, and he decided to get back into the race. His father said nothing, but was glad when Paul agreed to become a director of Minnehoma.

He again became a successful independent wildcatter while, at the same time, getting more closely involved in the family enterprise. In 1923, his father had a serious stroke and Paul felt it was both his right and his duty to take charge of the business. Some of the executives objected, but what really surprised him was that Getty Senior took their side when he recovered. The old man was not, after all, ready to retire. A new company, George F. Getty Inc, was set up to oversee the various interests, with Getty Senior as president. Paul was hurt by the rebuff, but later asserted that 'it was with overwhelming joy that I watched him improve slowly as the pressure he took upon himself mounted'.

Paul, meanwhile, embarked on the first of his five ill-starred marriages. His bride, Jeannette Dumont, was only eighteen and they got married without telling anyone. The Gettys were upset, but they took to Jeannette when they met her and all was forgiven when the couple had a son, who was christened George Franklin Getty II, in honour of his grandfather. The marriage, though, soon ran into trouble. Paul was away too much, and he still had a keen eye for other young ladies. Jeannette got a divorce on the grounds of mental cruelty and infidelity. Soon afterwards, he married again – this time, the seventeen-year-old daughter of a wealthy Texas rancher. Within months, both came to the conclusion that they had made a terrible mistake. Paul tried to keep the match a secret, but his father found out and, angered by his son's stupidity, changed his will without telling anyone, leaving the bulk of his estate to his wife, Sarah.

In the summer of 1928, Paul had a third go at marriage. Again he had fallen for a teenager, a German girl he had met in Vienna. For once, he took the precaution of asking his parent's permission. Getty Senior was so pleased by this gesture that he offered him a one-third interest in George F. Getty Inc. He was seventy-three and wanted a rapprochement with his son. Another child, Jean Ronald, was born in December 1929.

The following April, Getty Senior suffered a second stroke and this time it was fatal. He had not changed his will and Paul was shocked when he heard that, although he had been left $500,000, most of the $15.5 million estate (including control of the Getty oil interests) had gone to his mother. He became president but did not have the final authority which he had thought his father always wanted him to have.

Paul had revered the old man, despite their differences, and many years later wrote in his autobiography that his death was 'the heaviest blow, the greatest loss, I had suffered in my life'. He was also fond of his mother, but they soon disagreed about the way the business should be run. She and the executors, mostly old friends of the family, were worried about the economic situation and advised retrenchment. Paul took the opposite view: he felt that the time to expand was when prices were low. He thought the company should be turned into a major integrated oil giant which refined, transported and sold gasoline as well as producing crude oil. He no longer wanted to be at the mercy of the big oil companies which could squeeze an independent producer by blocking access to storage capacity, to pipelines, and to markets. To achieve this he proposed buying up other enterprises. His vision was to be triumphantly vindicated in later years, but at the time it set him in sharp conflict with his mother and the other directors. They rejected his approach and he eventually resigned from the board. He retained his interest as a one-third stockholder, but he wanted to be free to pursue his long-term objectives.

While all this was happening, Paul also went through another divorce and re-marriage to a woman half his age. They had two sons, christened Eugene Paul Getty and Gordon Paul Getty. This union, too, fell apart (his new wife complained, as the others had, that he was more concerned with his business than with his family). But there was a consolation: in 1933, he finally succeeded in persuading his mother, then eighty-one, to give him control of the family firm. In a complex deal, she got more than a million dollars in cash and another three and a half million in interest-bearing notes payable at agreed dates in subsequent years. She later relinquished the bulk of the notes, but stipulated that they should be committed to an irrevocable trust and that Paul should contribute one million dollars of his stock in George F. Getty Inc. He was to be the first beneficiary. After his death, the trust income would be shared between three of his four children. (Ronald was excluded on the grounds that he would one day inherit his maternal grandfather's substantial fortune.) These arrangements would eventually lead to bitter disputes, setting one Getty against another, but in 1933 it gave Paul the chance to make his dreams come true.

The story of how he turned the Getty interests into a vast organization, and in the process turned himself into the 'richest man in the world', has been told so many times and is so well known that there is no point in going over it all again. Let us, instead, consider his failure to build a dynasty.

His fifth marriage, which lasted considerably longer than the others, gave him another boy, Timmy. He now had five sons – enough, certainly, for what he had in mind. But it all ended badly. Getty wrote in his autobiography, published posthumously in 1976, that his father's influence and example were the principal forces that formed his nature and character. 'Unfortunately,' he said, 'I had no like degree of influence and control over the lives of my sons.' This was also what he had told me two years earlier. He blamed it all on his disastrous marriages. His wives were the plaintiffs in every divorce suit and were invariably awarded custody. He had visiting rights, but his sons saw very little of him in their formative years. Paul was always too busy, always chasing another deal. Perhaps it might have turned out differently if he had found time to build a better relationship with his children – as his father had done in his own case – but he didn't. He wanted a dynasty, but he was not prepared to put in the necessary effort. He seems to have thought that, if he concentrated on building up a big enough business empire, everything else would fall neatly into place. He was wrong.

At one time or another, each of the four older boys tried their hand in the family business. Two dropped out after relatively brief periods. Ronald went into the movie industry: Gordon chose to follow artistic and intellectual pursuits. Eugene Paul showed early promise (to please his father, he even changed his name to J. Paul Getty Jr) but lost interest after a spell with Getty Oil Italiana and left. Timothy, the youngest, never got the chance to try: he died at the age of twelve, after undergoing several operations for removal of a brain tumour. George, the eldest, was the only one who looked like a potential successor and was, accordingly, groomed to take over.

As a child, George had seen very little of his father. (Even at the age of thirty-three, when he had three daughters of his own, he reckoned that he had spent no more than six weeks with him since he was one year old. To him, Paul was always 'Mr Getty'.) George served in the United States Army and then took a one-year crash course at Princeton University. His aim, at that time, was to become a lawyer. But when he left Princeton he announced that he had changed his mind: he would go into the oil business. Paul, remembering his own father's advice, urged him to start as an independent producer, with his financial help. The experiment did not turn out as well as his own had done, all those years before, but Paul persuaded himself that his son had a natural aptitude for the industry and welcomed him into the Getty empire. Promotion was swift. In 1949, he sent the 24-year-old George to the Middle East as his personal representative. The Getty interest had the Saudi Arabia oil concession in the Neutral Zone, and this was an important job. George did his best to prove that he was worthy of his father's confidence. But the Neutral Zone was a bleak place, with few comforts and diversions. Then, as now, the Saudi authorities had strict rules against certain kinds of pleasure that the West takes for granted. After more than a year there, George was found drunk at one of the drilling camps and rushed out of the country in the hope of avoiding a scandal.

By the time the Saudis heard of the incident, he was safely back in California and they decided to forget the matter. But George was reprimanded by his father and exiled to the company's office in Texas.

If one or more of the other sons had stayed the course, the episode might have dealt a nasty blow to his chances of eventually taking the helm. But they did not, and at the age of thirty-six George became president of Tidewater Oil, one of the principal companies, and heir apparent to the emperor's throne. By all accounts, he did a competent job. Paul, however, seemed to have forgotten the problems he had with Getty Senior when he thought he was in the same position. Or, perhaps, he remembered them all too well and did not wish to see his son mount a premature challenge. Whatever the reason, he denied him effective control. George had to consult his father every day by transatlantic telephone before he could clear company business. (Paul was, by then, living at Sutton Place, the grand old manor house near London which he had bought from the Duke and Duchess of Sutherland.) His frustration was made clear in a letter he wrote to him: 'You run your business,' it said, 'and I'll run mine. You supply the oil, and I'll refine it. The days are gone when one man can control every detail of a great oil company.'

In his autobiography Paul later claimed that he had only given *advice*: it had been up to his son to make the final decision. But that is not how it appeared to George at the time. His father declared that henceforth the group would concentrate on exploration and production (thus reversing the direction he had himself advocated so passionately after the death of Getty Senior) and sold Tidewater's western properties. Tidewater was merged with Getty Oil, with Paul as president and George as executive vice-president. Game, set, and match to the emperor.

Or so it seemed. George, convinced that he could never win however hard he tried to please, began to drink heavily and took medication in order to sleep. His marriage deteriorated. One evening in 1973, Paul was called at a dinner party in London and told that his eldest son was dead.

At first he was led to believe that George had suffered a stroke, but the next day an autopsy revealed that the cause of death was an overdose of barbiturates and alcohol.

He later said that he sat for hours staring into space. 'I remember only one thought – that it was untrue, impossible.' He had always believed that his first son would outlive him by at least thirty-five years, which would leave George plenty of time to make his mark. He ordered an independent investigation and was told what he wanted to hear: that it was an unfortunate accident. But he could not shake off one nagging question: was it possible that the pressures were greater for George than for other business executives because he strove too hard to live up to the images of his father and grandfather?

A few months later there was more bad news: his grandson J. Paul Getty III, had been kidnapped in Rome (see Chapter 13). But it was George's death which affected him most, and which caused him to abandon his efforts to build a dynasty. His interest in the business waned and he devoted more time to other things, including his autobiography and his pet project, the J. Paul Getty Museum in California. He told me that, perhaps, one of his surviving sons might return to the companies eventually, but I got the impression that he did not much care whether they did or not. He said that he had realized, belatedly, that a father should never expect too much from a son because he *is* a son. One cannot predetermine the careers of one's children or the pattern of their lives.

The museum, opened in 1974, is likely to keep his name in the public eye for longer than anything else he ever did. The idea of building a replica of a Roman villa to house his large art collection first came to him in the 1960s. He had always been fascinated by Roman history and had been particularly impressed by the Villa dei Papyri at Herculaneum, which was engulfed by lava in the eruption of Vesuvius in AD 79 and rediscovered in the eighteenth century. Architects were commissioned and construction began on the site of Getty's Malibu ranch in 1970. He did not supervise it himself, but followed progress from his London home. Photographs, films, and detailed reports were sent to him every week. He talked about it constantly, but did not attend the opening ceremony and, in fact, did not live to see his creation. When he died, he was buried in a nearby mausoleum, shared with the oldest and youngest of his sons.

The museum has, inevitably, attracted a good deal of criticism. But Getty felt it was money well spent, and he left many millions to ensure its future. His surviving sons were also well provided for but quarrelled over *their* millions. In the manoeuvring that followed the old man's death, Getty Oil was sold to Texaco for $9.9 billion.

John Paul Getty II, who became a dollar billionaire, had a well-publicized period as a drug addict. In 1973 he came to London, where he has lived ever since. At first he was reclusive and did not leave his house in Chelsea's Cheyne Walk. But a neighbour, Mick Jagger, introduced him to cricket and he made many new friends. He has a box at Lord's and is a member of Britain's most distinguished cricket club, the MCC. He also owns a 1,700-acre estate in Buckinghamshire. Getty has become well known for his charitable work. He has given £100 million to various causes, including the National Gallery and the British Film Institute. His generosity was recognized by an honorary knighthood in 1986. His annual income is so vast that he can well afford to go on using a large part of it in this way – which, you will agree, is one of the better aspects of the extraordinary Getty saga.

18

Will Power

Wills are a major source of family strife: the rich are often at their worst when they fight over the fortunes left behind by parents and other relatives, even if they have done nothing whatever to deserve them. One might have thought that people have an undisputed right to decide what should happen to their money after they have gone. But their wishes are often challenged in the courts, and the outcome may be quite different from the one intended. In the course of these disputes a lot of dirty family linen tends to get washed in public, and in many cases the principal victim of the abuse is the person who made the will. He or she is no longer in a position to answer back, so everyone feels free to make all kinds of charges which the relatives – including the children – would never have dared to utter during the lifetime of their benefactor. The most common argument is that those who made the will did not know what they were doing because they were ill, or unduly influenced, or senile, or even insane.

Some rich people, knowing what a scramble there is going to be among their legal heirs and claimants, simply refuse to make any will at all. Pablo Picasso, for example, died intestate. He told a friend before his death: 'It will be worse than anything you can imagine.' He was right. Howard Hughes, too, failed to leave a valid will and the chaos that followed made headlines round the world.

Others do their utmost to cover every possible loophole, with the help of a small army of lawyers. H. L. Hunt, the Texas oil billionaire, had what may strike you as the simplest answer of all:

his will said than anyone who disputed it would automatically lose and forfeit all right to any benefit and all right and title to any property. It was his way of trying to ensure that his various offspring would continue to obey him; even so, some members of the family seriously considered challenging the will in court.

Henry Ford II, who died in 1987, left a meticulously prepared 55-page document setting out who was to get what and made a videotape in which he explained his reasons. Nevertheless, a bitter power struggle developed almost immediately.

As so often happens in cases where the benefactor has been married more than once, the battle involved his late wife and widow, Kathleen duRoss Ford, and Henry's children from his first marriage. Kathleen, who inherited the bulk of the $350 million estate, had never been on good terms with the Ford children, Edsel, Anne, and Charlotte. Edsel was understandably upset about his father's will and started a legal battle. He and his lawyers said they wanted to protect their father's trust fund from Mrs Ford, who they claimed wanted to administer it 'for her personal gain' without consideration for his grandchildren. The latter, not surprisingly, took Edsel's side.

More often than not, the various parties involved in such battles eventually manage to reach some kind of settlement. Sometimes the court, faced with the unenviable task of deciding between the different claimants, makes a swift decision in favour of one or the other. It may conclude that the benefactor was indeed of 'unsound mind' when the will was written, or it may judge that he has been unjust. It may also throw out the claim.

When Conrad Hilton died at the age of ninety-one, his daughter Constance contested the will, contending that her father had renounced her because he was guilt-ridden over having married her mother, Zsa Zsa Gabor, without having his first marriage annulled by the Catholic Church. She lost. There was also the bizarre case of a woman-hating American who stipulated that his estate should go into a trust fund for seventy-five years. At that time the accumulated interest would bring it up to $3 million, to be used for building a womanless library which would bear his name. The words 'No Women Admitted' must be cut in stone over the main entrance of the library; only books by men would be allowed; magazines would be censored to eliminate articles by women. Nothing in the design, decoration, or appointments must suggest feminine influence. His daughter, who had been left a mere $5, challenged the will but failed.

Relatives of Cornelius Vanderbilt, who left a fortune of over $100 million, had no more luck when they argued that his will should be set aside because he was mad when he made it. The basis for the claim was the fact that he believed in messages from the dead and in supernatural visions. The judge ruled that such a belief in spiritualism did not in itself establish proof of insanity.

Sometimes the battle drags on for years, to the delight of lawyers, who stand to earn enormous fees. This is one of the main reasons why so many rich people give away most of their money in their lifetime: they hope it will avoid future hassle.

The word 'trust' has come up repeatedly in this book, and it needs to be mentioned again because it so often appears in wills. Parents take pride in pointing out that they have already taken care of their children and that they therefore have no need to fight. Joseph Kennedy, the patriarch of the Kennedy clan, established a series of trusts for his family over a period of several decades. When he died in 1969, his will said that 'having provided during my lifetime for my children and grandchildren, and having made other arrangements for my household help and employees, I intentionally omit to make further provision for any of them'. It was a neat solution to the problem, which has been adopted by many others since. Another answer, also mentioned earlier, is the setting up of a family foundation. But even these ploys often lead to disputes – the beneficiaries may challenge some of the clauses, or object to the way trustees discharge their responsibilities.

The question of 'undue influence' is often one of the most difficult to resolve. Many people have walked into fortunes by showing kindness to wealthy old people who have become estranged from their children or other relatives. A perfectly legal, straightforward will, long taken for granted, may be scrapped late in life because someone has come along who is more friendly, more interested in the benefactor's problems. It may be a doctor, a lawyer, or a distant relative who has been forgotten by the children.

When Alice B. Atwood, granddaughter of the founder of the King Ranch in Texas, died at the age of eighty-five a Chicago policeman who had befriended her was the sole beneficiary. She specifically disinherited her relatives. They fought a long court-room battle, but the policeman walked off with the millions. The same thing happened in a case in Britain, though the amount involved – £200,000 – was more modest. An eighty-year-old widow left it to a policeman who, as the judge put it, 'came roaring up the drive on his motorcycle and into her life'. Her relatives said he 'made up to her' because he knew she was wealthy, but the judge ruled against them. It might have been a hopeless love, he said, but she was of sound mind when it happened.

Children who neglect their parents, you may feel, have only themselves to blame when this kind of thing happens. They can be remarkably callous. It is not unusual for sons and daughters to squabble quite openly about the estate of an ageing relative while he or she is still alive. Everyone not only feels entitled to a major share but also makes plans for spending it long before the poor soul has decided to give up. Anyone who tries to be nice to the rich old father, aunt or uncle is regarded as a threat and has to be dissuaded from saying a kind word – let alone performing some kind of service – in case the prospective benefactor goes berserk and changes the will. I have actually heard people arguing bitterly in front of an elderly relative, as if his views and feelings were unimportant.

Some of the rich amuse themselves, in their final years, by changing their wills at frequent intervals. They usually let it be known that they are in the habit of doing so, because it gives them a satisfying sense of power and makes at least some of their relatives eager to please. It is an effective way of getting attention.

Sometimes hate dictates the will rather than love. It may be worded in such a manner that the children are *certain* to turn on each other. Or it may disinherit them and make plain, in harsh language, that the motive was revenge. The entire estate may be left to charity or to some eccentric cause. Pets may be preferred to them: dogs, cats, and even parrots often benefit from wills.

But wills may also be used to pass on some final words of well-intentioned advice. A classic example is the one dictated two months before his death in 1960 by John B. ('Jack') Kelly, the wealthy father of Grace Kelly, who became a Hollywood star and later married Prince Rainier of Monaco.

'This,' he said, 'is my last Will and Testament and I believe I am sound of mind. Some lawyers will question this when they read my will; however, I have my opinion of some of them, so that makes it even.' He went on to list various bequests to his wife, children, and servants. 'In the case of my daughters' husbands,' he said, 'they do not share and if any of my daughters die, her share goes to her children, or if there are no children, then that share goes back into my own children's funds. I don't want to give the impression that I am against sons-in-law – if they are the right type, they will provide for themselves and their families and what I am able to give my daughters will help to pay the dress shop bills, which, if they continue as they started out, under the able tutelage of their mother, will be quite considerable.

'I hope,' he continued, 'that it will never be necessary to go into Court over spoils, for to me the all-time low in family affairs is a court fight, in which I have seen some families engage. If you cannot agree, I direct that the executor or trustees will be of my choosing or yours.' Then came some other advice. US Government bonds, he said, were the best investment even if the return was small. 'As the years gather you will meet some pretty good salesmen who will try to sell you everything from stock in a copper or gold mine to some patent that they will tell you will bring you millions, but remember, that for every dollar made that way, millions have been lost. I have been taken by this same gentry but that was perhaps because I had to learn from experience – when my father died, my hopes were high, but the exchequer low, and the stock market was on the other side of the railroad tracks, as far as I was concerned.

'To Kell' (his son, John Brendan Kelly) 'I want to say that if there is anything to this Mendelian theory, you will probably like to bet on a horse or indulge in other forms of gambling – so if you do, never bet what you cannot afford to lose and if you are a loser, don't plunge to try to recoup. That is wherein the danger lies. There will be another deal, my son, and after that, another one. Just be moderate in all things and don't deal in excesses. (The girls can also take that advice.) I am not going to regulate your lives, as nothing is quite as boring as too many "don'ts". I am merely setting down the benefit of my experience, which most people will admit was rather broad, since it runs from Port Said to Hawaii, Miami Beach to South America.

He went on: 'As for me, just shed a respectful tear if you think I merit it, but I am sure you are all intelligent enough not to weep all over the place. I have watched a few emotional acts at graves, such as trying to jump into it, fainting etc., but the thoroughbreds grieve in the heart. Not that my passing should occasion any "scenes" for the simple reason that life owes me nothing. I have ranged far and wide, have really run the gamut of life. I have known great sorrow and great joy. I have had more than my share of success. Up to this writing my wife and children have not given me any heartaches, but on the contrary, have given me much happiness and a pardonable pride, and I want them to know I appreciate that. I worked hard in my early life, but I was well paid for that effort. In this document I can only give you things, but if I had the choice to give you worldly goods or character, I would give you character. The reason I say that, is with character you will get worldly goods because character is loyalty, honesty, ability, sportsmanship, and, I hope, a sense of humour.'

If only all wills could be like that! Alas, such a combination of common sense and wit is rare: most of them are dry, pompous legal documents in which children are called 'issue' and which concern themselves almost entirely with the distribution of money and power.

The Polish Woman

This was certainly the case when lawyers drew up the Last Will and Testament of J. Seward Johnson, of the Johnson & Johnson pharmaceutical empire. Some of his children later complained about the fact that it was so perfunctory, but the legalese did not upset them nearly as much as the terms: Johnson, it emerged, had disinherited his offspring, left nothing to his grandchildren, and even cut out his favourite charity. Virtually his entire $500 million estate had been left to his Polish-born third wife, Barbara, a woman who had once been employed as a cook/chambermaid by his second wife.

The six Johnson children held a council of war and decided to go to court. (Their ages ranged from forty-one to sixty, but in the courtroom they were always referred to as 'the children'.) They charged that Johnson, who had made more than thirty wills over the years, was senile when he executed the final document. They also brought charges of undue influence, fraud and duress against their stepmother and her lawyer. The battle that followed was one of the most sensational, and expensive, in American legal history. More than two hundred lawyers had a hand in it, and their fees were estimated at a staggering $24 million. The trial lasted for seventeen weeks, and there were accusations of bribery and intimidation of witnesses, death threats against the judge, and even a riot in court.

The key issue was the personality and behaviour of the stepmother, the 'Polish woman'. Johnson had divorced his second wife to marry her in 1971: she was thirty-four, he was seventy-six. Thirty-three witnesses for the children painted a picture of a senile Johnson suffering from twenty-three ailments, including cancer of the prostate. His life with Barbara (called Basia, pronounced 'Basha') was described as a nightmare existence of isolation, coercion, physical violence, and mental torture.

Their lawyer said that, within a year of her arrival in the household, she had destroyed the old man's marriage. What, he asked, was the attraction that caused her to embark on matrimony? One is drawn unmistakably to the conclusion that the real attraction for Basia was his money . . . 'As tools to achieve her goal of dominion over Seward's entire estate, Basia relied not only on her ability to enchant and captivate Seward, but also on her violent temper and fierce outbursts which Seward, by nature a reserved person, became too weak to resist as time wore on. Against his will, or without his realisation, he placed virtually his entire estate under her control. A few weeks short of his 88th birthday, Basia succeeded to virtually his entire estate, undoubtedly becoming one of the world's richest women.'

Basia's lawyers told a different story. Her husband, they said, had left her the bulk of the estate because he was madly in love with her, because he wanted to avoid paying unnecessary taxes, and because he had become increasingly disillusioned with the profligate and wasted lives of his children. They had brought suit through 'disappointed greed and envy'. Johnson, the lawyers maintained, did not want them to have any more money because the vast fortune he had bestowed on them in earlier years had not been used wisely. They produced forty-one witnesses who testified that Johnson was competent, kind, sentient to the end, aware of current events, and grateful for the love of his wife, who cared for him with the utmost devotion.

The court had to decide which version was the truth. It proved to be more difficult than either of the parties had envisaged. In the process, reputations (including that of the benefactor) were attacked with a viciousness that surprised even the sensation-hungry press. In the end the two sides, weary of four months of courtroom argument, did what they surely ought to have done in the first place: they reached a settlement.

Basia, the central character in this bizarre drama, came to America as a refugee. As a child in Poland, she had suffered the horrors of the Nazi invasion. She later received one of the first Vatican scholarships to study art in Rome and Florence and, she subsequently claimed, became an expert art historian. Her father then encouraged her to emigrate to the United States, where she arrived on Labour Day in 1968. Friends in the Polish community introduced her to a cook at the Johnsons' farm in New Jersey and, through her, she was hired as an assistant. Johnson, who was known for his strong sexual appetites (he had even seduced his daughter Mary-Lea), soon made advances. She did not respond at the time, and when she had saved about $3,000 from her salary she left to enroll in an English class at New York University. But Johnson called her a few weeks later, invited her to his office to look at some paintings, and said that he intended to collect art. He wanted to use her expertise as a curator. He could also, he said, foresee a future for her in the oceanographic institute he was supporting. He took her on trips to Rome, Paris, and London, where they bought various works of art. They became romantically involved and by 1970 he had installed her in a New York apartment, paid for by him. He proposed on a trip to Brazil, after telling her that he planned to divorce his wife, and she accepted.

While preparing for the divorce, Johnson made a will leaving the bulk of his estate to charity. He bought the apartment for Basia, and, on the eve of their marriage, he signed a pre-nuptial agreement with her, granting her $250,000 outright plus the income from a $10 million marital trust. His children were not invited to the wedding.

There is no doubt that, at the time, he was indeed madly in love with his new bride. Like so many old men, he was flattered and delighted that a lovely young woman should be attracted to someone of his age. She rejuvenated him. In the years that followed, he made several new wills and Basia's share of the estate steadily grew. In 1972 her marital trust was increased to $50 million and a year later to $100 million, with the proviso that she receive the income but upon her death the principal would go to a charitable foundation selected with her approval. This proviso was dropped in yet another will he made a few months later. When his lawyer raised objections, he was fired.

The children later testified that they did not know the contents of any of their father's wills. Nor, in the early years of his marriage to Basia, did they seem greatly concerned with the subject. They, as well as the grandchildren, had all been provided for in trusts set up by him. These trusts ranged in value up to more than $100 million each, and gave them a handsome income.

During the trial, one of the questions most frequently asked was why, when they were already so rich, they had to fight for still more. One answer was that, because they could not touch the principal, some of them felt that the money was not really their own. But they also gave other reasons: a sense of family honour, a natural desire to take care of their own children, a wish to stand up for what had been their father's favourite charity. They simply were not going to allow Basia to walk away with all that cash.

According to Basia, her relationship with the children, during those early years, was cordial. Her husband had not wanted to see them, but she had made sure that he did. They had even been invited to go on trips with them. The children did not dispute this assertion. They said that they had been given to understand that, in the event of their father's death, Basia would share his fortune with them. They had only begun to get angry when they found out that she had been left everything – and that she intended to keep it for herself.

'I think,' Basia's principal lawyer said in court, 'you'll find the real question that the children are asking of their father in this case is "what have you done for me lately, Pops?"' He and his team produced all kinds of 'evidence' to show that Johnson Senior had good reason to be disillusioned with the behaviour of his children, including tales of messy divorces, drug addiction, and suicide attempts. They also went to great lengths to prove that the old man had been of sound mind when he made his will and that the marriage had been a happy one. One of their witnesses was an angelic nun in a flowing white habit, who had nursed him during his illness and who testified that 'Mr Johnson always knew his identity, his relationship with his wife and children, his wealth – he was mentally competent and functional. He was never confused.' Other witnesses said that the marriage had given him 'a new lease of life' and that Basia had been a loyal, considerate, and caring wife.

The children's lawyers countered by producing 'evidence' of Johnson's senility. They cited examples of his eccentric behaviour. He had suggested that the assets of the Harbor Branch Oceanographic Institute should be converted into gold and buried in a vault under his Princeton mansion. He had said that he was considering a plan whereby, upon his death, he would be lashed to the table in the main salon of his yacht and sunk with the ship. Were these the actions of a mentally competent man?

They also noted that the nun had received an $850,000 donation for her home from the Johnsons, implying that her testimony was of dubious value, and alleged that 'extraordinary sums' had been paid by Basia's lawyers 'to some witnesses who became beholden to them' and that they had threatened and intimidated others who did not. They attacked Nina Zagat, who as legal counsel to Basia had helped to draw up Johnson's later wills and codicils, and who stood to gain substantially from executor and trustee fees.

The head of the team insisted that Basia had 'bullied and terrorised' her enfeebled husband. 'She did not give him a new lease of life, she taught him a new servitude. Her tirades were terrifying and lasted literally for hours. She often shrieked in anger for so long that she became hoarse and could barely even talk.' She 'manipulated and controlled' her husband and 'exerted a psychological influence over him. She threatened him with abandonment, public humiliation, with the most common fears of all elderly and infirm people regardless of their wealth – isolation, loneliness, and embarrassment in front of others.' She called him 'ga-ga', 'stupid old man', 'senile old fool', and 'stupid American'.

To support these allegations he introduced a woman who had worked in the household as a cleaner and who, on the stand, confirmed that Basia had 'yelled at her husband constantly', slammed doors so hard that the plaster fell off the walls, and called him an 'idiot'. He then produced a bombshell: his witness had made a tape recording of one of the incidents. Despite the objections of Basia's lawyer the tape was played in court: it was indeed a terrifying tirade in Polish. Other witnesses also testified that Basia would have prolonged screaming fits during which she called her husband 'ga-ga' and 'stupid American'.

It all added up to a devastating blow to the image of a kind and loving wife. Basia, astonishingly, claimed that it was the work of KGB agents, who were out to get her.

Some time after this the judge had mysterious phone calls threatening to kill her if she did not declare a mis-trial, and there were also calls that there were bombs planted. They may well have been the kind of hoax warnings that are often made during much-publicized events, but the judge took no chances: she told the FBI, who provided her with a bodyguard.

Basia herself never took the stand. She said she was perfectly willing to do so, but her lawyers were against it: they felt that they could not predict what she would say or how she would react. The judge urged both sides to find some way of settling out of court, and Basia eventually made a settlement offer of $140 million. The children made a counter-proposal of $180 million. Their lawyers wanted to fight on, but they did not care for the prospect of spending further months, perhaps years, in the courts. Nor did Basia, who agreed to hand over a total of $180 million and who made a separate settlement with the charity. It still left her with more than $350 million.

It is easy to be disgusted by the whole affair, which need never have happened at all if there had been a little more goodwill and understanding on both sides. Basia should have realized that, with so much money at stake, there would be a fight if the children and grandchildren were disinherited. They should have tried harder to convince her that it was in her interest, as well as theirs, to share the fortune instead of forcing them to launch a lengthy and expensive court battle. They had been friends once: would it really have been so difficult to come to an agreement?

J. Seward Johnson may have been senile (though it was never proved) but it is significant that he had not included the children in his many previous wills, made over a period of several decades. He felt that they had been taken care of already, which by any normal standards they certainly had. This is what convinced Basia that she could win. She knew that he did not have any particular affection for them, and that he had the right to decide what should happen to the rest of his fortune. She certainly influenced him, but that is not unusual: wives *do* have an influence on their husbands. The problem for the court, as always in such cases, was to decide what constitutes 'undue' influence. There is no doubt that she was temperamental, but the occasional row does not add up to 'terror' and if every wife were to be condemned for calling her husband 'stupid' there would be few marriages left.

None of the participants emerged from this sorry episode with dignity, including the lawyers. Basia and the children were made to look foolish in public, and it is not hard to imagine how other members of the Johnson family must have felt about it. The lesson seems obvious: stay out of court.

19

Rich Losers

There is no law of nature which says that a talent for making money is, or can be, transferred to one's children. That is one of the reasons why the rich are so keen on trusts: you can never be sure that, left with a free hand, some dumb son or daughter will not throw it all away. If he or she cannot touch the principal, the risk is substantially reduced.

All business ventures involve risk, and there are many examples of people who have made a mess of things before going on to greater glory. Walt Disney, J. C. Penney, H. J. Heinz and many other well-known empire builders all faced bankruptcy earlier in their careers. But most of us seem to derive particular pleasure from the failure of inheritors: somehow, the news that a rich kid has blown it seems to make us feel better about our own shortcomings.

The problem for people with inherited wealth is that the Old Money code so often tends to leave them ill-equipped to deal with the sharks who cruise around the real world, waiting to take their money away from them. Tax collectors. Relatives. Fund-raisers. Friends. And, of course, promoters of business schemes which may or may not have genuine merit.

Rich inheritors are constantly bombarded with propositions from the New Rich and the Would-be Rich, and because they have been taught all those rules about honesty, sportsmanship, and loyalty they often fall for schemes which more experienced people would not dream of touching.

Some, of course, are quite capable of throwing away fortunes without any help. They fall in love with an idea of their own and charge ahead, convinced that it will work out for the best. Because they have the means to implement these ideas they tend to be less cautious than people who know that they are going to be in deep financial trouble if things go wrong.

One of the biggest Old Money bankruptcies in recent times was that of Lammot du Pont Copeland Jr, great-great-great-grandson of the founder of the world-famous chemical giant. When he went bust in 1970, the Harvard-educated scion of the immensely rich du Pont family listed liabilities of over $60 million against assets of only $26 million. He had become involved in a number of questionable business ventures and had incurred massive debts, largely by undertaking obligations on someone else's behalf. His hapless investments spanned newspaper publishing, toy manufacturing, real-estate development, film distribution, shopping centres, a car wash, insurance, proprietory colleges, and school dormitories. He had more than a hundred creditors, including Lammot du Pont Copeland Sr, who had advanced his son more than $8 million between July 1969 and June 1970 in a last-ditch attempt to stave off the inevitable. Copeland Senior was so embarrassed by his son's malfeasance that he resigned as chairman of du Pont.

It took four years to sort out the mess, with creditors finally settling for 10 to 20 cents in the dollar to be paid over a ten-year period. The only consolation for Junior was that, under Delaware law, they were unable to invade the trust established for him, which held about $14 million in securities. His father died in 1983, leaving more millions, so Junior is still quite prosperous.

During the bankruptcy proceedings, he depicted himself as the victim of 'a shrewdly conceived confidence game'. In the only statement he made to the press, he said: 'In recent months I have become aware of the character of some of my business associates. And I have become increasingly concerned over the consequences of my relationship with these unscrupulous individuals who have exploited me and the people who have placed their business trust in me.' The concern was a little late, but no doubt he has learned his lesson.

There are some sixteen hundred du Ponts and many have had more success in their endeavours. But one other member of the clan, Henry E. I. du Pont, also declared his insolvency a few years later. It was no mean feat, since he had inherited nearly $50 million from his father. Part of the money went on two lavish homes and three expensive wives, but like his cousin Lammot he lost many millions on business ideas which were not as good as he thought they were.

All such cases inevitably attract a lot of publicity. The press had a great deal of fun, in the 1970s, over the misfortunes of George Huntington Hartford II, grandson and namesake of the founder of the vast A. & P. grocery store empire.

The first George H. Hartford was a brilliant businessman who started as a clerk in a tea store and went on to build the largest grocery chain in America. His two elder sons, George and John, also turned out to be extremely able and the company continued to grow under their leadership. By 1951, A. & P. owned and operated 4,700 stores, most of them supermarkets.

The second George H. Hartford, born in 1911, worked for the business for a while, but was fired by his uncle John for taking off half a day to attend the Harvard-Yale football game. Eventually, though, he inherited $100 million and proceeded to spend it.

He gained early notoriety for his lavish lifestyle. He bought homes in Florida, California, New York, England and France, as well as a hundred-foot yacht. He married three times, which meant costly divorce settlements. But his ill-starred business ventures attracted even more attention. They included a magazine of the arts; a $100,000 investment to prop up a liberal New York daily, *PM*, now long defunct; an automated parking garage that was never built; a model agency that failed; a string of film and theatre productions that fared badly at the box office; a gallery of modern art in New York; an island resort in the Bahamas; and sundry other enterprises, including pamphlets and a book in which he characterized abstract art as a communist plot to bring down Western civilization.

The Bahamas resort *should* have worked. In fact it did, but only after he had pulled out with a substantial loss. The idea was not bad. The island he bought was in an excellent location and the price he paid, in 1959, was reasonable. He changed the name from Hog Island to Paradise Island, which was a smart move, and spent $20 million trying to make it look like paradise. But it did not catch on in the tourist trade and, after investing a total of $30 million in the project, he sold his interest for less than $2 million. The new owners managed to get a gambling licence and the resort took off.

'My tragedy,' he later said in an interview, 'was that I was not trained for anything. I knew nothing about business. When I got my capital I was suddenly rolling in so much money that I had a guilt complex about it. I didn't know what to do with all that stuff.' He now says that he is worth less than $10 million.

Hartford always maintained that he was trying to do something useful with his inheritance, instead of simply leaving it invested in the family business. One can hardly say the same for another venture which made even bigger headlines – the foolish attempt by the Hunt brothers, Nelson Bunker and Herbert, to corner the world's silver market.

The Hunts are an extraordinary clan, even by Texas standards. The founder, H. L. Hunt, was an Illinois farmboy who by the 1940s had become the richest man in America. He made his millions, as so many Texans have done, as a gambler and as an oilman. He was an irrepressible eccentric who lived in a replica of George Washington's house at Mount Vernon but wore cheap suits and carried his lunch to work in a brown paper bag. A great admirer of Senator Joseph McCarthy, he spent vast sums on a relentless propaganda campaign for the extreme right and wrote a Utopian novel called *Apalca* to spread his views. He also managed to run three families all at once: he fathered no fewer than fourteen children because, as he once confided to an associate, he thought he was carrying a genius gene and was doing the world a favour, providing the human race with its future leaders. He did create several very bright offspring, but he also fathered two children who suffered from incapacitating mental illnesses that even he sometimes feared were inherited straight from him. His genius, if that is what it was, consisted of an incredible talent for finding oil.

Nelson Bunker and Herbert Hunt are sons by his first wife, Lydia Bunker Hunt. They had a relatively easy childhood, because their eldest brother, H. L. Junior, was the heir apparent and got the toughest treatment. (He was one of the children who later developed mental illness and had to be sent to a psychiatric institution in New York State.) Bunker went to university but dropped out and joined the Navy in the later part of the Second World War. He later went to work for his father. But H.L. was not easy to please. He kept finding fault with his second son and eventually fired him. Bunker promptly went into oil exploration on his own and, after a shaky start, made a considerable fortune from oil concessions in Libya. Herbert, the next eldest son, gained a degree in geology and also joined his father. He made a more favourable impression and was given to understand that he would take over. Neither of them knew, at the time, that H.L. was keeping his two other families on the side.

The feisty old boy lived to the age of eighty-five, by which time he was a billionaire. Long before, however, he had transferred most of his money to the children, so that the estate was valued at only $50 million.

Bunker and Herbert were both immensely rich when they embarked on their silver play. In fact, that was a large part of the problem – they had so much money that, like Huntingdon Hartford, they did not know what to do with all that stuff.

Bunker had already bought five million acres of real estate in various countries, plus 20,000 head of cattle and an impressive string of racehorses. He also owned numerous oil and gas leases. But he was still left with a lot of cash, and a New York commodities dealer suggested that he should try the silver market. The idea intrigued him. Though always an optimist about his own business dealings, he took a pessimistic view of the world: everything, he felt, was getting worse. In Libya, Colonel Gadaffi was threatening to nationalize his oil field (which he eventually did). At home there were problems like crime and inflation. He had to find something that would protect his family in the turbulent times ahead. Silver looked like a good bet.

Herbert, it seems, came to the same conclusion after reading a book called *Silver Profits in the Seventies* by Jerome F. Smith. It was one of the many doomsday books, popular at the time, which argued that the world was 'on a collision course with chaos' and warned that 'only the individual can protect himself from the forces of destruction'. In Smith's view, the only way for an individual to do this was by converting paper money into 'real money', to wit, gold and silver. He also advised that it should be held in silver bars stored in Switzerland, as a precaution against a possible Soviet invasion of the United States.

Herbert thought the argument made sense and agreed to join forces with his brother. They bought slowly at first, making purchases in packets of 5,000 and 10,000 ounces. But Bunker felt that they ought to think big, as their father had done. They stepped up their buying and by early 1974 they had accumulated 55 million ounces. Bunker spelled out his reasoning in an interview with the financial journal *Barron's*. He said: 'Just about anything you buy, rather than paper, is better. You're bound to come ahead in the long pull. If you don't like gold, use silver. Or diamonds. Or copper. Buy something. Any damn fool can run a printing press.'

Their activities naturally pushed up the price of silver. It soon dropped back again, but the Hunts held on. The bullion was stored in Swiss vaults, as Jerome F. Smith had recommended. They were not getting any income from it, but they still believed that they could not go wrong. A third brother, Lamar, had stayed on the sidelines but now also began to invest heavily in the metal – reportedly after being teased by Bunker about 'missing out' on the big play. The Hunts even managed to persuade some prominent Saudi Arabian businessmen, who were close to the royal family, to become their associates. By 1979, they controlled a sizeable part of the world's supply.

The classic definition of a corner is an attempt to buy up the entire stock of a commodity in order to resell at a higher price. Few people have ever succeeded in doing it: the last time anyone cornered the market in silver was when the Bank of England accomplished the feat back in 1721. The Hunts were a long way from doing the same, but they were certainly in a position to influence the price. By January 1980, it was up to a record high of $50 an ounce.

But the brothers had forgotten (or never learned) one of the cardinal rules of the corner game: the supply must not be able to expand rapidly in response to a higher price. There were plenty of people with silver – not bullion, perhaps, but silverware and coins of all kinds. All over the world old ladies began selling their tea sets, candelabras, and other heirlooms. Coin collectors sold their collections. In a matter of weeks, an estimated 16 million ounces of silver coins and an additional 6 million ounces of scrap silver came onto the market. At the same time, the exchange decided to impose new restrictions on trade, which included a ban on dealing in futures.

The price fell, but Bunker remained optimistic. 'Why would anyone want to sell silver to get dollars?', he said. 'I guess they got tired of polishing it.' He boldly kept on buying, borrowing heavily from the banks and using his existing hoard as collateral. He also proposed to his Saudi Arabian partners that they should form a new investment group to raise a billion dollars or so to prop up the price. 'Silver is going to $200 an ounce,' he told them. 'This is only the beginning.' Before the new organization could get started, however, the metal took another dive. By March, it was down to just over $10. With so much of their hoard pledged as collateral on loans, which in turn had been used to buy massive quantities of silver, the partners were in trouble. The banks and brokers wanted more collateral. The head of one New York investment house called Bunker in Dallas and demanded instant payment of $135 million. He was stunned by the reply: 'We can't make it.' The Hunts were among the richest men in America; surely they could meet their commitments? He warned that they would have to begin liquidating their contracts. Bunker told him to go ahead.

The news spread fast, and had a devastating effect on the market. Silver plunged again and the brothers were faced with one of the biggest losses in US financial history. They were estimated to have lost more than $2 billion. A consortium of banks agreed to make a substantial loan, but they had to mortgage most of what they owned, including Bunker's racehorses, Herbert's collection of Greek and Roman statuary, and even Lamar's Mercedes-Benz and Rolex watch. They were also required to sell all their silver holdings. It was the end of the game – but not the end of the story.

In 1986, the Hunts filed a bankruptcy petition for Placid Oil, their flagship company, and three family trusts, as a precaution against having the assets seized by creditors. In 1988, a federal jury delivered its verdict in a civil case brought by one of the companies which had been hurt by the silver gamble. It said that the Hunts and their Saudi partners had conspired to corner the world market, and that Bunker and Herbert had committed fraud and violated commodities and anti-trust laws. The company was awarded $130 million in damages. Others promptly said that they, too, would seek damages. Bunker and Herbert responded by filing separately for personal protection under US bankruptcy laws.

In their attempt to prove that they were as good at making money as their father, the brothers had thrown away a vast fortune. Far from safeguarding themselves against 'the forces of destruction', they had brought disaster upon themselves and their families.

Their older sisters, Caroline and Margaret, were more sensible.

They stayed out of the play and kept a low profile. They had inherited almost as much as the boys, but had used it more wisely. Caroline, for example, had built up a diversified portfolio of oil and gas properties, ranch and timberlands, luxury hotels, and office buildings.

When I interviewed her for a BBC documentary in 1987, we talked about her own attitude to wealth. It was not there to be squandered, she said. 'If one has been blessed with so much, one has a duty to preserve it for one's children and grandchildren.' She nevertheless loyally said that she was proud of her brothers. They were 'wonderful people'. They were kind to their families and good citizens. They had given generously to charity. They had made 'an honest error'.

Others were not prepared to let them off so easily. Most commentators thought that they had been irresponsible, greedy, and stupid.

The brothers would no doubt argue that they were entitled to make an 'error': it was their money. But, as we have seen, when the scions of wealthy families make a mess of their business affairs many other people can get hurt.

The dangers involved in giving them too much money and power at an early age were highlighted in another dramatic case, this time in Australia. It centred round Warwick Fairfax, then twenty-six and heir to one of the country's oldest and greatest business dynasties. In barely six months 'young Warwick', as he had been known since birth, managed to bring it close to ruin.

The company, John Fairfax Ltd, was founded in 1831. It had been nurtured by generations of Fairfaxes and owned newspapers, television studios and radio stations throughout Australia, plus extensive interests in property, newsprint and telecommunications. Its publications included the highly regarded *Sydney Morning Herald* and the *Melbourne Age*. How could such a venerable institution run into serious financial trouble?

The saga is as bizarre as any soap opera. To understand it fully, one first has to consider a family row which took place many years earlier, because one of the reasons for young Warwick's extraordinary behaviour was a desire for revenge.

For several decades, the company was run in increasingly autocratic fashion by his father, Sir Warwick Fairfax. It prospered, but in 1959 he became embroiled in a scandal when a wealthy Sydney solicitor, Cedric Symonds, issued a writ alleging that his wife, Mary, had been induced to leave him by Warwick Fairfax and claimed damages of £100,000. Since Warwick was a prominent businessman, and still married to his second wife, the allegations caused quite a stir. Other members of the family were so appalled that he was asked to step down as chairman until the suit had been settled. A heated argument ensued, during which Warwick accused his eldest son, James, of betraying him. James Fairfax, the offspring of his first marriage, had only been elected to the board a few years earlier and his loyal support had been taken for granted.

Warwick finally agreed to step down, but quickly reached a settlement with Symonds. He divorced his second wife and married Mary. In 1960, they had a son of their own, 'young Warwick'. He was reinstated as chairman and presided over a period of considerable expansion. But in 1976 there was another challenge to his authority. His cousin, Sir Vincent Fairfax, and his son James decided that he would have to go. He was well into his seventies and appeared to regard the business as his personal fiefdom. They wanted James to take over. There were many emotional meetings and the pair eventually got their way. James became chairman and Sir Vincent's son, John, was made deputy chairman. Warwick Senior was furious, but he had to concede defeat.

The two victors had one thing in common: they detested Mary. She felt the same about them, and she resolved to repay them for what she regarded as treachery. Sir Warwick readily agreed. The chosen weapon was their son, but he was still too young to mount an effective challenge. He had to be groomed for the battle.

Young Warwick was educated at Sydney's elite Cranbrook School and then went to Oxford. This was followed by stints with various companies in America – an advertising agency, a Boston investment bank, the Chase Manhattan in New York, and a summer job with the *Los Angeles Times*. He also went to Harvard, where he got a master's degree in business administration. Thus armed, he returned to Australia. When his father died in 1987, at the age of eighty-five, young Warwick and his mother decided that the time had come to make their move.

James and John had applied themselves diligently to running the business in an increasingly competitive media environment.

The company had gone public in the 1950s, but control had been kept in the family. Warwick joined the board of directors and was appointed assistant publisher of the *Sydney Morning Herald*. He remained silent at board meetings, playing the role of meek newcomer, but secretly worked on an elaborate plan to gain power.

He already had 14 per cent of the shares and had assumed control of another 11 per cent which he was due to inherit from his half-brother. His mother held 1 per cent. He now borrowed $30 million to buy a further 1.5 per cent in the market. His motive, he explained, was to push the family holding above 50 per cent to protect the company from potential raiders like Rupert Murdoch, Robert Holmes a'Court or Kerry Packer. None of the other directors thought a bid was likely, but none of them was in the least suspicious of Warwick's buying spree. They ought to have been: his real intention was to put himself into a majority position within the family.

Soon afterwards the board decided to sell the television interests, which left the company virtually debt-free and well placed to gear up for further expansion in its traditional area of strength – print. It was then that Warwick decided to come out into the open. He announced a stunning $2.55 billion bid to privatize the business. It came as a total surprise to the other family shareholders except, of course, Mary. The whole deal had been put together with the help of friends, who used code-names on working documents to minimize the risk of leaks – John Fairfax Ltd was known as the 'Dynasty Corporation'.

James and John were dismayed by the news, and did their best to talk Warwick out of it. He remained unmoved. The purpose of the bid, he declared, was to 'provide stability for the Fairfax group'. His half-brother and cousin felt that it would have precisely the opposite effect. Their pleas became increasingly desperate, but he refused to change his mind. In the end, they felt that they had no alternative but to sell their shares, if the price was right.

To achieve his objective, Warwick had to borrow a lot of money – $2.6 billion – and then to start disposing of assets to pay the interest. To keep afloat, he had to sell property, a string of magazines, a network of radio stations, a chain of local newspapers, and the *Canberra Times*. Still unable to keep pace with his debts, he closed two of Fairfax's Sydney newspapers, throwing 500 people out of work.

Media analysts said the deal was ill-advised and unnecessary. The Fairfax empire, they collectively concluded, was 'vastly diminished'. John Fairfax told him: 'This is no longer a take-over, it's a fire sale. You're selling everything. What you are doing is tragic.' He issued a statement on behalf of his family pointing out that they had not initiated the bid and would have wished the company to have remained unchanged. Warwick simply said: 'What's got to be has to be.'

A few weeks later, the stock market crash blew his master plan to pieces. Analysts thought he would cancel or postpone, but it seemed that that was no longer a feasible option. Various parts of the deal collapsed, and he was forced to increase his borrowing. James and John resigned from the board. He replaced them with his friends, whose first act was to tell them to get out of the building by the end of the day.

Warwick refused all interviews, even to journalists from his own newspapers, who grew so alarmed by the actions of the new management that they staged a 24-hour strike and passed a motion of no confidence. The editor-in-chief of the *Sydney Morning Herald* and other senior employees decided to leave. Rumours soon began to circulate that the *Melbourne Age* was to be sold, perhaps to Robert Maxwell. Staff immediately began mobilizing to try and prevent such a move. T-shirts went on sale bearing Warwick's image and the legend: 'Never send a boy to do a man's job'. Journalists on the *Age* asked their young proprietor to tell them what was going on; he declined, explaining that he did not like 'talking to large groups of people'.

The setting next shifted to a courtroom. Two companies which had helped to organize his take-over of John Fairfax Ltd claimed $100 million in fees. Warwick filed counter-claims totalling more than $160 million, alleging that they had not done enough to earn their money. In court, counsel acting for the two companies described him as 'a young man in a hurry', a devious schemer who wanted control of the Fairfax empire 'whatever the risk and virtually whatever the cost'. He said that Warwick had labelled his family as 'fools' and that, during discussions with his advisers, he had declared: 'I am the intelligent one of the family. I have the ability. I have just completed a business degree at Harvard.'

Cross-examined, Warwick admitted that he had been less than candid with his half-brother and cousin. But he denied that he had called them 'a bunch of incompetents'; what he had said was that they did not have the required level of competence.

The Australian press made fun of him, but it was the least of his problems. The biggest worry was how to hold on to what was still left of his company. The clever Harvard business graduate had managed to transform a large, successful, debt-free business into a small, debt-laden enterprise that was struggling to survive. Despite the massive sale of assets, cash flows rarely covered interest and other costs. He turned to various banks for help, and after months of tough negotiations he announced a complex $1.5 billion medium-term refinancing agreement early in 1989. The package, which included $450 million in high-interest junk bonds issued in the US by Drexel Burnham Lambert, was described as 'the biggest corporate refinancing and restructuring in Australia's history'. It allowed the company to retain control of three newspapers – the *Sydney Morning Herald*, the *Melbourne Age*, and the *Australian Age*, and the *Australian Financial Review*. It also bought him a little more time in which to prove that he has learned from his mistakes. It will be fascinating to see how he uses it.

The sad thing about the whole affair is that, as the analysts said, it was all quite unnecessary. John Fairfax Ltd was a prosperous organization whose shareholders were content with the existing structure. He would have inherited the crown in due course. Why blow it through impatience and his mother's need for revenge?

20

Young and Old Boys

The Harvard Business School teaches its students that there is no room for sentiment in financial management, so one must suppose that Young Warwick had at least some idea of what he was letting himself in for. But clearly it also persuaded him that a degree in business administration gives one superiority over others, including the New Money types who never got beyond elementary schooling.

The enthusiasm for business schools is a phenomenon of our times. Earlier generations settled for a good all-round education culminating in attendance at a university. Old Money families in Britain felt that it was quite enough if their children could get a reasonable degree in history from Oxford or Cambridge. In America, they usually aimed for an Ivy League college, ideally Harvard or Yale. This is still the general practice, but postgraduate courses at a reputable business school have become increasingly fashionable, chiefly because industry nowadays demands a higher level of professionalism.

America has led the way and Europe has followed. Britain's two most prestigious business schools, in London and Manchester, were only set up in 1965. They mostly attract ambitious people who hope that an MBA (Master of Business Administration) will help them to climb to the top of the corporate ladder.

Not everyone shares the enthusiasm. Indeed, there is widespread prejudice against these specialized institutions. Many Old Money people dislike the emphasis on what they regard as ruthless commercialism. Self-made millionaires tend to be openly sceptical about the value of an MBA. They reject the notion that business can be taught in a classroom. Students, they say, have their heads filled with fancy theories which are of little use in the real world.

Nevertheless, business schools are here to stay. Many offspring of the rich attend them because they are determined to prove that they can be as professional as anyone else.

This, of course, comes at the tail-end of an elaborate process to maintain or secure membership of an elite. The rich may or may not care about business schools, but they certainly want to ensure that their children get a 'proper' education. It is an aim which both old and new families have in common. Even the self-made millionaire who questions the merits of a formal business training, and who proudly points out that he has grown rich even though he had to leave school at sixteen, is usually eager to send his children to a 'good' private school and to university. Ask him why, and he will probably tell you that he wants to do the best for them and that an expensive education is a good 'investment'. There may well be some truth in that, but it is seldom the only reason.

The plain fact is that most parents are snobs. Old Money people cannot bear the thought that their offspring may have to mix with children from working-class backgrounds and acquire their disgusting habits; New Money families feel that, having escaped from a humble past, they must do everything they can to ensure that their children do not slip back into it. The self-made millionaire does not want his son or daughter to talk and behave like the people in the street where he was brought up. Well-educated children confirm his family's new status.

In many cases, the process begins on the day the child is born. Demand for places in some of the more prestigious educational establishments is so high that its name is 'put down' while it is still howling in its cradle. Now that medical techniques make it possible to predict the sex of a child, some parents even try to register an embryo's name.

Snobbery helps to explain the popularity of prep schools like Hill House near Harrods in Knightsbridge, which never lets anyone forget that this is where Prince Charles started his education. The school's facilities leave much to be desired, and the emphasis is on sport rather than studying. 'Swimming,' says the eccentric former army colonel who owns it, 'is more important than reading and writing.' He is also keen on hockey and horses, and every year a group of children is taken to the permanent Hill House annex in Switzerland, where they practise mountain climbing. The Colonel vets every parent who applies and decides who is 'suitable' or not. He makes a point of drawing their attention to the Hill House motto: 'a child's mind is not a vessel to be filled but a fire to be kindled'.

One may question whether his form of kindling is really appropriate, but there is no doubt that it appeals to many wealthy parents. I have a friend who sent his son there. 'Hill House,' he says, 'may not be the best choice if you can't wait to get your son or daughter started on an academic career. But it teaches discipline and good manners. The place isn't perfect, but Peter enjoyed it. He made new friends and it helped him to cope with Eton.'

There are numerous prep schools all over Britain and new ones are being added every year. The ever-growing demand for private education is a direct reflection of the eagerness of New Money families to join what they believe to be the social elite. State schools often have better teachers, but classes are larger and you never know what kind of children are going to be in them. Nor can you be sure that your precious offspring will not be exposed to left-wing ideas. Why take the risk?

The heads of prep schools tend to justify their fees by arguing that the early years are most vital: this is the period when children have their first real contact with others and the attitudes they develop may well last for a lifetime. Small classes help teachers to discover what they are good at and steer them in the right direction.

Parents are generally grateful that someone who understands child psychology is willing and able to assume the burden. They realize that prep schools help to shape character. Young children like to have everything their own way, and rich families tend to spoil them. At school they discover that strangers cannot be manipulated so easily. They make demands and expect obedience. The child also learns that life is competitive. Other children may be brighter or better at sport and therefore win more praise.

Socialists tend to regard prep schools as playgrounds of privilege, and they have a valid point. It is precisely why so many parents like them. They do not mind the allegation that private schools are socially divisive; they would be more upset if they were not.

Snobbery plays an even bigger role in the choice of senior schools. This is the all-important stage when the children of the rich really establish their social credentials. A public-school education no longer guarantees admission to university, or even a well-paid job, but it secures their place in 'society'.

The heads of public schools insist that, nowadays, academic achievement has a high priority. Perhaps so. But pupils from independent schools account for less than half of the students accepted by Oxford and Cambridge. Many never bother to apply: making it through the 'right' school is considered to be adequate qualification for membership of the elite. Clever boys and girls from 'inferior' social backgrounds – working-class areas and state schools – may brandish their diplomas and may even grab the senior management posts in big corporations, but they will not be bona fide members of the upper class. That, at least, is the reasoning which comforts old and new families whose offspring lack the talent or determination to gain a university degree.

England's best-known and most prestigious school for boys is Eton, which ironically was founded in 1440 by King Henry VI to educate seventy poor scholars. The tradition has been maintained: Eton still selects seventy of the brightest children it can find and gives them special treatment. They live in College rather than in town and twenty-five pay nothing for their education; the rest contribute up to half the normal fee. But these King's scholars are vastly outnumbered by the children of the rich. Eton has 1,250 pupils and considers itself to be at the heart of the English establishment.

Prep schools equate admission to Eton with finding the Holy Grail. It has two waiting lists: parents with school connections write directly to the housemasters to enter their sons, while others place their children on the 'general list'. The system favours Old Money families who have sent their offspring to the school for generations. Forty per cent of the student body are sons of Etonians, the highest percentage of old boys of any school in the land. The list of old boys is long: the Duke of Wellington, victor at Waterloo; poets like Gray and Swinburne; economist John Maynard Keynes; Prime Ministers Gladstone, Douglas-Home, Macmillan; and writers Horace Walpole and George Orwell, to name a few. A recent list of the 200 richest people in Britain, compiled by the *Sunday Times*, showed that 55 were Old Etonians.

Eton, a neighbour of Windsor Castle, is deliberately old-fashioned, to the delight of class-conscious parents. Its dress code still requires striped trousers, black waistcoat, tails and stiff collars. (The latter cause chronic stiff necks; it is a sure way to spot an Etonian.) Tourists gaze in amazement at the sight of the quaintly attired boys as they go about their business. They are ignored: Etonians do not deign to pay attention to camera-toting members of the lower classes.

The school even has its own language, carefully preserved through the years. Eton does not have classes, it has 'divisions'. Teachers are 'beaks' and are called 'tutor' by the boys. You do not say that you are being taught by a certain teacher, you are 'up to' someone. Should your work be highly satisfactory, you are given a 'show up', which means that you show your work to all and sundry. If your work is poor you are given a 'rip', which is exactly what it says: your work is ripped and once again you show it to all and sundry. To be caught eating in a division is to be caught 'socking'. This crime could mean that you are put on the 'bill'. To be on the Headmaster's bill is not a pleasant experience. If found guilty you can be sentenced to a number of punishments, ranging from extra work to expulsion.

Each term is called a 'half' and three 'halves' make a whole school year. The ladies who take care of the domestic details in the boy's houses are called 'dames'. To be a member of the Library you do not have to be a book worm: it is the name given to the senior house monitors or prefects. Their juniors are members of Debate. The College Chaplain is known as 'the Conduct'.

Then there is 'Pop' – a small group of seniors which every boy longs to join. It is the school's premier social club and main prefectorial body. Its members wear flamboyant waistcoats and ornate collars and cuffs, which instantly makes their status known to the less fortunate. Membership of Pop is reckoned to guarantee social success: Old Etonians everywhere, remembering their own schooldays, retain considerable respect for what is, after all, only a society of self-important schoolboys.

Like other public schools, Eton is keen on games, which tends to make life difficult for children who do not have the physical capacity to excel at sport. Soccer and rugby are popular, but the school also has its very own Wall Game, a cross between football and rugby, and values skill in traditional English sports like cricket, archery, rowing and beagling. (The school keeps its own pack of dogs.) You may well ask what all this has to do with education: the answer is that it is considered to be an essential part of the Old Money curriculum which has produced so many outstanding soldiers and statesmen. The children can turn themselves into computer experts later on, if they so wish. Public schools are more interested in fostering the spirit that once built an empire.

Feminists, not surprisingly, have no time for places like Eton. Writing in a recent issue of the school's magazine, a public schoolgirl – signing herself Sarah – branded Etonians as arrogant male chauvinists who are interested in girls only for sex. 'Females are status symbols, thought of as intellectually inferior', she said. 'The single sex nature of Eton makes girls a rarity and a girlfriend therefore becomes a means of increasing your standing with your peers. Attempts at serious conversation are seen only to get in the way of the relationship's intended sexuality.'

Parents' day at Eton is a grand occasion. Etonians past and present gather to pay tribute to an institution which has withstood the onslaught of New Money 'progress' and rejoice in the certainty that they are the chosen people, upholders of all that is best in the English way of life. Gleaming Rollers and Bentleys line up on the playing fields, and everywhere families dig into the boots of their splendid cars, set up trestle tables, unfold chairs, and lay out champagne picnics on white linen cloths. The pupils are dressed in their upper-class uniforms: tails and white tie or Victorian boating gear. Old friendships are cemented and new alliances are formed. The day ends with the school's famous song:

> Jolly boating weather, and a hay harvest breeze
> Blade on the feather, shade under the trees
> And we'll all swing together, with our bodies between our knees.

Revolutionaries would dearly love to see them 'all swing together'. Not me. I am content to leave them with the illusion that they represent the ruling class. We know that it is no longer true; why spoil their fun?

The daughters of the rich have their own elite establishments – schools like Roedean and the Cheltenham Ladies College – whose primary task (at least as far as parents are concerned) is to turn them into glittering ornaments of society, fit to be the marriage partners of Etonians. But it would be unfair to suggest that they see it as their only joy. Not these days, they do not. Girls have become more eager to embark on a career and public schools have taken notice of the fact. The better ones are very conscious of the need to get a good percentage of their pupils into university.

One young lady of my acquaintance went to St Paul's in London. This is what she says about the experience.

It really didn't matter whether our families were rich or not, as long as they could afford the fees. There were a lot of girls from wealthy backgrounds, so no one boasted about having money. It was much more important, at St Paul's, to be a good student. The school was very proud of its record of academic achievement and set high standards. We didn't talk about our parents, and some of the girls were embarrassed when they turned up in their Rolls-Royces and showed off.

Old Money parents usually had more sense. You could always tell who had New Money: the mothers wore mink coats and the fathers flashed their Cartier watches. They didn't realize that these things didn't count. What we desperately cared about was proving that we could make it on our own. Some of the girls had a hard time because they simply weren't up to it. They were miserable.

If you go to a state school, your parents may not expect very much. But if you go to a school like St Paul's everyone expects you to do well. The family's pride is at stake. Your father is inclined to say, 'Look, I have spent all this money and you are letting us down. What are you going to do about it?' It can be a great motivation, but it can also make you very unhappy. You feel that you no longer matter as a person: you are someone who is expected to fulfil the ambitions of your family.

They assume that, because they have made a success of life, you must be able to do the same. Some of the girls didn't dare to go home with their school reports. I don't suppose that it mattered in the end. They probably ended up marrying some rich banker. I wonder if parents realize what they do to their children when they ask them to do more than they are capable of.

It is a fair question. A certain amount of pressure can be beneficial, but parents ought to know where to draw the line. Old Money families tend to be better at this. They do not mind giving a clever offspring a helping hand, but they would much rather have a glittering ornament than an unhappy daughter who has to fight hard to prove that she can compete with the striving classes.

The competitive young lady from St Paul's went on to Oxford and was glad that she had been to one of the more demanding schools. Britain's universities, these days, are a unifying force. There is more emphasis on merit than ever before. Fellow students, male and female, are more likely to be from a state school than from Eton or Harrow. A viscount may find himself sitting next to the son of a carpenter. Many students are from overseas, which adds another dimension. Young people from all backgrounds, and of all races, mingle, study, and often meet their future husbands and wives. The rich still have a financial advantage, but social class divisions have been eroded.

Many rich families find it difficult to come to terms with this. They still cling to the outdated notion that universities exist for their benefit. It seems to them inconceivable that institutions like Oxford and Cambridge – for so long regarded as an integral part of the establishment – should refuse to accept their children because they cannot meet the required academic standards and, instead, give places to the bright offspring of clerks and maids. They pull strings and offer financial aid to colleges; they may even try to bribe individuals who are in a position to help. I dare say that it works now and then (though the universities insist that it does not) but the power of money has its limits. By and large, you can't buy an Oxbridge degree for a stupid child.

Many parents also tend to revive the worries which, years earlier, made them so anxious to find the 'right' independent school. Will their children make friends with the wrong sort of people? Will they fall under the spell of tutors with left-wing ideas? Will they indulge in the kind of permissive behaviour which they would never have been allowed to get away with at a decent public school? Such concerns helps to explain why many do not bother to apply: why suffer needless embarrassment? A degree is a nice thing to have, but their children will manage well enough without one.

The children themselves, of course, may feel differently. They tend to welcome the greater freedom offered by the universities and, in many cases, relish the challenge that they represent. They consider themselves entitled to make up their own minds – which they are.

America is supposed to be less class-conscious, but its educational system is in many ways similar to that of Britain. Snobbery certainly plays a part in the choice of elementary schooling. The boarding schools of New England, heavily favoured by Old Money families and those who aspire to join their set, are just as determined to preserve patrician values as our own public schools. And, as in Britain, parents who send their children to them do so largely because they want to be sure that they fall among people who are, socially and aesthetically, good influences.

They also, of course, want to get their kids into Harvard or Yale. It has obliged the schools to raise their intellectual standards, but they are very much aware that academic achievement is not the sole objective. If it were, they would be much more inclined to go for talent rather than for social qualifications and they would be less concerned with teaching their pupils 'correct' behaviour.

Harvard itself is still trying to reconcile what it perceives to be its two basic functions: to confirm the standing of Old Families and to confer that standing on New Families. It wants to encourage the newly talented but it also feels that it has an obligation to Old Money. For admission officers it is very much a question of balance: between children of Old Money alumni and children of genuine ability. In recent years it has fixed the balance at around 20 per cent of alumni children. They are called 'legacies' and they have a distinct advantage: they can slip through the net more easily.

Colleges depend heavily on contributions from their alumni for their financial survival, so they find it difficult to reject a marginal applicant from a wealthy family that might someday be induced to contribute generously to the school. They are well aware that the children may not have the required intelligence and may well drop out before graduation, as some of the Rockefellers and Fords have done. But rejection may harm the commercial interests of the college, so they feel that they have to make allowances.

Harvard has managed to retain its prestige, but in a country as vast and prosperous as the United States there are plenty of alternatives. In California, Stanford has high academic standards and is known as the Harvard of the West. Parents who have made it big in Hollywood send their children here or to the University of South California – often called the University of Spoilt Children. The headmaster of Eton would probably hate the USC: students seem to be able to indulge in antics which would get them banned from his school. The atmosphere is casual, laid-back, liberal. If anyone turned up wearing a tailcoat and stiff collar it would be assumed that he was on his way to a fancy dress party. Many students have flashy cars and boast about their parents' wealth; New Money dominates at USC, which is reckoned to be one of the world's wealthiest universities. Some of the kids arrive each day in the company of beefy bodyguards with guns bulging under their jackets. Teachers are disturbed by the widespread use of drugs and the sexual high-jinks; many of the students are gay, which has created an AIDS problem.

The college's annual home-coming parade is an extraordinary affair, with noisy marching bands, troops of majorettes, and hordes of USC alumni in golf trousers and golf shirts who, when I was there, converged *en masse* on the Coliseum sports stadium for a football game against arch rivals Stanford. Football players command much more respect than brilliant academics; if you are good enough to play for the college team all your other shortcomings tend to be forgiven.

The USC produces a large number of graduates, so one must assume that its students also manage to do some serious work. Some of the alumni hold powerful positions in the state. Others have gone into the entertainment industry; they no doubt feel that the college did a better job of preparing them for life in the crazy world of showbiz than Harvard could have done.

21

Good and Bad

You may well feel by now that the critics of the rich are right after all – that they are a greedy, quarrelsome, and unscrupulous lot and that their children are not much better. I have certainly provided a great deal of ammunition for radicals who think that they do not deserve their wealth and who would like to see it taken away from them. One cannot help being appalled by the avarice, vulgar excesses, cynicism, and ruthlessness of so many of the species. The rich can be unbelievably callous in their dealings with others, including their own kind. This is particularly true of the New Rich, many of whom seem to regard the world as a jungle in which only the cruel and selfish can survive.

I hope, however, that I have also managed to show that there is another side of the picture – that many of the rich, and their offspring, have a strong sense of obligation to their families and to the community as a whole. Their drive, creative enthusiasm, and willingness to support worthy causes has been of benefit to us all. Most of the great innovations which have had such a profound effect on the way we live and work have been inspired by the desire for profit. I would not, for one moment, wish to associate myself with those who, either because of envy or because they genuinely believe in the merits of 'redistributing wealth', urge that the rich should be deprived of their fortunes. I believe in free enterprise because it is the only system that can uphold and protect individual freedom, which matters to me more than anything else. That freedom must include the right to make one's own way in life – to build business empires (if that is what one wishes to do), to preserve the family estates, to ensure a better future for one's children. Wealth has a positive side.

The twentieth century – now almost over – has seen great changes and there may be more to come. Wealth is already more widely distributed than it was in previous centuries, not only because it is taxed more heavily but also because the nature of business has changed. It has become increasingly dominated by giant corporations, run by executives who may or may not be rich themselves, rather than by the kind of people who used to build personal empires – men like Paul Getty, Henry Ford, Howard Hughes, Conrad Hilton, and Aristotle Onassis. These corporations distribute their profits in the form of dividends, not just to the inheritors of wealth but also to pension funds and the growing ranks of small shareholders.

There are, to be sure, still plenty of entrepreneurs who hope to emulate the Gettys and Hiltons. Many have already done so and more are well on the way. But there are also numerous families whose fortunes have gone into a steep decline, either because the founders and their offspring have mismanaged their affairs or simply because of the sheer force of changing circumstances. The past few decades have seen countless mergers and acquisitions, and many family companies have been absorbed by the new giants. The scions of the rich may have their dividends, but they can no longer count on being able to join their parents' business and rise effortlessly to the top. There is more emphasis, these days, on what you can *do* rather than on *who* you are.

This has, inevitably, influenced attitudes and careers. Children have become more aware of the need to 'make it' on their own. They have become more independent, more flexible, more conscious of the need to take account of the feelings of others. Modern methods of travel have also widened their horizons. It is quite common for children to be sent to other areas of the world, to learn how people in various countries conduct their affairs or to play a role in local operations. Business is now on a global scale, and they are part of it.

Another development has been the arrival of what is widely regarded as a new breed: the well-educated 'yuppie' who has no patience with the often elaborate business of building an empire and who seeks to make his fortune overnight through clever financial deals. There is, in fact, nothing new about it.

Earlier generations, too, had their share of wheeler-dealers. But the number of players has grown considerably and in today's turbulent markets many are astonishingly successful. It is not unusual for some bright young spark to make more money in a very short time than his parents have managed to do in a lifetime of work. I do not, myself, regard it as a laudable or even desirable trend, and I am glad that the authorities have tackled some of the more obvious abuses, but again it seems to me that, in a free society, 'yuppies' should have the right to make their own way within the limits set by the law.

Most of them tend to be male, which no doubt annoys the feminists but which can hardly be blamed exclusively on the business world's long-standing prejudice against the female sex. It is true, as noted earlier, that the cards are still stacked against women when it comes to taking over a family business, but the best and brightest certainly have a greater opportunity than ever before to 'make it' on the financial scene. They also have a better chance of getting promoted to the higher levels of big corporations. Many women have shown that it *can* be done.

As we have seen from some of the case histories mentioned in this book, the biggest obstacle is often the attitude of parents and brothers rather than that of outsiders. The male members of rich families still seem to find it hard to accept that women deserve an equal opportunity to show what they can do. I am sure that this, too, will change in the years ahead, but it will take much time and effort. It will also require courage: daughters will have to become much more determined to assert their rights. In many cases, the existence of trust funds gives them considerable power. Sally Bingham showed how it can be used, though the result was not what she had in mind when she started her famous fight.

The prime target must be the fathers. It is, as a rule, the father who is the dominent force in a wealthy family and who has the last word. He will have been influenced by his own upbringing, which in the past has generally emphasized the natural superiority of the male. His sons may turn out to be a disappointment, but he will still be inclined to take the view that a man (even a son-in-law) must succeed him. He has spent his whole life in a male-dominated environment and he tends to feel that women are simply no match for the sharks who inhabit it. A daughter has to try much harder than a son to convince him that she is more than capable of dealing with them in a bold and decisive manner. If, that is, she wants to. Many women do not.

Fathers tend to assume that their children are eager to play their assigned role as members of the dynasty he hopes to create or to perpetuate. It is not necessarily so; they are much more inclined, nowadays, to rebel against the whole idea. I am on their side. I find it puzzling that the urge to build dynasties should be so strong. I can understand the desire to preserve the family business and to keep one's name alive. But this can be achieved in many other ways. What I find difficult to understand is why some fathers feel that they *must* have their children in charge, even though the children may not wish it or are totally unfitted for the task. It so often leads to unhappy relationships without, in the end, reaching the hoped-for objective. It seems to me that Paul Getty, who learned this lesson so late in life, came to the right conclusion: you cannot predetermine your children's careers or the course of their lives.

The root of the urge, I suppose, is admiration for Old Money and the wish to be just like it. Dynasties are upper-class; business enterprises, on their own, are not. New Money has to be given the patina that most people still find so impressive. In America, the use of the founder's name, with the addition of Roman numerals, is meant to do the trick. In Britain, the dynastic process has long been aided by the acquisition of titles. New Money will give just about anything for a hereditary knighthood or peerage. Unfortunately for the New Rich, politicians are no longer willing to oblige. No new hereditary titles are being created, except in very special circumstances. Not surprisingly, the loudest protests have come from the New Rich, who would dearly love to perpetuate their names in this aristocratic fashion. Without it, they have to be content with being knights, lords, dames and ladies during their own lifetime: no amount of money can buy more. They cannot pass on what earlier generations managed to do with ease: a title which would be a lasting tribute to the standing and skill of the founder. All they can do is to leave their children the business, or a trust fund, and hope for the best.

Do the children *care*? Some undoubtedly do; though titles may no longer be passports to cushy boardroom jobs, they still carry considerable social clout. But I do not think it matters nearly as much to them as it does to their parents.

What really tends to count for much more is a sense of personal fulfilment. They do not want to be driven by the ambitions of their fathers and mothers. The money is welcome, but it is seen as a means to an end, and that end may well be quite different from the one envisaged by the parents. Again, I find myself on their side. I did not inherit a penny, but if I had I would have wished to be free to decide what direction my life would take. I have never had the slightest desire to create a dynasty, and I have never sought to force my children to do anything they did not want to do. I tried to guide them to the best of my ability when they were young, but after that they were pretty much on their own. I offered advice when it was sought, and still do, but I have always held the strong belief that we should all do our own thing. Perhaps that has made me a bad father – who knows? – but I like to think that they understand and appreciate my position.

There is, I think, much to be said for the technique used by George F. Getty Sr when he realized that his only son had a talent for business but did not want to play second fiddle. He suggested, you will recall, that he should spend a year trying his luck as an independent oil prospector and offered to help him financially, with the proviso that they should share the profits. He did not try to apply pressure, and his proposal that they should share the profits (which Getty Senior certainly did not need) put the deal on a proper footing: the son was not being treated with patronizing generosity but was given the kind of help that he might also have got from a banker. The father guessed, correctly, that if he turned out to have some success on his own he would be hooked and would, in time, want to take over the family firm. A variation of this ploy was used by Frank Mars, the founder of the candy empire, who in 1932 gave his only son Forrest a cheque for $50,000, plus the foreign rights to Milky Way and several other trademarks, and told him to start his own business in another country. Forrest went to Britain, set up a confectionery company, and eventually returned to run Mars Inc. In each case the heir had a chance to acquire experience and test his skills without constant parental supervision. He was able to establish a sense of personal worth before going into the family business. He could say to his father and his colleagues: 'Look, I have shown that I am as good as anybody else.'

Sometimes, of course, the experiment does not turn out in

quite the way it is supposed to. Having tasted independence, the offspring may decide to go on running his own enterprise. (Nothing wrong with that, but the dynasty builders tend to get rather upset.) Or the son may not be as good as either he or his father thought he was. It is probably best that both should make this discovery outside, away from the critical attention of the family firm's staff. Mistakes are less embarrassing if they are not made at the home base. They may also be less expensive. A son who is given too much power at an early age – as often happens in a family business – can cost the company a frightening amount of money. It is better to let him feel his way in a more junior role at another firm, where his scope for causing damage is much more restricted.

For many children, one of the most awkward problems is how to tell their parents that they have decided to do something entirely different – that they want to be actors, or pop stars, or fashion designers, or writers. 'But,' the bewildered father is liable to protest, 'this isn't a *real* job.' The most effective counter is to tell him what some of the people in these fields earn; casually drop in names like Johnny Carson, Harold Robbins, Pierre Cardin, and Mick Jagger.

He may, of course, know already. Indeed, he may be in the same line of business, in which case it will probably cause more surprise if a son or daughter wants to go into trade or manufacturing. Whatever the circumstances, it pays to be calm, rational, considerate. Parents do not have the right to decide what their children should do with their adult lives, but if they support them financially, and are expected to go on doing so, they are entitled to ask that their views should be respected.

Many relationships are wrecked, or put in abeyance for years, because both sides stubbornly refuse to compromise. They dig in, shout, write angry letters, make threats which they cannot easily withdraw, and end up in court. I find it both sad and ridiculous that the Guccis could not settle their differences among themselves – that the eighty-year-old patriarch had to go to prison because he and his son Paolo felt compelled to fight to the finish.

It is easier to see why broken marriages lead to disputes, especially if the parents remarry. The children are generally drawn into the warfare, which creates unhappy situations all round. They then have to come to terms with a new stepmother or stepfather. In many cases, there is instant and mutual hostility. The children resent the newcomer and refuse to take orders from him or her; in turn, the new stepmother or stepfather regards them as disruptive holdovers from the past and tries to put them in their place. It happens in families everywhere, but the rich are more prone to it because they often go through more divorces and because money becomes an important additional factor. Paul Getty blamed his five failed marriages for the problems he had with his sons. Aristotle Onassis must have recognized the difficulties his daughter had with Maria Callas and, later, Jackie Kennedy.

This is a problem which is getting worse, not better. The divorce rate has risen sharply in recent years, so there is greater disruption of family life. It creates conflict not only among parents and their children but also between brothers and sisters, especially if one or the other parent starts a second family.

Some parents abandon their progeny completely and often end up living to a lonely old age. Others try to make amends by wrapping them in a cocoon of material goods. Their children tend to grab all they can get, and grow up lacking any shred of self-discipline. Many become drug addicts. It is hard to feel sympathy for the princely German couple who got hooked on drugs and killed themselves, leaving a young son in someone else's care. They wanted only to have fun, fun and more fun, until long after it was not fun any more.

The abuse of drugs is a worldwide problem among the young, but again the rich are more prone to it because they can afford to indulge themselves. More and more children of the rich are using cocaine, crack, marijuana, and heroin to escape from boredom, lethargy, and depression – or simply for pleasure. They talk carelessly about 'getting high', meaning euphoric, happy. There are many other ways of achieving highs (like falling in love or winning a race) but drugs can do it powerfully and immediately. Like alcohol, they can provide a quick lift. It does not last, but users maintain that even a temporary lift is better than nothing at all.

Parents generally find it difficult to decide what to do about it. Some may be hooked themselves, which hardly qualifies them to give advice – unless they have seen the error of their ways. If you cut off the children's supply of money, they will seek to raise it elsewhere. If you notify the police, you will create embarrassing headlines. So most of them tend to settle for stern lectures, which may or may not do any good. In many cases, fortunately, the children sooner or later decide on their own that their habit is self-destructive and do their best to end it.

Another feature of modern life which causes widespread concern is homosexuality, not just because parents find it hard to come to terms with the fact that their son or daughter is gay, but also because homosexuals are said to be particularly exposed to that great scourge, AIDS. Wealth does not guarantee immunity from this or any other illness, though it can obviously buy the finest medical treatment. Parents, inevitably, feel even more helpless in such cases than they do when they discover that their children have become addicted to drugs. They have all this money, but they cannot save their children.

Let me end on a more cheerful note. Prosperity brings benefits as well as problems. Most of us – not just the rich – are better off than our ancestors were. We have more comforts (even the poor can count on more help than they had in previous centuries) and we tend to live longer. In Shakespeare's day, people considered themselves lucky if they made it to the age of forty. A hundred years ago, the life expectancy of most people was no more than fifty or sixty. Today we can reasonably look forward to seventy, and the way things are going the average should be close to eighty by the end of the century. The next generation may come to regard a hundred as the norm.

I have always been immensely grateful for the tremendous advances in medicine during my own lifetime. I have also thanked God that my children have been spared another war. I was a young boy during the last world war and I still vividly recall the horror of it all: the wholesale killing, the mindless acts of brutality, the sense of utter helplessness as we huddled in the cellar during an air raid, praying that the bombs would fall somewhere else. War, like illness, hits rich and poor alike. A bomb does not discriminate. We lost our home; others lost their lives. Rich and poor lost fine children as well as their possessions. I was one of the lucky ones: I survived. But I can never forget that dreadful childhood experience, and I fervently hope that nothing like it will ever happen again.

My children, to be sure, face a *potential* horror: nuclear weapons. I am well aware of their power, but I firmly believe that they have been a blessing: they have ensured peace in Europe for a longer period than ever before and I have little doubt that they will continue to do so in the foreseeable future. It is always easy to devise frightening scenarios, but I draw comfort from the fact that, so far, the doomsayers have been proved wrong – not only about nuclear weapons but about everything else.

The 'flower children' of the 1960s were haunted by the spectre of a holocaust. In the 1970s and early 1980s we were told to worry about an 'inevitable' economic collapse. It induced the Hunt brothers, among others, to invest in silver and other supposedly stable commodities which they thought would protect their wealth from certain destruction. Young 'survivalists' headed for remote mountains, where they erected barricades against the rampant starving hordes who, it was said, would pour out of the cities to live off the land. It has not happened. The world economy has suffered setbacks, but it has not collapsed. The stock market may not be what it was, but hardly amounts to the predicted apocalypse. The oil has not run out; there is a glut.

I doubt if in the decades ahead the major industrialized countries will see the kind of growth they are accustomed to, but that is more likely to be a consequence of the proliferation of such factors as modernization, literacy, affluence, birth control, and government and private policies reflecting different values and priorities.

Economic change will continue to be accompanied by social change. The class system will be further eroded by the advance of the meritocracy and the New Rich. Children already mix more freely than in the past – in the classroom, at work, in politics, in sport, in clubs. Eventually, social class may well become irrelevant. It is, surely, the task of today's parents, whatever their station in life, to prepare their children for the challenges of tomorrow.

Index